Microsoft® Publisher

D1303033

Microsoft® Publisher

Luisa Simone

PUBLISHED BY
Microsoft Press
A Division of Microsoft Corporation
One Microsoft Way
Redmond, Washington 98052-6399

Library of Congress Cataloging-in-Publication Data
Simone, Luisa, 1955–
     Microsoft Publisher / Luisa Simone.
        p.   cm.
     Includes index.
     ISBN 1-55615-375-9
     1. Desktop publishing--Computer programs.   2. Microsoft Publisher.
  I. Title.
  Z286.D47S5965 1992
  686.2'2544536--dc20   92-7987
                                               CIP

Printed and bound in the United States of America.

1 2 3 4 5 6 7 8 9   MLML   7 6 5 4 3 2

Distributed to the book trade in Canada by Macmillan of Canada, a division of
Canada Publishing Corporation.

Distributed to the book trade outside the United States and Canada by Penguin
Books Ltd.

Penguin Books Ltd., Harmondsworth, Middlesex, England
Penguin Books Australia Ltd., Ringwood, Victoria, Australia
Penguin Books N.Z. Ltd., 182-190 Wairau Road, Auckland 10, New Zealand

British Cataloging-in-Publication Data available.

Adobe Type Manager and PostScript are registered trademarks of Adobe Systems, Inc. TrueType is a registered
trademark of Apple Computer, Inc. Bitstream is a registered trademark and Dutch, Facelift, and Swiss are
trademarks of Bitstream, Inc. Arts & Letters is a trademark of Computer Support Corporation. HP and LaserJet
are registered trademarks of Hewlett-Packard Company. Brush Script and Park Avenue are trademarks of
Kingsley-ATF Type Corporation. Helvetica and Times Roman are registered trademarks of Linotype AG and/or
its subsidiaries. Microsoft and MS-DOS are registered trademarks and Windows is a trademark of Microsoft
Corporation. Harvard Graphics is a registered trademark of Software Publishing Corporation. PC Paintbrush is a
registered trademark of ZSoft Corporation.

Acquisitions Editor: Marjorie Schlaikjer
Project Editors: Nancy Siadek, Sally Brunsman
Technical Editor: Jerry Joyce

To J.V.S.— otherwise known as Mom.

CONTENTS

ACKNOWLEDGMENTS

The author would like to extend her thanks to the product support team at Microsoft, including David Perry and Karen Fries.

The editors who worked on this project provided a steady stream of help and patience, both of which I appreciated. Thanks to Marjorie Schlaikjer, Nancy Siadek, Sally Brunsman, Jerry Joyce, and the Microsoft Press team; and Michelle Neil, Justin Cuyler, Joan Houlihan, Hiyaguha Cohen, and the Editorial Services of New England team.

The wonderful clip-art images of edible flowers and beautiful fish are part of the Totem Color PostScript Art collection and appear courtesy of Totem Graphics. For more information contact Totem directly at 6200 Capitol Blvd. SE #F, Tumwater, WA 98501, (206-352-1851).

Finally, my personal thanks must go to friends Alan Richardson and Robbin Juris, both of whom contributed their artistic skills to various design projects in the book.

INTRODUCTION

You're about to work with Microsoft Publisher, an affordable desktop publishing program that is so easy to use and understand that you'll be producing professional-looking documents in no time at all. And you don't need to be a graphic designer to create first-class documents — Publisher's unique intuitive interface actually guides you through the design process.

Publisher can help you bring your everyday documents to life with pictures, decorative borders, and distinctive typefaces. Take a quick look at the variety of projects and publications — for business and home — that you can produce with Publisher.

- A company newsletter published for the employees — by the employees
- An original logo for your company or community organization
- Buttoned-down business forms for everyday use
- Eye-catching advertisements and brochures
- Professional-looking stationery that reflects your personal style
- A technical report integrating spreadsheets, charts, and diagrams
- Paper airplanes that really fly

What Microsoft Publisher Offers

With Microsoft Publisher you can create high-quality publications that integrate words and pictures. Publisher's built-in word processing and drawing tools let you create any publication from scratch. And you can change the appearance of text and graphics by using Publisher's powerful formatting features. The program even offers a spelling checker for eliminating typographical errors.

Best of all, Publisher provides a built-in tool — PageWizards — that can automatically create standard publications, such as newsletters, brochures, and business forms. You simply answer a few commonsense questions, and then watch as the PageWizard builds a document based on your responses. You can also use a PageWizard to create special effects — such as a fancy first letter or a coupon — within your publications.

The WordArt and BorderArt tools make it easy to add type effects and graphical accents to your designs. With a click of the mouse button, you can create the perfect decorative touch, such as a fancy patterned border or slanted and rotated headlines.

Publisher can also convert text and graphics files from a variety of other popular application programs. So you can continue to use your favorite word processor or paint program and import the files directly into your Publisher document.

Microsoft Windows

Microsoft Publisher takes advantage of the Microsoft Windows operating environment. For example, Publisher shares many interface conventions with other Windows-based programs, such as English-language commands that appear in drop-down menus and a Toolbar that displays icons. Publisher also offers a high degree of integration with other Windows-based programs. On the simplest level, this means you can copy words and pictures between programs by using the Clipboard — a utility available only to programs running in the Windows environment.

On a more sophisticated level, you can use another Windows feature — Object Linking and Embedding (OLE) — to integrate Publisher with other programs, such as Microsoft Works, Word for Windows, and Excel. Two commands — Paste Special and Insert Object — rely on the power of OLE. Using the Paste Special command, you can create Publisher publications that are automatically updated each time you open the file. Using the Insert Object command, you can launch any of the mentioned programs from within Publisher — making it easy to incorporate spreadsheets, sophisticated drawings, and graphs into your designs.

The Microsoft Solution Series

Microsoft Publisher is part of the Microsoft Solution Series, which includes two other programs: Microsoft Works and Microsoft Money. Microsoft Works offers all the standard business applications — word processing, spreadsheet, and database functions — in one integrated package. Microsoft Money helps you manage all your financial transactions.

You can use each of these programs alone, but you'll be surprised by the synergy among them. The Solution Series programs were designed to work together, so if you own Microsoft Works as well as Publisher, you can use the drawing program that comes with Works from within Publisher. Likewise, you can insert a Works spreadsheet into a Publisher document. By doing so you can create a desktop published quote form and complete the math in the quote by using the Works spreadsheet features.

Why Read This Book?

This book is not a substitute for Microsoft Publisher's manual, which provides clear descriptions of the program's various features. Instead, this book teaches you about Publisher's tools within the context of a typical small business environment. Most chapters in this book focus on a single design project for a fictitious business called Epicurean Delights. You'll discover how the owner of the store, Elizabeth Jarmen, uses Publisher's design tools to improve her business and impress her clients.

For example, with the help of Publisher, Elizabeth upgrades her business correspondence by designing a unique logo for the store's stationery and by creating quote sheets she and her employees can fill out electronically. In addition, she keeps in touch with her customers through a promotional news-letter and adds value to her catering services by supplying customers with printed invitations and menus.

Each project illustrates some general rules of good design. After all, publica-tions aren't effective when they're cluttered or hard to read. Your publications will be much *more* effective when you've learned to present your ideas and information in a clearly understandable, highly readable — and even enjoyable — format.

Each project also demonstrates the most important rule of good design: form should follow function. To show you how content drives design, each project contains text and pictures that relate to the small gourmet shop. All the copy was written specifically for Epicurean Delights and reflects real-life business situations. The clip-art illustrations were researched to fit the content and are all part of a wonderful collection of PostScript images available from Totem Graphics at 6200 Capitol Blvd. SE #F, Tumwater, WA 98501 (206-352-1851). The photograph in the newsletter in Chapter 9 was digitized using a standard desktop scanner. You can complete the exercises by substituting your own text files and Publisher's clip-art images for the ones shown in the book.

How This Book Is Organized

This book is divided into four sections, each with its own purpose.

Section I, "Quick Start," provides a quick start for novice users. Newcomers who learn how to manipulate a mouse in Chapter 1 will be producing a newsletter by Chapter 4 — honest!

Chapter 1, "A Window of Opportunity," covers the basic skills necessary for working in the Windows environment, including how to choose commands and fill in dialog boxes.

Chapter 2, "Microsoft Publisher Basics," introduces you to several key concepts in Microsoft Publisher, including customizing your work area by using formatting attributes to change the appearance of text and picture elements.

In Chapter 3, "Desktop Publishing Wizardry," you use a simple PageWizard to create a business form. Because the PageWizard takes care of designing the document, you can concentrate on learning about text entry.

In Chapter 4, "The Power of PageWizards," you employ a more sophisticated PageWizard to create a two-page newsletter. By watching the PageWizard at work, you can learn quite a lot about the design process. And by completing the newsletter, you will practice importing both text and picture files.

Section II, "Do-It-Yourself Design," concentrates on publications you create from scratch. The step-by-step instructions will help you master all phases of the design process. In addition, each chapter explores a particular subset of Publisher's tools. Chapter 5, "Planning a Publication," leads you through what are admittedly the more mundane aspects of creating a publication — in this case a small mail-order catalog. You'll learn to build the foundation for a publication by choosing the printer, setting the page size, creating an underlying grid, and managing multiple pages.

Chapter 6, "Focusing on Type," addresses the issue of text formats. In the course of designing a letterhead and formatting a letter, you'll learn the difference between display type and body copy.

Chapter 7, "Designing with Type," uses WordArt to create a dramatic headline for a sample advertisement, proving that special type effects can be as visually appealing as a picture.

Chapter 8, "Accent on Graphics," teaches you about Publisher's internal drawing tools. You'll discover that you can combine — and format — simple geometric shapes to create an effective illustration for a sample menu.

Chapter 9, "Picture Perfect," concentrates on Publisher's picture-handling features. A flexible newsletter layout gives you the opportunity to work with pictures of different sizes, shapes, and even different file formats.

Section III, "Advanced Tips and Techniques," contains only two chapters, but they are full of advanced tips and techniques. Chapter 10, "Ten Hot Tips for Type," presents ten text-handling techniques. You'll learn how to dress up a list with decorative bullets and how to insert special characters, such as accented foreign language letters, copyright symbols, and international monetary signs for a professionally typeset look.

Chapter 11, "Ten Hot Tips for Pictures," taps into sophisticated features that let you automatically update the pictures in your publications from external files or launch other Windows-based programs from inside Publisher. Other work-saving techniques present ways to speed up screen redraws and include nonprinting reminders in your publication files.

Section IV, "Appendixes," contains important reference material. Appendix A, "Installing Microsoft Publisher," gives you detailed instructions for Publisher's installation procedure. Appendix B, "Keyboard Alternatives," explains the ins, outs, and combinations of Publisher's keyboard shortcuts. Appendix C, "Printing with Microsoft Publisher," goes beyond the basic print commands in Publisher to explore the nuances of printing your designs. This appendix includes a discussion of fonts, color output, and the default settings of the Windows Control Panel. Appendix D, "Glossary of Terms," is a handy reference tool that defines words and technical phrases that might be new to you. This glossary helps you understand the lingo associated with computer-based graphics, desktop publishing programs, design theory, typography, and commercial printing processes.

In one important organizational sense, all the chapters in this book are identical. Each chapter contains hands-on exercises that let you put design theory into practice. The step-by-step instructions explain how to create a wide variety of publications, and Helping Hand notes clarify difficult points and help you avoid potential mistakes.

What You Need to Begin

In order to run Microsoft Publisher, you need the same basic hardware configuration required by Microsoft Windows 3 to operate in Standard or 386 Enhanced mode: an 80286 or higher processor, a hard disk, at least 1 MB of memory, and at least an EGA graphics monitor and adapter. For Publisher, you also need a mouse and, if you want to print your works of art, a graphics-capable printer.

To become a competent designer, you need a little something extra — a willingness to experiment. You can rely on PageWizards, templates, and special effects like BorderArt and WordArt to jump-start the design process and to serve as a source of visual inspiration. And Publisher lets you test out your designs ad infinitum.

This book is intended to encourage you to exercise your creativity and develop confidence in your own design judgments. In the final analysis, it doesn't matter if your design sensibility is whimsical, notoriously new-wave, or the essence of elegance. Your publications are sure to be successful if the design clarifies and enhances your message.

QUICK START

Chapter 1

A WINDOW OF OPPORTUNITY

When you use a desktop publishing program like Microsoft Publisher, you open a "window of opportunity." Publisher can help you create snazzy newsletters, dazzling invitations, and buttoned-down corporate reports. With such well-designed documents you not only inform your readers — but you can influence and entertain them as well. However, you cannot tap the benefits of Publisher until you learn how to open its window of opportunity in a very literal way.

The window of opportunity is Microsoft Windows of course — the graphical environment in which Publisher operates. Windows enhances and extends the capabilities of MS-DOS, which is your PC's standard operating system.

Unlike the MS-DOS screen, the Windows screen shown on the following page presents you with icons — or symbols — each of which initiates a particular function. You don't need to remember commands because the appearance of each icon provides a visual clue about its use. Notice how the icon for Microsoft Write (one of the programs packaged with Windows) is a writing pen. Likewise, the telephone icon is linked to a communication program, and the clock icon invokes a display of the current time. These icons are easy to understand because they look — and behave — like their real-world counterparts.

In addition, drop-down menus, accessible along the menu bar at the top of the screen, provide you with plain English descriptions of their functions.

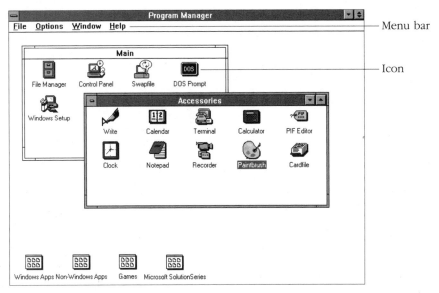

Menu bar

Icon

In this chapter, you will explore the Windows environment. Every program that runs under Windows uses the same basic interface conventions. For example, applications always appear on the screen within a program window, and all Windows applications use both icons and menus to issue commands. If you become comfortable with these conventions, you will find it easier to learn Publisher and other Windows-based programs.

You must develop a visual vocabulary to work with Windows successfully. And so the following discussion includes almost as many pictures as words. Also, be prepared to do a few hands-on exercises that will help you to master mouse movements and manipulate icons.

> **NOTE:** *If you are already familiar with Windows, you can proceed directly to Chapter 2, "Microsoft Publisher Basics."*

The Windows Environment

In addition to a visually oriented interface, Windows provides several features not found in MS-DOS:

■ Two utilities — Program Manager and File Manager — to help you load programs and manage files

- Accessory programs such as Calendar, Calculator, Clock, and Card File, that simulate an actual desktop

- A suite of programs, including Microsoft Write and Paintbrush, that lets you create documents immediately

- The ability to switch between programs almost instantaneously or to run more than one program simultaneously

- Several mechanisms, such as the Clipboard, that help you share information between programs

- Easy access to all the extended memory installed in your computer

Sometimes the only way to start a journey is to take a step backward. In this case, we have to use MS-DOS to open the Windows program.

 Hands On:
Opening Windows

1. If you are not currently in the Windows directory, type the following command at the C> prompt:

   ```
   cd\windows
   ```

2. Issue the command to load Windows by typing

   ```
   win
   ```

   The Windows Program Manager appears on the screen.

Note: *If Microsoft Windows resides in a directory other than WINDOWS, substitute the name of the correct directory when you use the CD command. If another application program starts as soon as you turn on your computer, you might want to alter the computer's startup directions. See your MS-DOS documentation about altering the AUTOEXEC.BAT file.*

The Program Manager is the heart and soul of Microsoft Windows because it is the easiest way to visually organize and launch other applications.

While your screen might not look exactly like the screen that follows, it will contain the same elements: program icons (used to launch applications), program groups (used to organize program icons), and program group icons (used to open and close program groups).

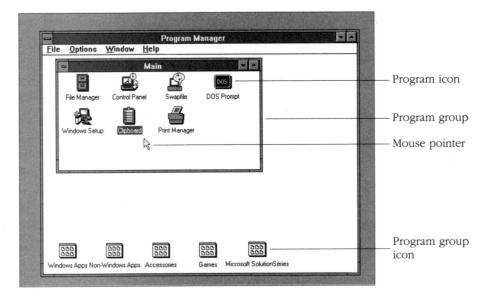

Program icon

Program group

Mouse pointer

Program group icon

Among all the objects on the screen, one element plays a particularly important role: the pointer. Its arrow shape provides a clue to the active role it plays within Windows. The pointer moves across the screen in response to motions that you make with a mouse.

The Mouse

A mouse, like a keyboard, is simply an input device. Instead of typing information as you would with a keyboard, you move the mouse to point at objects on the screen and click a mouse button to indicate a selection. As you can see in Figure 1-1, most mice have two buttons. It is not uncommon to

Helping Hand: Pointer Shapes

Pay attention to the shape of the pointer. It changes appearance as you perform different operations. We will encounter several different pointers as we explore Windows.

For example, the arrow pointer selects various screen elements. The two-headed arrow lets you resize window borders. The four-headed pointer moves objects.

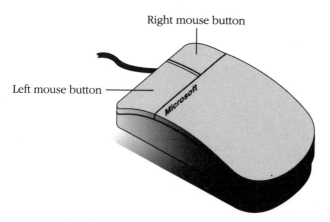

Right mouse button

Left mouse button

Figure 1-1.
Use the mouse to move the pointer around the screen.

have a three-button mouse, but usually you will use only the left button. With few exceptions, the exercises in this book use the left button. Be sure that the left mouse button fits comfortably under your right index finger.

> **NOTE:** *If you prefer using the mouse with your left hand, you can use the Windows Control Panel to reverse the mouse button assignments. See your Windows documentation for details.*

Using the mouse is different from using the keyboard in a number of ways. For example, with the keyboard, you use arrow keys to make selections and move the pointer. This restricts your motions to either up or down, or left or

Helping Hand: Mousing Around

As you work through the following exercises, you might run out of maneuvering space on your desk. Just pick up the mouse and reposition it. The tracking ball on the bottom of the mouse must be in contact with a surface for its movement to register. So picking up the mouse temporarily interrupts the movement of the pointer on screen but doesn't change its position.

right. In contrast, the mouse lets you move the pointer in any direction and along any path. This flexibility lets you use the mouse to choose items from a menu, move objects, or even draw lines.

To work fluidly in Windows, you must practice moving the mouse and learn several kinds of button actions. At first, you might find it difficult to coordinate the way your hand moves the mouse across your desk with the way the pointer moves across the computer screen. But have patience. With a little bit of practice you'll find that you can use a mouse with a great deal of precision.

Mastering the Mouse

You'll need to learn three mouse operations before you can work efficiently in Windows — point and click, drag, and double-click.

Point and Click

To point and click, you must position the arrow-shaped pointer over a Windows element, and then press and release the left mouse button. This is the most basic mouse action in Windows. Use the point-and-click operation to select icons and choose items from menus.

To try your hand at a simple point-and-click operation,

1. Move the pointer until it is positioned over the Minimize button (the downward-pointing arrow in the upper right corner of the Program Manager window).

2. Click the Minimize button.

Your screen should change dramatically to match the screen that appears on the following page. Note that the Program Manager, which is still loaded in memory, now appears as an icon in the lower left corner of the screen. The blank area is your Windows Desktop. Also notice that the pointer, in the form of an arrow, is still active.

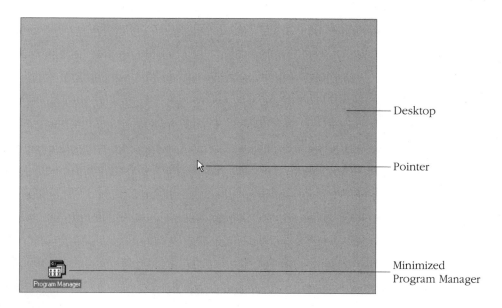

Desktop

Pointer

Minimized
Program Manager

Drag

If you select an icon by pressing and holding the left button without releasing it, you can drag the pointer (and the icon beneath the pointer) to a new location. Move the Program Manager icon to a new location on the desktop by completing these instructions:

1. Point the arrow-shaped pointer at the Program Manager icon.

2. Press the left mouse button and without releasing it, drag the icon to the center of the screen.

3. Release the mouse button.

Double-Click

A double-click is similar to a point and click, but instead of clicking and releasing the left button only once, you click twice with hardly a pause between clicks and without moving the mouse. Double-clicks are often used as a shortcut to bypass menus. For example, in the following steps, you can use a double-click to restore the Program Manager window to its former size.

1. Move the pointer over the Program Manager icon.

2. Double-click the left mouse button. Remember to press and release the left mouse button twice in quick succession without moving the mouse.

You have just used the mouse in three different ways. You pointed and clicked to minimize the Program Manager. You dragged the Program Manager icon to a new location. And you double-clicked the Program Manager icon to restore it to a usable size.

Though the primary goal of this chapter is to practice using a mouse, you can also operate Windows using the keyboard. Keyboard equivalents are sometimes faster when you must perform repetitive tasks. And some people simply feel more comfortable typing than using the mouse. See Appendix B, "Keyboard Alternatives," for a complete list of keyboard equivalents and short-cuts. With some experimentation, you'll soon develop an individual working method that combines both mouse and keyboard input.

Properties of a Window

In this section, you will see how to use the mouse to activate each element in a window. You will work almost exclusively with the Program Manager because it displays elements that are common to all program windows. You can apply the skills you learn here not only to Publisher, but to other Windows-based programs as well.

The Title Bar

As you can see in the illustration on the next page, the program window title bar displays the name of the program, and the program group title bar displays the name of the program group. The title bar changes color to indicate when the window is active. You can move a window by selecting the title bar and dragging it to a new location by using the mouse, as follows:

1. Click anywhere within the Main program group window to make it active.

2. Drag the Main program group window to a new location within the Program Manager window. (Remember to keep the left button depressed while you move the mouse.)

3. Release the mouse button.

The Maximize and Minimize Buttons

You've already used the Minimize button to reduce the Program Manager window to an icon. You can use the Maximize button to increase the size of the window so that it fills the entire screen. The up arrow maximizes the window, and the down arrow minimizes the window.

1. Point to the Maximize button (the up arrow).

2. Click and release the mouse button.

   Notice that when the Program Manager fills the entire screen, the Maximize button changes into a button that contains both an up arrow and a down arrow. This is the Restore button. It returns the window to its original size.

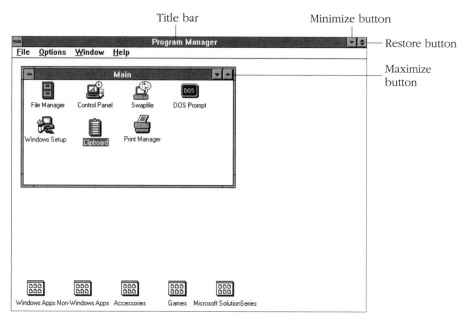

Title bar   Minimize button

Restore button

Maximize button

   Try out the Restore button now.

3. Click the Restore button.

The Window Border

The window border offers another way to control the size and the shape of the window. When you position the pointer over the window border, the pointer changes into a two-headed arrow to indicate that you can now resize and reshape the window. The following instructions allow you to test this out for yourself.

1. Move the pointer over the window border until it changes into a two-headed arrow.

2. Using the two-headed arrow, drag the border of the window to a new position. (Remember to keep the left mouse button depressed as you move the border.)

3. Release the mouse button.

Scroll Bars and Scroll Boxes

When all the information contained in an application cannot be displayed in the window at once, scroll bars appear. Scroll bars and scroll boxes allow you to move the information on the screen up, down, left, or right so that you can see the off-screen parts of the file. You can use scroll bars to move through a file in small increments or use the scroll box to move in long sweeps. Follow the steps below to try out both methods:

1. If necessary, use the window border and the two-headed arrow to reduce the Program Manager window until scroll bars appear.

2. Click the up, down, left, or right scroll bar arrows. Notice that each click moves you across the file only a small distance.

3. Drag the scroll box to move quickly through the contents of the window. The position of the scroll box always indicates your relative position in the file. For example, when the scroll box is at the midpoint of the vertical scroll bar, you are approximately halfway down the contents of the window.

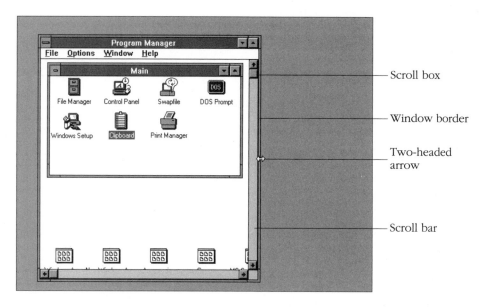

Scroll box

Window border

Two-headed
arrow

Scroll bar

Menus, Commands, and Tools

Until now, you have used the pointer only to manipulate windows. But moving windows around the screen and resizing them can hardly be considered
productive work. To do real work — such as writing letters, totalling numbers,
or searching through business records — you must access the functions of an
application program. In Windows, you access a program's functions by clicking the commands and tools as they appear in menus, dialog boxes, and
toolbars.

The Control Menu

Every window has a Control menu, which appears as a boxed dash in the
upper left corner of the window. The Control menu contains the commands
that allow you to manipulate the size and position of a window.

When you click the Control menu box, you can access commands to maximize, minimize, move, size, or close the window. To maximize the Program Manager window,

1. Click the Control menu box to display its commands.

   Take a moment to study the menu choices listed in the Control menu box. Like all other menu choices in Windows, they appear either as white text on a black bar, as black text on a white background, or as gray text.

   ◻ White type against a black bar indicates that the menu choice is selected. Click on a selected command to execute it.

   ◻ Black text on a white background indicates that a menu choice is available. You can select the command by dragging the selection bar down through the various options, or you can execute the command by clicking it.

   ◻ Gray text indicates that the menu choice is not currently available.

2. Choose the Maximize command.

The Menu Bar

All programs running under Windows also display a menu bar containing the commands specific to that program. Though the actual commands vary from program to program, all menu bars use the same conventions and work the same way.

Each program's commands appear as menu selections under general headings. Think of the menu bar as the top level of an outline. Related commands appear under each heading when you point to the heading and click the mouse. Try it.

1. Point to the Program Manager menu bar and click the first item, File.

2. Point and click the second menu item, Options.

3. Point and click the third menu item, Windows.

4. Click anywhere on the screen to close the Windows menu.

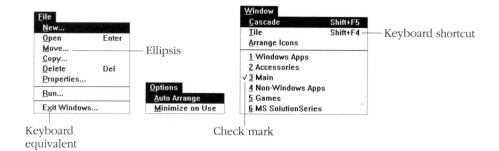

Notice how the commands on each menu relate to the heading that appears on the menu bar. For example, commands that allow you to open a new file, move or copy a file, and delete a file are grouped logically under File.

The three Program Manager menus shown in the previous illustration — File, Options, and Window — invoke different program functions. However, they share certain conventions, including the following:

■ Underlined letters let you use the keyboard to invoke the associated command. For example, on the File menu, notice that the *x* in "Exit Windows" is underlined. If you press the *x* on your keyboard, you will exit the Program Manager. Notice that the keyboard alternative isn't necessarily the first letter of the command.

■ A key or key combination listed after the command is a keyboard shortcut. These keystrokes let you invoke the command without ever opening up a menu. For example, the Window menu indicates that you can automatically tile windows by using the Shift-F4 key combination. Of course, there isn't a keyboard shortcut for every command in every program, but whenever one exists, it is displayed to the right of its associated menu item. To learn keyboard equivalents, try using the mouse to find the command you need and then take an extra second to read through the menu. Soon you can bypass the menu, using a keyboard shortcut instead. Refer to Appendix B, "Keyboard Alternatives," for a listing of Publisher's keyboard shortcuts and Windows keyboard equivalents.

■ A check mark next to a command signifies that the command or program group is currently selected, or active. The check mark acts as a toggle to turn it on or off. When no check mark appears, the command or program group is inactive. In the sample Window menu, the Main program group is designated as the active window.

- A triangle (not shown) always brings up a secondary, cascading menu that presents you with more choices.

- An ellipsis (. . .) signals that the command cannot be completed until you have supplied more information to Windows.

Dialog Boxes

Whenever a program needs information from you to complete a command, it uses a dialog box. The simple dialog box shown in the following illustration pops up when you choose the Run command from the File menu:

In this example, Windows cannot run an application until you supply its name in the text box. Use the following instructions to display and then close the Run dialog box:

1. Click the File menu.

2. Click the Run command.

3. Click the Cancel button to close this dialog box without running an application.

Dialog boxes appear within their own window. This dialog box, for example, contains a Control menu (the dash) and a title bar. As in any other window, you can use the Control menu to move or close the window and the title bar to move the window around the screen.

In addition, this dialog box has three ways of requesting information from you:

- The text box requires you to type the necessary information — in this case, a program name. When you click this box, the mouse pointer changes into a text insertion point — or I-beam — indicating that you can type normally.

- The check box lets you load and run the application in minimized (icon) form. You can turn the box on or off by clicking the mouse. If an *x* appears in the box, the Program Manager will load and run the application in minimized form.

- Command buttons allow you to select a command, cancel an operation, or call up additional options. The information you supply and the choices you make won't take effect until you click the OK button. In this case, you can choose to load the program whose name you typed into the text box by clicking OK, or you can close the dialog box by clicking Cancel.

The Run dialog box contains only three items, but other dialog boxes can be very complex, as the following illustration shows:

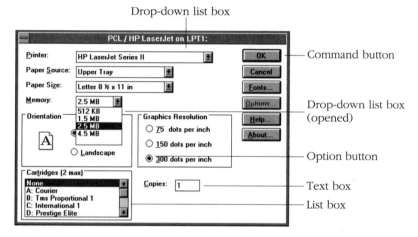

This complex dialog box requests information using these additional methods:

- List boxes or drop-down list boxes that present you with all of the available choices. If the entire list does not appear, you can use either the scroll bar or the downward pointing arrow to see the remaining items. Before you can complete the command, you must highlight one or more items.

- Option buttons that you can turn on or off with a mouse click.

Toolbars

Toolbars (sometimes called toolboxes) are common to desktop publishing programs like Publisher and to illustration programs like Paintbrush. Instead of using words to describe commands, toolbars represent a program's functions with pictures. Toolbars work in much the same way as menu items: you click a toolbar choice to invoke a particular drawing or design function. Like menus and dialog boxes, toolbars give you easy access to a program's functions.

However, because toolbar functions are used so frequently, it is more efficient to display the tool icons in the application window rather than hiding them away on a menu. For example, Publisher's Toolbar contains the Text Frame tool because you must create text frames frequently in order to type or input copy.

Text Frame tool

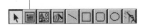

Program Manager

As you have seen, Program Manager provides many functions to you via icons. In this section, you will learn how to use icons to launch applications. In addition you will learn how to organize the desktop with program groups and program group icons.

Icons

If you have been following the exercises in this chapter, you should have the Program Manager on screen and the Main program group should be active, as shown:

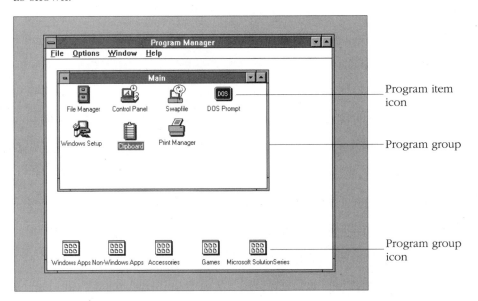

As you can see, the Program Manager screen is filled with icons. Each of the icons in the Main program group represents an application that comes packaged with Windows. Each icon's appearance, as well as its label, suggests the function of its associated program. You choose a program item icon to launch the application it represents.

When you double-click a program icon, the Program Manager retrieves the relevant information and loads that icon's associated program. Try it now on the Clipboard icon.

1. Position the pointer over the Clipboard icon.

2. Double-click the mouse button.

The Clipboard appears in its own window. You can move the window to any position on screen. Because the Clipboard is a separate application, it can overlap or move outside the border of the Program Manager. In the following illustration, notice how the Clipboard window overlaps the Program Manager window:

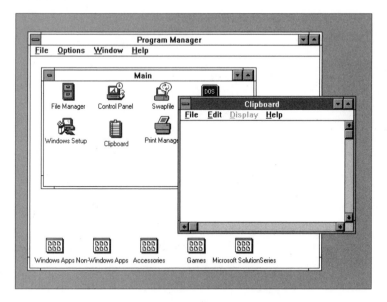

The Clipboard program provides a special area where you can temporarily store data from other Windows applications. You'll use the Clipboard later in this chapter session to share information between programs. You could close the Clipboard now and reopen it later, but Windows gives you a more convenient way to free up system resources like screen space and memory. You can minimize the program rather than close it completely.

1. Position the pointer directly over the Minimize button located in the upper right corner of the Clipboard window. (Be sure you are working with the Clipboard window and not with the Program Manager window.)

2. Click the mouse button. The Clipboard window changes to an icon in the lower left corner of the Desktop:

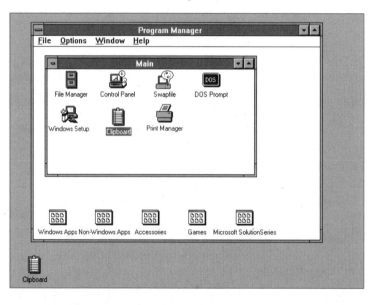

Helping Hand: Finding a Lost Icon

If you can't see the Clipboard icon on the Desktop, either you have closed the Clipboard application inadvertently, or the Program Manager window fills the entire screen.

To return the Program Manager to its intermediate size and reveal the Desktop, click the Restore button (the two-headed arrow button at the upper right corner of the Program Manager window). The Desktop should now be visible, along with the Clipboard icon.

Notice how the Clipboard icon now appears in two places: within the Main program group window and on the Desktop. If you try to invoke the Clipboard now by double-clicking the Clipboard icon in the Program Manager, Windows will tell you that the Clipboard is already running. That's because you haven't closed the Clipboard yet. You've simply miniaturized it and put it aside. To activate it again, click the Clipboard icon that's now located on the Desktop, and then choose Restore.

Program Groups

The Program Manager lets you work more efficiently by organizing program item icons into logical groups. For example, the Windows installation program automatically creates several program groups, including Accessories, Games, and Main. In addition, Publisher's installation program automatically creates a program group titled Microsoft Solution Series. (If you purchase other Solution Series programs, such as Microsoft Works or Microsoft Money, they will also be installed in the Microsoft Solution Series program group.)

Program groups let you control your working environment in a number of ways. You can rearrange groups by adding and deleting program item icons, or you can move program item icons between groups. You can also create new program groups as you need them.

You can minimize program groups into program group icons, transforming a cluttered Windows Desktop into a neat arrangement of clearly labeled icons. To gain access to a program group, you simply maximize the icon and reopen the window. Practice minimizing program groups and maximizing program group icons in the following exercise.

> **NOTE:** *Before we begin the exercise, be sure that Microsoft Publisher is properly installed on your computer. If you need help installing Publisher, see Appendix A, "Installing Microsoft Publisher."*

 ### Hands On:
Working with Program Groups

1. Double-click the Microsoft Solution Series program group icon.

    The Microsoft Solution Series program group appears on screen and overlaps the Main program group. Notice in the following illustration that the Microsoft Solution Series program group contains icons for Publisher, Works, and Series Info. In subsequent exercises you will use both Publisher and Works to see how grouping program icons together can increase your productivity.

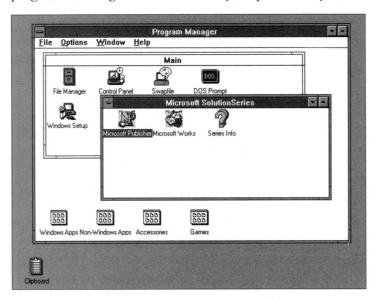

2. Click anywhere in the Main program group to make it the active window, and then click the Minimize button (the downward arrow) in the Main program group.

   The Main program group is now reduced in size to a program group icon and appears at the bottom of the Program Manager window.

Microsoft Publisher and Windows

Your Windows education won't be complete until you experience, first hand, how Microsoft Publisher benefits from the Windows environment.

You will discover, for example, that you can keep Publisher open while you work with other programs, like Works or Write, because Windows allows you to load several programs into memory at one time. Windows also lets you organize multiple programs on screen and switch among them with a simple mouse click. You can also access the Clipboard from within Publisher. This allows you to copy or paste information between Publisher and other Windows-based programs.

Windows even lets you start other programs from within Publisher. On the simplest level, this means that you can launch the Publisher Help program from within Publisher and keep a handy reference to all Publisher's commands and functions on screen in a discrete window.

In the following exercises we will work with a number of different Windows applications, including Publisher, to see all these features in action.

Managing Multiple Applications

In this section we will keep several application programs open on the Desktop at once, learn how to switch among them, and learn how to organize them for maximum efficiency.

Learning to manage multiple windows is a lot like learning how to swim. You plunge in and flail around a bit before you master the technique. Though you may not realize it, you already have your big toe in the water because you have two programs running right now — Program Manager and the Clipboard.

Even though the Clipboard appears on your Desktop only as an icon, it is still loaded into memory. In fact, minimizing programs lets you straighten up the Desktop but still keep all of the applications you need within a working session handy.

Before you can learn how to manage multiple windows, you must open a few more programs. Let's load two programs from the Microsoft Solution Series program group: Publisher and Works.

> **NOTE:** *If you do not have Microsoft Works installed, you can complete the following exercises using Windows Write or any other Windows-based word processor.*

Hands On:
Loading Application Programs

1. Double-click the Microsoft Works icon in the Microsoft Solution Series program group.

2. When the opening screen for Works appears, click the Word Processing icon at the far left.

3. Move the pointer to the title bar of the Works window. Drag the window about halfway down the screen. You should see the Publisher icon in the Solution Series program group.

Helping Hand: Adding a Program Item to a Group

You can still complete all the exercises in this book even if you don't plan to use Works for Windows as your word processing program. Follow these instructions to add the program icon for Write (a simple word processing program that is packaged with Windows) to the Microsoft Solution Series program group:

1. Double-click the Accessories program group icon to open the window.

2. Click the Window menu, and then click the Tile command to display the Microsoft Solution Series program group and the Accessories group side by side.

3. Point to the Write icon in the Accessories program group.

4. While holding down the Ctrl key, drag the Write icon over to the Microsoft Solution Series program group.

NOTE: *If you drag the icon without holding the Ctrl key you won't copy the icon, you'll move it.*

When you release the Ctrl key and the mouse button, a copy of the icon appears in the Solution Series program group and the original is still in place in the Accessories program group window. Now you can launch the Write program from either the Microsoft Solution

4. Double-click the Publisher icon to open the program. Publisher's
   Start Up screen offers you several options.

5. When you see Publisher's Start Up dialog box, click the Blank
   Page icon.

6. Click the OK button.

7. Click Publisher's Restore button.

   If you scrutinize the illustration on the following page, you will see
   that at this point you have four programs open on the Desktop:
   Publisher, Works, Program Manager, and the Clipboard (minimized).

Series window or the Accessories program group window.

5. Click the Minimize button in the Accessories program group
   window to reduce it to an icon and clean up the Program Manager
   window.

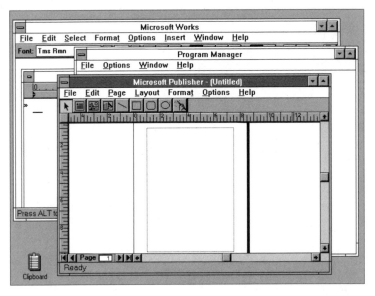

Because Publisher was the last program you opened, it appears on top of the stack with its title bar highlighted to indicate that it is the active window. The rather haphazard arrangement of the other windows creates a visually cluttered working environment. You could organize your Desktop by minimizing all the programs to icons, as you did earlier with the Clipboard. Although that solution looks neat, it isn't appropriate in this case.

Luckily, the Windows Desktop comes with a handy utility called the Task List Manager that lets you organize program windows and switch between various applications. The Task List Manager dialog box contains six command buttons and a list of the programs currently loaded in memory.

Helping Hand: Keyboard
Shortcut to the Task List Manager

Even if the program windows on your screen overlap and completely obscure the underlying Desktop, you can still invoke the Task List Manager by pressing Ctrl-Esc — the keyboard shortcut.

Hands On:
The Task List Manager

1. Double-click any exposed surface of the Windows Desktop to open the Task List Manager.

   The Task List Manager pops up on screen wherever you double-clicked the mouse. As the following illustration shows, the Task List becomes the active window. It sits on top of all the other windows, and its title bar is highlighted.

2. In the list box, move the highlight from Publisher to Works.

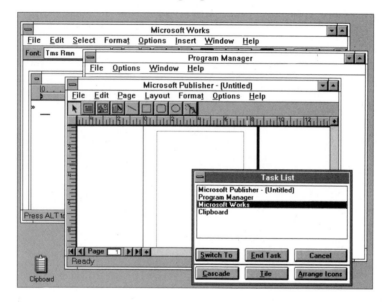

3. Click the Switch To button.

   Works now moves to the foreground and becomes the active window.

   You can also use the Task List Manager to organize the windows on screen. You can cascade windows so that they overlap or tile windows so that each takes up an equal amount of screen space. After you've organized the windows, switching between programs is as simple as clicking an open window.

4. Invoke the Task List Manager by double-clicking the Desktop or by using the Ctrl-Esc keyboard shortcut.

5. Choose the Tile command.

   The three program windows appear on screen side-by-side. Tiling gives you a simultaneous view into all of your windows — a useful feature. You can arrange the windows differently by using the Task List Manager once again.

6. Invoke the Task List Manager.

7. Choose the Cascade command.

   Now the program windows overlap so that the title bar of each window is visible. Cascading allows you to keep a large number of windows open on the Desktop, and to maintain a decent working size for each window. To bring any program window to the top of the stack, just click its title bar.

The Cascade and Tile commands make it easy for you to organize program windows on your screen. However, you shouldn't feel constrained to work only with these preset arrangements. You might find it better to create custom sizes for each window, because then you can allocate the correct amount of space for each application.

Hands On:
Customizing Windows

1. Click the Program Manager title bar to make it the active window.

2. Minimize the Program Manager window.

3. Double-click the Clipboard icon (the one on the Desktop) to restore it to a working window size.

4. Invoke the Task List Manager by double-clicking anywhere within the Desktop.

5. Choose the Tile command.

6. Resize and move the three windows by dragging the window borders and title bar. Try to duplicate the arrangement of windows

shown in the following illustration, with Publisher occupying most
of the screen and Works and the Clipboard taking up less space.

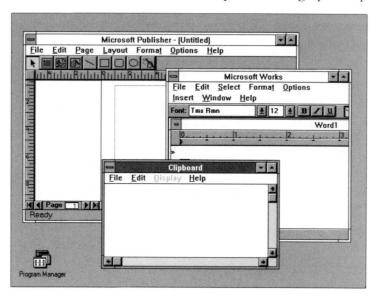

The current arrangement of program windows allows you to switch quickly among programs and, at the same time, to see what is happening in all
the windows. Because you have now sized each program window appropriately, you will not have to interrupt your workflow to maximize or minimize
windows.

Sharing Data Through the Clipboard

Think of the Clipboard as a temporary storage area where you can stash text,
numbers, and even pictures until you need them. You can access the Clipboard from most Windows applications by selecting the Cut, Copy, or Paste
command on the program's Edit menu.

In the following exercises, you will learn how the Clipboard interacts with
other Windows programs. You will generate text in Works, copy it to the Clipboard, and then paste it into Publisher.

Hands On:
Copy and Paste With the Clipboard

1. Click the Works window to make it the active program.

   Throughout the exercises in this book, you'll create a variety of sample documents for a fictitious gourmet food shop called Epicurean Delights. Begin now, by using the name of the store as a sample line of text.

2. Type the following:

   `Epicurean Delights`

3. Highlight the text by placing the pointer (now an I-beam to indicate text mode) at the beginning of the line and dragging it across all the text:

4. Open the Edit menu in Works.

5. Click the Copy Command.

   If you switch to the Clipboard window by clicking on it, you will see that the Copy command placed a duplicate of the text on the Clipboard, as shown at the top of the next page.

6. Make Publisher the active window by clicking anywhere within its boundaries.

   Note that you cannot import the copy from the Clipboard into Publisher until you draw a text frame — which functions as a container for the words.

7. To draw a text frame, click the Text Frame tool (the second icon from the left) on the Toolbar.

   When you bring the pointer down to the working area you'll notice that it changes into a crossbar. The crossbar (which resembles a plus sign) lets you draw objects with great precision because the intersection of the cross exactly marks the position of your mouse.

8. Move the pointer to the position for the upper left corner of the text frame. Then, without releasing the button, drag the crossbar diagonally to draw a box approximately 1 inch deep and 2 inches wide. Don't worry about exact measurements or positioning.

   The text frame appears as an empty box with eight small squares (or handles) around its perimeter. The handles indicate that the text frame is selected and that you can import text into it.

9. Open the Edit menu.

10. Choose the Paste Text command.

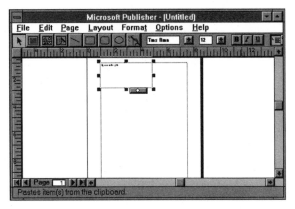

Publisher pastes the contents of the Clipboard into the selected text frame. Because you are in Full Page view it might be difficult to read the text. However, you can magnify the text frame to actual size.

11. Open the Page menu and choose Actual Size view.

Now you can read the type as it appears in Publisher:

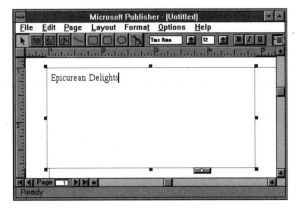

You can see from the previous exercise that even though you have pasted the text into Publisher, a copy of it remains on the Clipboard. Whatever you copy to the Clipboard remains there until new material replaces it. However, many Windows users forget that the Clipboard stores items only temporarily and lose track of text and pictures that they meant to save. The following exercise will show you that it is quite easy to accidently overwrite the contents of the Clipboard.

Hands On:
Replacing the Contents of the Clipboard

1. Make Works the active window.

2. Type the following line of copy:

   `Catering Services`

3. Highlight the text.

4. From the Edit menu, select Copy.

5. Switch to the Clipboard window.

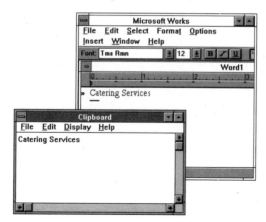

The Clipboard window reveals that the new text replaced the previous contents of the Clipboard. Keep in mind that you can't append items to the Clipboard. To permanently save the contents of the Clipboard, you must either paste the contents into another application or use the File command in the Clipboard to save the contents to disk.

You don't need to display the Clipboard in order to use it. When you use any Windows-based program, you have access to the Clipboard whether or not you specifically invoke the Clipboard utility.

To see how this works, close the Clipboard and continue with the Paste operation.

6. Since you no longer need the Works program, close the Works window by choosing the Exit Works command from its File menu.

7. When asked if you want to save the changes to the current document, click No.

8. Double-click the Clipboard's Control menu icon to close the Clipboard.

9. Make Publisher the active window.

10. From the Edit menu, select the Paste Text command.

The text phrase appears on the screen. Even though you closed the Clipboard, Publisher has access to its Cut and Paste functions.

The Help Program

The Windows Help facility shows how easy it is to launch and use a secondary program along with Publisher. Publisher (and most other Windows-based applications, including the Program Manager itself) contains a separate on-line Help program that you can invoke from the Main menu bar. Because Publisher's Help is a separate program, you can treat it like any other program window. You can resize it, minimize it to an icon, and even tile it so that Publisher and Help appear on screen side-by-side. You can leave the Help program open on the Desktop for handy reference.

Best of all, if you learn how to use Publisher's Help, you will know how to use the Help program for all Windows-based applications. Windows Help, for example, uses the same structure and commands to explain the Program Manager.

In the last exercise, you pasted text from the Clipboard into a text frame that we created in Publisher. In the following exercise, we will try to locate more information about Publisher's text frames by using the Help program.

Hands On:
Using the Help Index

1. Open the Help menu in Publisher.

2. Choose the Index command.

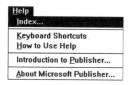

The Help program appears on screen.

3. Enlarge the Help window by clicking the Maximize button.

   As you can see in the next illustration, the Help Index uses an outline structure and provides a short list of general topics. To locate information you must select a general topic, and then work your way down through the outline by selecting more specific topics. For example, to find information about text frames, select the closest match, which is the item titled Adding and Changing Text.

4. Move the pointer to the topic titled Adding and Changing Text.

5. The pointer changes from the standard arrow to a pointing hand to indicate that you can select a topic. Select the topic by clicking the mouse.

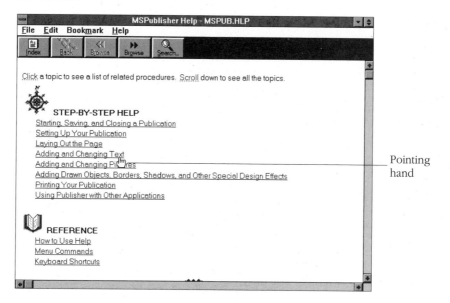

Pointing hand

6. When a more detailed topic list appears on screen, choose the item titled Adding Text.

   The Help screen appears, containing a thorough description of text frames. You can read through the information on the screen to learn how text frames work.

7. Click the up and down arrows on the scroll bar to move through the topic.

   Remember that you can move quickly through the topic by dragging the scroll box to a new position on the scroll bar. You can also use the Browse button on the Toolbar to read through related topics that precede or follow the current topic.

   As you read, you'll notice that some words have a dashed underline. Words with a dashed underline have an associated box that contains a definition of the word.

8. To read the definition, first move the pointer to the underlined word.

9. Click the mouse button to invoke the definition box:

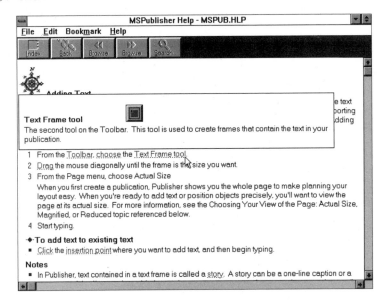

Note that as long as you keep the mouse button depressed the definition will remain on screen.

10. When you finish reading the definition, release the mouse button. The box disappears from the screen.

The Help Index's biggest drawback is that it requires you to have a good sense of which general heading contains the information you need. But Publisher's Help offers a more efficient way to find information. In the following exercise, you will take advantage of the Help program's Search function.

Hands On: Using Search

1. Select the Search button from the Toolbar that runs along the top of the screen.

2. A dialog box appears. You can type a search phrase in the box. Since you want information about text frames, type *text frame* in the text box.

   As you type, Help searches for categories that match the text you enter, and then it lists the best matches.

3. Move through the list box of matching categories by clicking the down arrow in the scroll bar.

4. Double-click the closest match to your original search phrase, "text frames: creating."

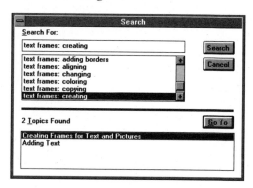

As you can see from the previous illustration, when you double-click the key phrase, you select and confirm it in one motion. As a result, the Help program conducts a search and displays a second list containing even more specific topics.

5. Since Creating Frames for Text and Pictures is highlighted, click the Go To command.

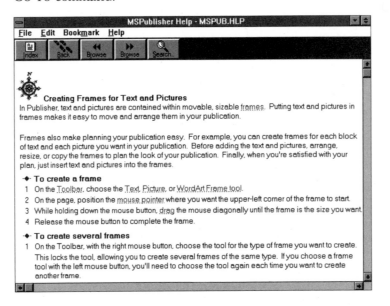

A screen appears with information about drawing frames. Interestingly, by using the Search command instead of the Index, we found different (and more specific) information about Publisher's text frames.

You can locate the information you want in the Help Program even more easily if you use two other commands found on the menu. Annotate, located on the Edit menu, allows you to add your own personalized notes to the Help program. And the Bookmark command lets you put an electronic placemarker in the text so you can quickly find information that you look up frequently. Experiment with these two functions on your own.

6. When you finish reading the information on the screen, exit the Help program by double-clicking the Control Menu box or by selecting the Exit command from the File menu.

Quitting Windows

The time has come to end your first very productive session with Microsoft Windows. But before you can close the Windows program, you must close all the open application windows, which means closing Publisher.

You are already familiar with two ways to exit an application program: You can use the Exit command on the File menu, or you can invoke the Close command in the Control menu. Let's take this opportunity to learn a keyboard shortcut that accomplishes the same thing.

Hands On:
Closing Publisher

1. Use the keyboard shortcut Alt-F4. (Remember to press both keys simultaneously.)

   When you exit the program without first saving your work, a dialog box appears and asks you whether you want to save or abandon the changes to the current document. Whichever method you use to quit the program, Publisher asks you to decide the fate of the sample file you created in the previous exercises.

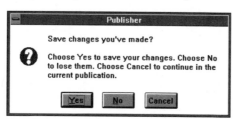

2. Click the No button to abandon this file.

   You have seen that Windows offers an extremely flexible working environment, providing several ways to invoke any command.

For example, to exit Windows (which should appear on the desktop as an icon) follow these instructions:

3. Click the Program Manager icon.

4. When the Control menu box appears on screen, choose the Close command.

However, you can also exit Windows using any of the mouse actions or keyboard alternatives in the following list:

- Double-click the Control menu box of the Program Manager.

- Open the Control menu by pressing Alt-Spacebar, and then choose the Close command by pressing C.

- Open the Program Manager File menu, and choose the Exit command.

- Open the File menu by pressing Alt-F, and choose the Exit command by pressing X.

- Press Alt-F4.

In each case, Windows presents you with a dialog box that asks you to confirm that you want to quit Windows and save the current settings for the desktop. You don't have to save the current arrangement, but you might find it easier to continue with the exercises in subsequent chapters if you do so.

1. Be sure the check box is selected to save the current Desktop.

2. Click the OK button.

What's Next?

In this chapter you've learned quite a lot about Windows. You practiced basic mouse movements and manipulated program windows. You also discovered how to load programs using icons and how to invoke commands using menus and the Toolbar. In addition, you learned how to take advantage of the Windows interface by accessing the Clipboard and employing the Help facility. These essential skills will help you to use all Windows-based programs.

In the next chapter, you will explore Publisher's unique commands and tools. You will learn how to customize the workspace, and you'll begin to work with the basic building blocks of desktop published documents — text, pictures, and graphic objects.

Chapter 2

MICROSOFT PUBLISHER BASICS

Look at the drafting table of any professional art director and you'll find a collection of tools — such as T-squares and X-Acto knives — within easy reach.

Microsoft Publisher also provides design tools, in the form of electronic rulers and computerized cut-and-paste functions. You'll find Publisher's tools even easier to reach than the ones on a drafting table because they are only a mouse click away. And you can customize Publisher's design tools to your individual preferences — a significant improvement over conventional tools.

Because you learned about Windows-based programs in Chapter 1, you will recognize many of Publisher's features. The Publisher program window, for example, displays all the usual Windows paraphernalia, including a title bar, a Control menu box, Maximize and Minimize buttons, and scroll bars. In addition, most of the program's functions and commands are located on the menus and the Toolbar.

Chapter 1 taught you the basic skills you need to navigate the menu choices, Toolbar options, and dialog boxes common to all Windows-based programs. In contrast, this chapter focuses on features unique to Publisher. In the following exercises, you will learn how to customize your work area. You will also learn to recognize and manipulate text (words), graphics (drawings created in Publisher), and pictures (artwork imported into Publisher). These elements are the building blocks of any desktop published document.

The first step is to open Publisher.

Hands On:
Opening Publisher

1. If Windows is not already running, start it by typing

   win

   If you worked through the exercises in the previous chapter, Windows should start with the program group for the Microsoft Solution Series on screen. This program group contains program item icons for Publisher and Works:

Helping Hand: Keyboard Alternatives

Although Publisher's menu commands work optimally with a mouse, you can also issue commands using keyboard equivalents or keyboard shortcuts.

Keyboard equivalents allow you to open menus and execute commands by typing. For example, to print a file you can first type Alt-F to open the File menu, and then press the P key to invoke the Print command. (See Chapter 1, "A Window of Opportunity," for more information on keyboard equivalents.)

Keyboard shortcuts are similar to equivalents, except that they let you by-pass menus altogether. For example, you can press Ctrl-P to print a publication without opening the File menu. Publisher's keyboard shortcuts are always displayed at the right of their associated menu item. (See Appendix B, "Keyboard Alternatives," for a complete list of Publisher's shortcuts.)

If the Microsoft Solution Series program group window is not open, simply double-click its program group icon to open the window.

2. Open Publisher by double-clicking the Microsoft Publisher icon in the Microsoft Solution Series program group.

The opening screen of Publisher presents a number of options.

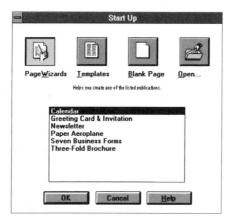

Each of the four buttons arranged along the top of the Start Up dialog box contains an icon:

☐ PageWizards, which can automate the design process for standard publications like greeting cards and newsletters.

☐ Templates, which offer a host of ready-made designs.

☐ Blank Page, which lets you design a publication from scratch.

☐ Open, which lets you call up a document that you previously created and saved.

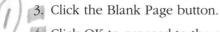

3. Click the Blank Page button.

4. Click OK to proceed to the actual work area, which should resemble the illustration on the next page.

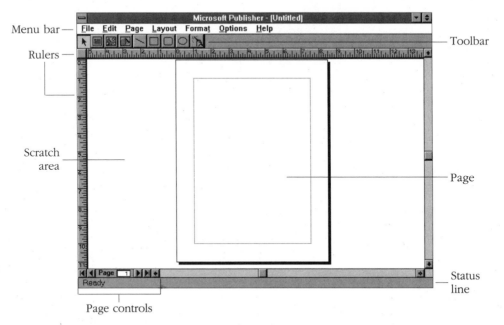

Menu bar — Toolbar

Rulers —

Scratch area — Page

Status line

Page controls

Modifying the Work Area

Microsoft Publisher's electronic page mimics a blank sheet of paper on which you can place text and pictures. The visual metaphor is realistic down to the shadow that simulates a piece of paper sitting on a desktop.

However, Publisher's electronic page offers significant advantages over mere paper. For example, the page is always shown in relation to rulers that appear along the top and left sides of the screen. Notice how the 0 point on both rulers automatically aligns to the upper left corner of the page.

You can also move through the pages of your publication more easily when you do it electronically. The graphic on the next page shows a detail of the page controls located at the bottom of your screen. The controls contain direction arrows that let you move forward or backward through the pages of a document. The text box actually performs two functions. It displays the current page number — but you can type a new page number in the text box to quickly move to any page of your document.

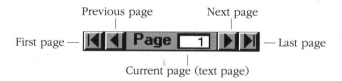

Best of all, you can change the appearance and function of the work area by using menu commands and preference settings. The following are some of the modifications you can make:

- Display or hide the rulers.

- Change the unit of measurement of the rulers to inches, points and picas, or centimeters.

- Move the rulers to measure objects anywhere on the page.

- Switch the nonprinting guides on or off.

- Assign a magnet-like pull to either the guides or the ruler marks to align objects easily.

- Switch among eight different views of the current page, including an over-view of the design (Full Page) and a magnified view suited to precision work (200% Size).

You could easily modify the work area several times in the course of a long design project. However, for the exercises in this chapter, you will make only two small changes to the work area: you will switch your view of the page and modify the way the rulers work.

You *could* find the commands to make these changes by browsing through the menus. You would simply click each item on the menu bar in turn and then read the choices. But instead of using this hit-or-miss approach, you can look for the command you want by searching under the most logical heading. For example, the commands for viewing the page at different levels of reduction and magnification appear on the Page menu.

Hands On:
The Working Screen

1. Open the Page menu, and choose Actual Size.

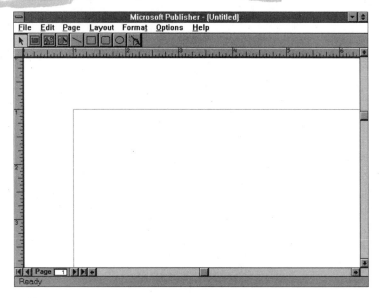

In the Actual Size view, only a portion of the page, starting at the upper left corner, fits onto the screen.

Notice how the rulers are rescaled to accurately measure the page in this view. You can also make the rulers more powerful by assigning a magnet-like pull to the ruler increments or divisions. This option — called "Snap to Ruler Marks" — aligns objects on the screen to the tick marks on the rulers.

2. Open the Options menu, and choose the Snap to Ruler Marks command.

This command is a toggle command, which means you turn it on or off by choosing it. To see how toggling works, open the Options menu again.

```
┌──────────────────────────────────┐
│ Options                          │
│ Check Spelling...                │
│ Hyphenate...          Ctrl+H     │
├──────────────────────────────────┤
│ √Snap to Ruler Marks             │
│  Snap to Guides       Ctrl+W     │
├──────────────────────────────────┤
│  Hide Pictures                   │
│  Hide Rulers          Ctrl+K     │
│  Hide Status Line                │
│  Hide Layout Guides   Ctrl+G     │
│  Hide Object Boundaries Ctrl+Y   │
├──────────────────────────────────┤
│  Settings...                     │
└──────────────────────────────────┘
```

Notice that a check mark appears to the left of the command name, indicating that Snap mode is turned on. You can turn Snap mode off and remove the check mark by clicking the command again. Instead, click anywhere on the page to close the Options menu and leave Snap to Ruler Marks turned on.

As you proceed in this chapter, you'll appreciate the changes you made to customize your work area. You'll find it easier to see elements displayed at their true (or actual) size, and you'll find it easier to design your page when the elements you add automatically align to ruler divisions.

Recognizing Text, Picture, and Graphic Objects

When you look at a desktop publishing document on the screen, you see words and pictures. When Microsoft Publisher considers the same page, it sees a collection of objects. Typical Publisher documents contain three kinds of objects:

- Text objects are made up of words. You can either type text directly into Publisher or import a word processing file.

- Picture objects include any visual material imported from an external source. Scanned photographs, technical diagrams, clip-art images, and pie charts are all picture objects.

- Graphic objects are simple accents that Publisher generates. They include rules, decorative borders, and geometric shapes such as rectangles and ellipses.

In the exercise in the next section, you will create and import text, picture, and graphic objects. And you will learn how to change an object's appearance by using Publisher's formatting tools.

Creating Objects

To create an object from scratch in Publisher, you must activate the appropriate tool on the Toolbar. The Toolbar, which is found just below the menu bar, contains nine task-specific tools. As you can see in the following list, each tool has an associated icon.

Icon	Description
	The Selection tool allows you to select an object or a group of objects.
	The Text Frame tool draws special boxes that hold words. You must draw a text frame before you can type or import text into a Publisher document. When you draw a text frame, the Toolbar changes to include additional icons. Each icon represents a text formatting option, such as typestyle and point size.
	The Picture Frame tool creates boxes that hold artwork. When you activate the Picture Frame tool, the Toolbar changes to include additional icons, each of which represents a formatting option, such as shading or fill pattern.
	The WordArt tool allows you to generate special type effects, such as rotated text and text wrapped along an arc.
	The drawing tools (Line, Rectangle, Rounded Rectangle, and Oval) produce simple geometric shapes. The formatting options that pop up on the Toolbar when you select a drawing tool include icons for line width and fill pattern.
	The Wizard button invokes Publisher's automated design functions for creating special design elements, such as fancy first letters, coupons, and tables.

As the illustration on the next page shows, the formatting options always appear as icons on the right side of the Toolbar.

Text Frame tool selected
(and text frame drawn)

Text formatting options

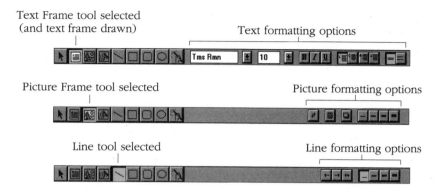

Picture Frame tool selected

Picture formatting options

Line tool selected

Line formatting options

You'll learn about each tool's formatting options as you proceed with the exercises in this chapter. For the moment, let's work with the Rectangle tool.

Hands On:
Using the Rectangle Tool

Begin by drawing a simple rectangle.

1. Select the Rectangle tool by clicking it.

    The icons that appear on the right side of the Toolbar represent different formatting options. To change the width of the rectangle's border, you can click one of the four icons that represent line thicknesses. Clicking the icon that shows a tiny rectangle with a shadow behind it automatically adds a shadow to the rectangle you have drawn. And the icon that shows a box filled with diagonal lines lets you choose a shading pattern for your rectangle.

    When you bring the mouse pointer to the actual work area, you will notice that it changes into a crossbar. The intersection of the cross indicates the exact position of the mouse — so it helps you to draw with greater precision.

2. Place the crossbar pointer 1 inch from the top and left side of the page. Drag the pointer diagonally until you form a box approximately 2 ½ inches wide by 1 ½ inches deep.

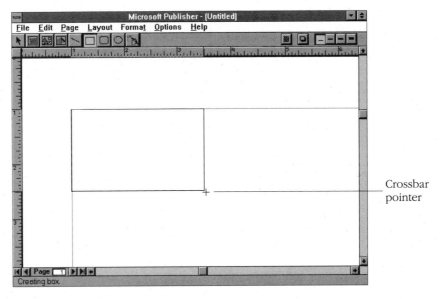

Crossbar pointer

As long as you keep the mouse button depressed, you can change the size of the box. Move the crossbar as you draw to feel the pull of the Snap feature. The Snap to Ruler Marks command lets you easily increase the size of the rectangle in measured, $\frac{1}{16}$-inch increments. Note that when you complete the rectangle, eight small, square handles appear around it, indicating it is the currently selected object.

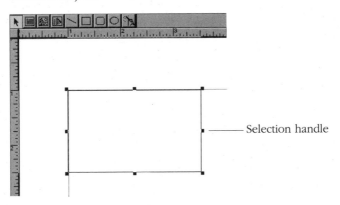

Selection handle

Selecting Objects

You cannot manipulate or format any object unless you first select it. You select an object by clicking it. When you create an object, it remains selected until you click another object or click any blank area of the screen.

Once you select an object, you can perform a host of operations on it. For example, you can use the selection handles to resize and reposition the rectangle you drew. In addition, you can change the rectangle's appearance by applying formatting commands.

Hands On: Resizing Objects

1. Be sure the rectangle is selected.

2. Position the selection pointer on the selection handle at the right side of the rectangle.

   The pointer changes from the selection pointer to the resize pointer.

3. Drag the handle to the right approximately ½ inch.

Helping Hand: Pointer Shapes

Most Windows applications use a two-headed arrow to resize objects and a four-headed arrow to move objects. However, Publisher lets you substitute more descriptive pointers instead.

If the resize pointer appears as a two-headed arrow, but you want to use Publisher's Helpful Pointers (and match the screens shown in this book), follow these instructions:

1. Open the Options menu, and then choose the Settings command.

2. In the Settings dialog box, click the Helpful Pointers check box.

3. Click OK.

When an X appears in the Helpful Pointers check box, the move pointer appears as a moving van, the resize pointers indicate direction, and the cropping tool looks like two pairs of overlapping scissors.

Don't worry if your rectangle is slightly larger or smaller because you can always resize it later.

4. Now position the selection pointer along the edge of the rectangle, but not directly over a handle.

   The pointer changes from the selection pointer to become a pointer that indicates you can now move the rectangle — in this case a moving van.

5. Drag the rectangle to a new position.

   As you resize and reposition objects on a page, you might make mistakes or change your mind. For example, you might grab a handle and inadvertently change the size of an object when you meant to grab the object's edge. Publisher doesn't make you tediously recreate the object's previous state. Instead, you can undo your last action by choosing the Undo command. However, you must undo the action before you execute any other command.

6. To return the rectangle to its previous position, open the Edit menu and choose Undo Move Object(s).

Formatting Objects

In the real world, objects are defined by their properties or attributes. A chair, for example, is an object that has a seat, a back, four legs, and a function — namely, supporting you when you sit. Publisher is an object-oriented computer program. All objects in Publisher — text, pictures, and graphics — also have attributes. For example, boldfacing is a text attribute. A 50-percent gray fill pattern is a rectangle attribute. The true power of desktop publishing lies in the fact that you can easily alter the appearance of objects by changing their attributes. This process is called *formatting*.

As shown in the illustration on the next page, you can change the appearance of your sample rectangle — without redrawing it — by assigning a shadow attribute and a 4-point rule to the border.

Content + Formatting = Appearance of object

| Rectangle | Shadow attribute | 4-point border rule | Graphic element as it will print |

And you'll find reformatting the rectangle convenient because Publisher places the formatting tools you need right on the Toolbar. Let's make the necessary changes.

 ### Hands On:
Formatting Options

1. Be sure the rectangle is selected.

2. On the Toolbar, click the shadow icon.

3. Now click one of the line-weight icons. The thinnest line represents a 1-point rule, and the thickest line represents an 8-point rule. For this example, use the 4-point rule by clicking the icon second from the right.

Frames

In order to work with text or pictures you must understand how Microsoft Publisher employs frames. To start, think about the relationship between a picture and a picture frame. Simply stated, a picture frame is a receptacle for artwork. It surrounds the artwork with a decorative border, but it also serves a function because it allows you to hang the art in position on the wall.

Publisher's frames, which can contain either words or pictures, function in a similar way. You can, for example, assign a decorative border to a Publisher frame. But more importantly, Publisher's frames let you position words and pictures wherever you want on the page so that you can create complex designs. In fact, you can design an entire publication by using empty frames, and then you can import text and pictures from external sources into your layout to create a document.

In the following exercises, you will work with both text frames and picture frames. You'll import artwork from a file stored on disk into a picture frame, and then you'll type a simple phrase directly into a text frame. Next you will use Publisher's formatting options to complete the design.

Hands On:
Importing a Picture

1. Choose the Picture Frame tool.

2. Using the crossbar pointer, draw a vertical box (or frame) 1 inch wide by 1 ½ inches deep. The picture frame box should overlap the right side of the rectangle that already appears on the screen.

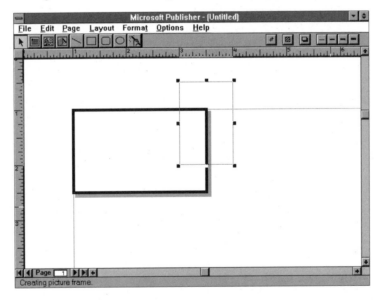

3. Open the File menu and choose the Import Picture command.

The Import Picture dialog box appears on screen. Before you can import a picture you must locate it on the hard disk. Publisher stores all the pictures that come packaged with the program in a directory called CLIPART.

4. Double-click the CLIPART directory to select it.

5. In the Picture Name list box, use the scroll bars to locate the file CHEF.CGM.

6. Click the filename. The name appears in the text box.

7. Click the Preview button to take an advance look at the CHEF.CGM image.

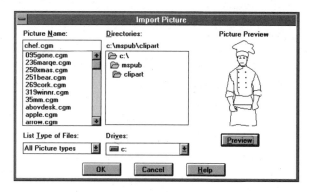

The Preview feature lets you confirm the contents of a file before you actually import the picture into your publication.

8. Click OK to import the picture.

Now, use the formatting commands on the Toolbar to assign a shadow and a 2-point rule to the picture frame.

9. With the frame containing the picture of the chef still selected, click the shadow icon.

10. Select a line weight from the icons on the Toolbar. To match the illustration that follows, click the 2-point rule, which is the second line-thickness icon from the left.

Remember that as long as the picture frame remains selected you can use the resize and move pointers to change the shape and location of the picture.

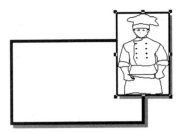

Now that your picture is in place, it's time to add your text and then format it.

Hands On:
Working with Text Frames and Formatting

The last object you will add to your design is the name of our fictitious gourmet food store. But first, you must create a text frame.

1. Select the Text Frame tool.

2. Use the crossbar pointer to draw a box approximately ¾ inch deep by 2 inches wide. This box will contain the text. As you can see in the illustration on the next page, the text frame should overlap both the rectangle and the picture frame.

After you release the mouse button, the text frame is automatically selected. A selected text frame always contains an active text-insertion point — so you can begin typing immediately. A selected text frame also contains an I-beam pointer that allows you to move the text-insertion point or to highlight portions of a text block.

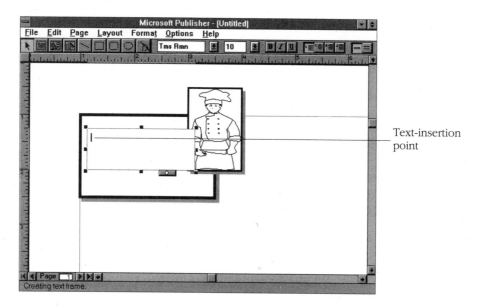

Text-insertion point

3. Type the following text:

Epicurean Delights

At the moment, the text looks rather weak against the heavily ruled boxes. That's because it appears in Publisher's default typeface — 10-point Times Roman. But you can easily reformat the appearance of the text without changing its content. You can find all the formatting commands you need on the Toolbar.

Notice the three buttons on the Toolbar that are identified only by letters. They might seem cryptic, until you realize that the letter B is shown in a bold typeface, the I is italicized, and the U is formatted with an underline. You click the appropriate button to boldface, italicize, or underline your text.

The Toolbar also contains icons that depict alignment and spacing options for text blocks. You can choose among icons for left, center, right, and justified alignments, as well as for single-spacing or double-spacing. If you have trouble distinguishing among the admittedly small drawings, you can refer to the mnemonic initial letter for each button. For example, the left-aligned icon displays an L.

It would be impossible for the Toolbar to contain icons for all your installed typefaces and all the available point sizes, so typeface and point-size options are listed in drop-down list boxes. Clicking the downward-pointing arrow will reveal the available options. Or you can type the font name or font size in the text box.

4. Move the pointer into the text frame and drag the I-beam pointer to highlight the text in the frame.

5. On the Toolbar, open the drop-down list box to reveal the available typefaces by clicking the arrow to the right of the default typeface — Tms Rmn (Times Roman).

6. Choose a bold, blunt typeface like Swis 721 BT (Bitstream Swiss).

   Note that your typeface choices might vary depending upon the hardware and software fonts installed on your system. For a more detailed discussion about font technology, see Appendix C, "Printing with Microsoft Publisher."

7. Change the point size by opening the drop-down list box and choosing 14.

8. Click the B button to boldface the text.

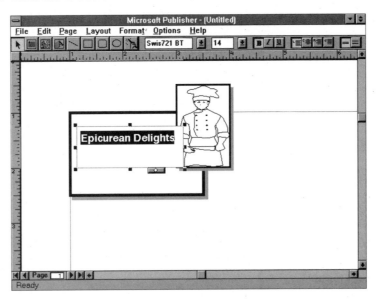

Working with Multiple Objects

It's easy to locate the current text frame because it has selection handles around its perimeter. However, you might find it difficult to identify individual objects on the screen when you work with multiple objects in a complex layout. This is especially true when the objects overlap so that you can't tell where one object ends and the next begins.

Microsoft Publisher allows you to change the way in which objects overlap one another. You can bring objects from the back of the stack to the front, and vice versa. You can even work with several objects simultaneously by selecting them as a group. You will now finalize this design by employing these techniques.

The Layout menu contains all of the commands that let you rearrange objects on the page. Follow the instructions in the next exercise to rearrange the layering of the objects on the current screen.

 **Hands On: Layering**

1. Click anywhere on the picture to select the picture frame.

2. Open the Layout menu, and choose the Bring to Front command.

   The picture of the chef moves to the front of the design once again.

Although the objects on the screen are arranged perfectly in relation to one another, they aren't positioned optimally on the page. If you move each object individually to a better location on the screen, you will need to recreate the entire design.

Helping Hand: Text Wrap

When you bring the picture frame to the front of the stack, you might find that all or some portion of your text moves or disappears. Publisher does not allow a picture to overlap text, and so it wraps the words around the picture frame.

To display the text once again in its original position, use the move pointer to drag the picture slightly to the right or the text frame slightly to the left.

Luckily, Publisher lets you move, copy, paste, and delete objects as a group. Let's move these three objects as a group from their current position to the center of the page.

Hands On:
Group Select

1. Be sure the selection pointer is the current tool.

2. Instead of clicking an object, place the selection pointer above and to the left of all three objects. Drag the pointer down and to the right to create a box that surrounds the three objects.

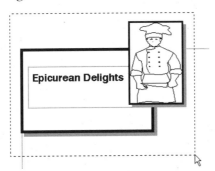

Epicurean Delights

When you release the mouse button, the rectangle, text frame, and picture are selected as one group.

3. With the objects still selected, open the Page menu and select the Full Page command to change the view.

4. Use the move pointer (which appears as a moving van in the following screen) to drag the group to the center of the page. Only the outlines of the objects move with the pointer — the objects are repositioned when you release the mouse button.

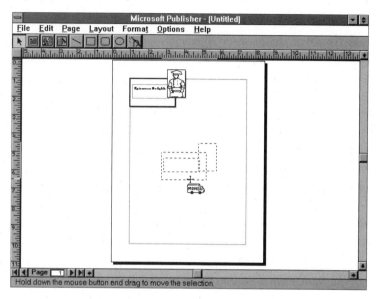

Print Preview

Microsoft Publisher gives you a WYSIWYG (What You See Is What You Get, pronounced wizzywig) screen display. WYSIWYG means that the screen image of your design reflects the way it will look when it is printed. You can make the screen preview look more like the printed page by adjusting the work area settings to hide the object boundaries.

Hands On:
Previewing the Printed Page

1. With your design selected, open the Page menu, and choose Actual Size view.

2. Click the mouse anywhere on the page — except on the objects in the design — to deselect them.

3. Open the Options menu, and choose Hide Object Boundaries.

Object boundaries appear as dotted lines around the perimeters of text frames, picture frames, and geometric shapes. Object boundaries are useful because they let you clearly see where objects begin and end. However, object boundaries never print. Hiding the object boundaries makes your display a more accurate preview of the printed page.

Saving Files

Although your practice file isn't an aesthetic achievement, it is a true desktop publishing document because it integrates both words and pictures. For that reason (and also for the practice), save it to disk.

Helping Hand: Directories List Box

Many programs, including Publisher, assume that you want to save files to the same directory where the program is stored. If you want to store your files in a different directory, use the Directories list box to change directories or the Drives drop-down list box to save your files to a different disk drive.

- The current path information appears in the Directories list box in outline form, with each level of the directory structure indented from the initial drive letter.

- The highlighted open file folder icon always indicates the current directory location.

- To move down one level in the directory structure, double-click the folder or the name of a directory indented from your current position in the directory outline.

- To move up one level in the directory structure, double-click the file folder or directory name that is outdented from the current position.

- To change to a different drive, click the scroll arrow at the right of the Drives list box, and then select the drive you want from the list.

 ***Hands On:***
Saving a Document

1. Open the File menu, and click the Save As command.

   A dialog box appears prompting you to supply a filename.

2. In the Publication Name text box, type *objects*. Publisher will automatically add the PUB extension, which identifies the file as a Publisher document.

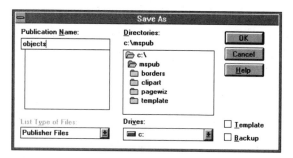

3. Click OK.

   You can end the current work session by closing both Publisher and Windows.

4. From Publisher's File menu, choose Exit.

5. Use the Alt-F4 keyboard shortcut to exit Windows.

What's Next?

In the course of completing the exercises in this chapter, you have experimented with many of Microsoft Publisher's features. You used menu commands to optimize the work environment, and you employed the Toolbar to create and format objects.

In the next chapter, you will use Publisher's unique PageWizard technology to create a business form almost automatically. The essential skills and concepts you've learned here will let you complete the Wizard's preliminary design and produce a professional-looking business form that is both aesthetically pleasing and highly functional.

Chapter 3

DESKTOP PUBLISHING WIZARDRY

In the course of an average week, you are sure to encounter numerous desktop publishing opportunities. At work, you could improve business letters by adding high-quality typefaces. At home, you could add a personal touch to birthday cards.

Elizabeth Jarmen, the fictitious owner of our imaginary gourmet shop, is so busy with her booming catering business that she often lets desktop publishing opportunities pass her by. For example, she doesn't yet have a way to properly court new customers. In fact, she often finds herself scribbling estimates on paper bags.

Elizabeth bought preprinted forms from a stationery store to make her estimates look more professional. But the forms had extra columns she didn't want and item descriptions she didn't understand. Worse, if she attempted to type the estimate, she had to painstakingly line up the preprinted form in the typewriter and try to fit her words into the allotted space. Elizabeth needs a quote form specifically designed for Epicurean Delights. Unfortunately, she doesn't have the time or the training to design an estimate sheet from scratch.

In this chapter, you will use Publisher to create a quote form for Elizabeth, and in the process, you will see how simple creating a customized form can be. Microsoft Publisher offers a unique feature to help beginning designers overcome the biggest obstacle they face at the start of any project — a blank page. That's why you don't see an intimidating blank screen when you first open Publisher. Instead, you see a dialog box that gives you the option of working with PageWizards. Publisher's PageWizards help you to create well-designed publications almost magically. PageWizards don't really use sorcery, of course. Instead, they run mini-programs that ask you for information and then create a design based upon your answers.

Types of Wizards

The PageWizard icon appears both on the Toolbar and in the Start Up box shown below. You can create any of the following complete documents using the PageWizards that you access from the Start Up dialog box:

- A calendar

- A greeting card and an invitation

- A newsletter

- A paper aeroplane

- Seven different business forms

- A three-fold brochure

PageWizards
icon

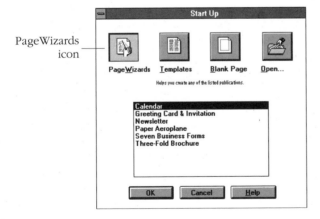

In contrast, the PageWizard icon on the Toolbar allows you to create design elements that fill only a portion of a page. You can use the PageWizards on the Toolbar to create:

- An advertisement

- A calendar

- A coupon

- A fancy first letter

- A newsletter banner

- A Note-It

- A paper aeroplane

- A table

PageWizards Versus Templates

Many desktop publishing programs allow you to jump start the design process by providing preformatted documents, called templates. Publisher also includes templates for everything from business cards to catalogs. But PageWizards are superior to templates in a number of ways.

Design Flexibility

Templates are static. If a template doesn't meet your needs, you have only two choices. You can try to squeeze your information into the preformatted design (and produce a document that looks like a square peg shoved into a round hole). Or you can try to modify the template's design without destroying it.

In contrast, PageWizards are flexible design tools. PageWizards don't present you with a preformatted design. Instead, they engage you in a conversation about your specific project. By answering a PageWizard's questions, *you* determine the final appearance of your publication. You can decide which elements to include in your document and which elements to exclude. And, as shown in the illustration at the top of the next page, you can choose among different design styles.

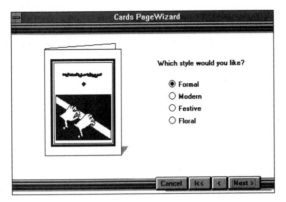

Automated Design

As you become more experienced with Publisher, you may find that you prefer your own designs to those offered by either the PageWizards or the templates. However, you will always find some aspects of desktop publishing more tedious than creative. And PageWizards can take care of some of these repetitive tasks for you.

For example, the Business Forms PageWizard shown in the following illustration creates a complex table by calculating the correct column widths for your project and then drawing and aligning all the text frames.

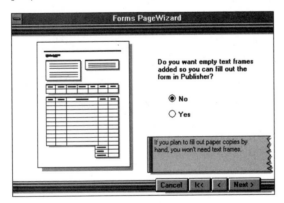

Inclusive Design Process

In the course of asking you questions about your project, PageWizards can also remind you to include important items that you might otherwise forget. In some cases, PageWizards prompt you to include items — such as inventory control numbers or tax exemption identification — that are a part of the content of your publications. In other cases, the items in question — such as fancy first letters and pictures — have a design function. For example, if you tell the Brochure PageWizard to create a brochure for mailing, the PageWizard will create and position text frames for a mailing label and a return address.

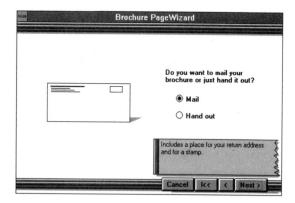

Helping Hand: PageWizards and Printers

PageWizards assume that you will use the default printer you designated in the Windows Control Panel. If you plan to print your document on a different printer, change the default printer in the Windows Control Panel — before you start the PageWizard. See your Windows documentation for details on how to change the default printer.

If you create a publication using a PageWizard and then use the Print Setup command on Publisher's File menu to change printers, your publication may not print correctly.

Educational Design

PageWizards teach, as all good instructors do, by example. You can watch a
PageWizard create a document and, in the process, get a good idea of how
Publisher's Toolbar functions. In fact, a special dialog box provides a running
commentary on every operation that PageWizards perform. This dialog box
also contains a scroll bar that allows you to set the speed at which the
PageWizard completes the design. If you slow down the process you can follow along as the PageWizard adds new pages, draws text frames, imports pictures, and types sample text.

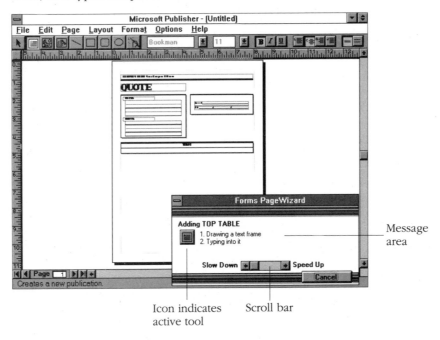

Message
area

Icon indicates   Scroll bar
active tool

Working With the PageWizard

Throughout the exercises in this book, you will work with PageWizard technology whenever it's appropriate. In subsequent chapters, you'll employ
PageWizards to create a newsletter, as well as to generate coupons and fancy
first letters. For now, let's use a PageWizard to create a straightforward business form.

To use PageWizards, you need only the most basic Windows skills. If you completed the exercises in Chapter 1, you'll have no trouble filling in text boxes, turning on check boxes, or choosing options. After the PageWizard does the preliminary work, you'll complete the document by using Publisher's Toolbar and menus to format both the text and text frames.

Hands On:
The Business Form PageWizard

Now you'll try your hand at designing a business form.

1. Start Windows if it is not already running. Load Publisher by double-clicking the program icon.

   Publisher presents a dialog box that lets you start a new publication. You can choose among the PageWizards, Templates, or Blank Page icons. In addition, you can use the Open icon to retrieve publications you have already worked on and saved to disk.

2. Click the PageWizards icon.

   When you choose PageWizards, all the available PageWizards appear in the list box.

3. Highlight the entry Seven Business Forms.

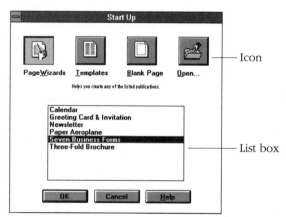

4. Click OK.

A dialog box appears to describe this particular PageWizard. There isn't much happening in this dialog box, so your first impulse might be to skip over it quickly. But instead, slow down and scrutinize this screen.

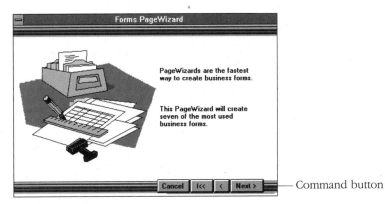
— Command button

Like all windows, the Forms PageWizard window contains a title bar, a Control menu box, and several command buttons. The Cancel button lets you close the PageWizard at any time. In addition, the three direction command buttons let you move back and forth between dialog boxes so that you can review or change your answers before the PageWizard creates the business form.

5. After you read the opening message, click the Next button.

The next dialog box asks you to choose among seven different business forms.

6. As an experiment, click each of the buttons in succession.

As you choose each option, the sample page displayed at the left side of the window changes. This is the preview area, which shows you how your current choice affects the final design.

7. For now, select the Quote option and move on to the next screen.

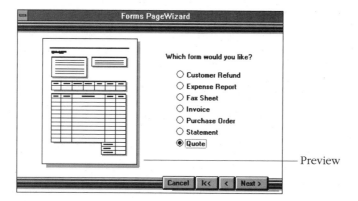

— Preview

8. When the program asks you to choose between a portrait (vertical) or a landscape (horizontal) orientation, click the Portrait button. (You may or may not see this dialog box, depending on your printer setup.) Remember to click the Next button to advance to the next screen.

9. In the next dialog box, click the Traditional design button if you want your final printout to match the illustrations in this book.

   The Traditional design scheme employs a serif typeface. Most printed documents use serif faces because the short decorative lines (or serifs) at the ends of the main strokes of the letters make text more readable. The traditional design is conservative in other ways as well. For example, simple rules highlight each text area. For

---

Helping Hand: The Active Window

When a PageWizard dialog box is on the screen, its title bar is highlighted to show that it is the active window. Unlike other windows, however, you must respond to the PageWizard's dialog boxes before you can either proceed or return to Publisher.

To terminate a PageWizard, you must either click Cancel or use the Control menu to close the window.

comparison, look at the other available styles, which use heavier rules or sans-serif type. If you choose one of the other styles, you will produce a quote sheet that contains the same information as the sample document in this chapter but displays a totally different look.

After you decide on the style you like best, click Next.

Now that you've seen how easy it is to answer the PageWizard's questions, you should feel comfortable moving a little more quickly. The next few screens will query you about the kinds of information to include in the quote sheet.

10. When the Wizard asks if you use a Customer ID number, answer no, and then click the Next button.

The PageWizard now asks you what information you want to include in the top row of the form. Each item on the list is preceded by a check box. Click an unchecked box to fill it with an X and include the item (Yes), or click a checked box to remove the check and exclude the item (No).

11. Click the check boxes so that your choices correspond to the following list:

Your #	No
Our #	No
Sales Rep	No
FOB	No
Ship Via	No
Terms	Yes
Tax ID	No

After you enter all the information as it appears in the table, click the Next button.

The next dialog box asks which items to include in the main portion of the estimate sheet.

12. Respond to each item as follows:

Qty	Yes
Item	No
Units	No

Description	Yes
Dsc %	No
T (Taxable)	No
Unit Pr	Yes
Total	Yes

Remember to click the Next button in order to proceed with the questions.

13. The next screen lets you choose which items to include in the table summary. Follow this list to complete the screen:

Subtotal	Yes
Tax	Yes
Freight	No
Misc	Yes
Balance Due	Yes

Click the Next button to move on.

14. In the next dialog box, choose to have the PageWizard create empty text frames by clicking the Yes button. (Remember to click Next.)

By choosing Yes you instruct the PageWizard to handle the truly tedious job of generating and aligning text boxes for each item in this quote form. All you need to do is fill in the text boxes with your information.

15. Epicurean Delights is (hypothetically) located in Chicago, Illinois. So English is obviously the language of choice for your sample form.

However, don't dismiss the other language options. Even small businesses like Epicurean Delights deal with overseas companies. For example, suppose that Epicurean Delights special orders smoked salmon from Norway. At the very least, it is courteous to use the native tongue of your business associate. Doing so might also avoid any language-based misunderstandings. So, generating a facsimile cover sheet or Purchase Order in Norwegian, French, or Spanish suddenly makes sense.

After you click the Next button, a final dialog box appears to inform you that you have answered all the relevant questions.

However, the PageWizard will not compose the document until you issue the Create It command.

At this point, you can backtrack through the previous dialog boxes to review and revise your answers. For this exercise, however, you will keep the choices you have already made.

16. Click the Create It button.

Magicians use secret incantations and sleight of hand to accomplish their tricks, but Publisher's PageWizards explain every operation they perform. They do so by displaying messages in a special dialog box and highlighting the currently selected tool on the Toolbar.

You can observe the PageWizard at work more easily if you slow it down.

17. Slow the PageWizard by clicking the left arrow on the scroll bar, or move the scroll box to the left.

18. When a dialog box appears telling you the PageWizard has finished the design, click the OK button.

After you click OK, the PageWizard closes. You can now complete the document using Publisher's standard tools.

Analyzing the Design

After the PageWizard has finished its work, take a moment to analyze the design. First think about the design rules behind a successful document. For example, each section of the quote form is highlighted by a rule and offset by a shadow. Although these elements are decorative, they also help to organize the page — making the form easier to read and complete.

You should also look for areas within the design that need improvement. In your sample form, a few category headings should be replaced with more accurate and appropriate text. For example, you'll need to replace the sample text that reads "COMPANY NAME Your Company Address" with Epicurean Delight's name and location. And you should change the "MISC" heading in the summary section to "DEPOSIT" as a reminder to get some cash up front. You should also change "Invoice #" to "Quote #" and "TERMS" to "DESCRIPTION OF SERVICES."

It's easy to change these text phrases; as you'll see in the next section, you'll simply select the text frames and replace the copy. As you make the edits you will use several text-entry methods.

Text Entry

Unless you intend to produce desktop published documents using pictograms, entering text is the single most important function for you to master. When you select a text frame in Microsoft Publisher, you can begin typing immediately. When the pointer is positioned within the selected text frame, it becomes an I-beam pointer. You can use the I-beam pointer to position the text-insertion point anywhere within the text. When the pointer is outside the boundary of the selected text frame, it appears as the standard arrow pointer and allows you to select other objects.

Publisher lets you enter text using one of two modes: insertion mode or replace mode. Entering text in insertion mode is like straightforward typing — you add words to the copy already on screen. The backspace and delete keys erase characters to the left and right of the insertion point.

Replace mode automatically deletes highlighted text and replaces it with any new characters you type. You choose the text-entry mode that you want in the Settings dialog box on the Options menu.

Let's see how both text-entry methods work.

Helping Hand: Object Boundaries

Complex documents, such as this Quote form, consist of numerous objects. Publisher helps you see where one object ends and another begins by displaying a dotted line around each text, graphic, or picture element. This line is called an object boundary.

If your screen does not display dotted lines around the text frames, open the Options menu and select the Show Object Boundaries command.

Hands On:
Text Insertion

Until now, you have worked in Full Page view. Although you can enter text in this view, the small size of the text makes catching typing errors difficult. Therefore, before you attempt to enter text, you'll switch to Actual Size view.

1. Select the first text box that runs along the top of the business form. When you change views, Publisher assumes that you want to display the currently selected object and magnifies that portion of the page.

2. Open the Page menu, and choose Actual Size.

   You should now be working in Actual Size view. The text frame that contains information about the company name and address should be selected.

   Notice in the illustration on the next page that the PageWizard has chosen an appropriate typeface and point size for the address line — 10-point Bitstream Dutch.

   The PageWizard might use a different typeface for your document depending on which fonts are installed on your system. For more information about fonts, see Appendix C, "Printing with Microsoft Publisher." For more information about Bitstream's Facelift font utility, see Appendix A, "Installing Microsoft Publisher."

3. Position the I-beam at the end of the line, and click the mouse to move the text-insertion point to the right of the last letter.

4. Use the Backspace key to delete all the text to the left of the insertion point — one letter at a time.

5. Type the following information on one line, duplicating the capitalization.

   EPICUREAN DELIGHTS 100 South Riverside Plaza Chicago IL 60606
   312-999-9999

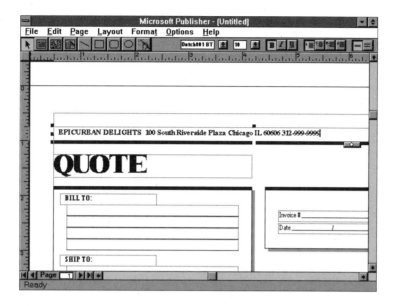

6. Select the text frame that contains the Invoice # item.

7. Position the I-beam at the beginning of the line of text.

8. Type *Quote.*

   Notice that the text you are adding to the line appears where you placed the text-insertion pointer.

9. Use the delete key to remove the word "Invoice" (to the right of the insertion point), one letter at a time. The new line of copy should now read "Quote #."

Helping Hand: Keyboard Shortcut

Like all Windows-based programs, Publisher provides several keyboard shortcuts that let you bypass the menus. For example, the F9 key toggles between Actual Size view and the previous view (Full Page).

Hands On:
Typing Replaces Text

Publisher assumes that you want to work with text-insertion mode, as you did in the previous exercise. You can also configure the program so that whatever you type will replace highlighted text. To do so, follow these instructions:

1. Open the Options menu and choose Settings.

2. When the Settings dialog box appears, click Typing Replaces Selection to turn it on.

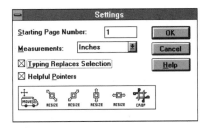

3. Click the OK button.

4. Without changing from Actual Size view, use the scroll bars to move down until the text frame that contains the word "Terms" appears on screen.

Helping Hand: Undo

The Typing Replaces Selection option can make editing text easier, but it can also cause problems. You might accidentally delete more text than you intended. And sometimes, instead of dragging a highlight over the text, you will inadvertently drag the text frame itself to a new location.

You can recover from either of these mistakes by immediately choosing the Undo command from the Edit menu.

5. Select the text frame.

6. Highlight the word "Terms" by positioning the I-beam at the beginning of the word and dragging the I-beam until all the letters in the word appear as white characters on a black background.

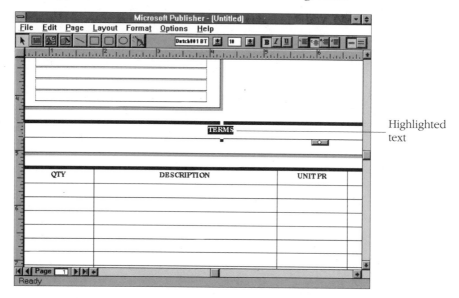

Highlighted
text

7. Type the phrase *DESCRIPTION OF SERVICES* (all in upper case). The highlighted text disappears.

    Now you will use replace mode to transform the "MISC" category into a line item for deposits. Of course you can use the scroll bars to move to the bottom of the page. But this is a good opportunity to practice a keyboard shortcut.

8. Press the F9 key to return to Full Page view.

9. Choose the MISC text frame in the table summary.

10. Press F9 to zoom in on the selected text frame.

11. Be sure the MISC text frame is selected, and then highlight the copy.

12. Type the new category name, *(DEPOSIT)*, in the MISC text frame. Be sure to include the parentheses because they indicate that the amount of the deposit should be deducted from the running total. Standard abbreviations like this one can help you fit a lot of information into a narrow column.

Now that you have finished modifying the quote sheet, print a copy as a quality check.

13. Open the File menu. Choose the Print command and accept the defaults by clicking OK in the Print dialog box. Your printout should look like the one shown in Figure 3-1.

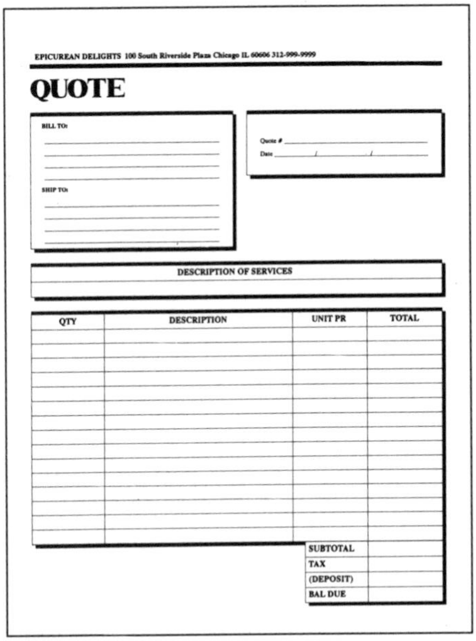

EPICUREAN DELIGHTS 100 South Riverside Plaza Chicago IL 60606 312-999-9999

QUOTE

BILL TO:

Quote #
Date

SHIP TO:

| DESCRIPTION OF SERVICES | | | |

QTY	DESCRIPTION	UNIT PR	TOTAL
		SUBTOTAL	
		TAX	
		(DEPOSIT)	
		BAL DUE	

Figure 3-1.
The modified quote form.

If you are satisfied with the Epicurean Delights Quote form, you can put it to work. But first save the file.

Saving a Template

Instead of saving this business form as a standard Publisher document, you will save it as a template. When you save a document as a template, Publisher automatically stores the file in the TEMPLATE subdirectory. More importantly, the next time you open your template file, Publisher will leave the original file undisturbed and make a copy of the document for your use. This guarantees that the original copy of the template is never inadvertently changed or destroyed.

Hands On:
Saving and Opening a Template

1. Open the File menu and select Save As.

2. Activate the Template option by clicking the check box in the lower right corner.

3. Type an appropriate filename in the text box. For this example, QUOTE would be a simple but descriptive filename.

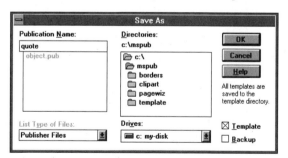

Currently, the file on screen is the original Quote form template. To use a copy of the template, you must start a new publication.

4. Open the File menu, and choose Create New Publication.

5. When the Start Up dialog box appears, click the Template button.

6. The list box that appears includes the filenames of all available templates. Use the scroll bars to find the Quote template, and then highlight it.

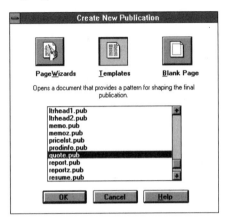

7. Click OK.

Publisher opens a copy of the Quote template as an untitled publication.

Formatting Options

You can practice your text-entry skills by completing the template form. Switch back to Actual Size view, select each text frame, and then type the text that appears in Figure 3-2 on the next page. As you type, notice that the new text appears on the screen in the correct typestyle, as shown in the illustration at the top of page 88. In Microsoft Publisher, even empty text frames can be formatted with complex typestyles.

EPICUREAN DELIGHTS 100 South Riverside Plaza Chicago IL 60606 312-999-9999

QUOTE

BILL TO:

Harry Smithson

Smithson Public Relations, Inc.

200 South Riverside Plaza

Chicago, IL 60606

SHIP TO:

(Same)

Quote # 1093

Date : 4/10/92

DESCRIPTION OF SERVICES

A buffet luncheon is tentatively scheduled for April 20, 1992. Thirty-four (34) people will attend.

QTY	DESCRIPTION	UNIT PR	TOTAL
15	Brie, Avocado, and Watercress Sandwich	4.00	60.00
20	Smoked Salmon with Cream Cheese Sandwich	5.50	110.00
3 lbs.	Pasta Primavera	8.50	25.50
2 lbs	Waldorf Salad	6.25	12.50
1 lb.	Chocolate Chocolate-Chip Cookies	15.00	15.00
1	Homemade Carrot Cake	9.00	9.00
3 doz.	Beverages, assorted fruit spritzers and mineral water	1.85	66.60
3 doz.	Place Settings: plates, glasses, napkins, and utensils	2.00	72.00

SUBTOTAL	370.60
TAX	29.65
(DEPOSIT)	(50.00)
BAL DUE	350.25

Figure 3-2.
The final document.

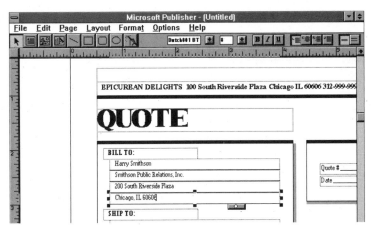

In addition to designating typeface and point size for your text frames, you can set margins, assign decorative borders, and format large blocks of copy into multiple columns.

You can use the menu commands and dialog boxes to assign complex formats to a text frame. However, the Toolbar offers the fastest way to apply typestyles to highlighted text and to text frames. Remember that text formatting options appear on the Toolbar whenever you select a text frame. These formatting options appear at the right side of the Toolbar:

- Drop-down lists that show the currently available fonts and point sizes

- Icons that let you choose bold, italic, or underlined typestyles

- Icons that let you choose left, center, right, or justified alignment

- Icons that let you designate whether to single-space or double-space lines of text

Hands On:
Changing Text Attributes

1. Select the text frame directly below "DESCRIPTION OF SERVICES."

   As soon as you select the text frame, the Toolbar displays the associated typestyle. Read the Toolbar options from left to right. You will see that this particular text frame is formatted for 10-point

Bitstream Dutch bold, right-aligned and single-spaced. (Your font and point size might differ, depending on the printer and fonts you have installed.) As long as you haven't typed anything into this text frame, you can change the default formats.

2. Be sure that selection handles appear around the text frame. Click the B button to deselect boldfacing.

3. With the text frame still highlighted, click the left-alignment icon.

4. Now type the following text on one line:

```
A buffet luncheon is tentatively scheduled for April 20, 1992.
Thirty-four (34) people will attend.
```

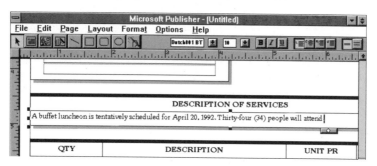

Once you type text into a frame, merely selecting the frame and changing the Toolbar attributes will not affect the appearance of the text that is already in the frame. To change the appearance of text that is already on the page, you must first highlight the text and then change the typestyle. This method allows you to apply different typestyles to various lines of text within the same text frame. Try it now.

5. Scroll up and over to the text frame that contains "Quote #," and select it.

6. Highlight the empty line where the quote number should appear.

If you try to enter copy, you'll discover that the "blank" line consists of a tab that has been formatted with the underline attribute. This makes it difficult to type in a legible ID number.

7. Turn off the underline attribute by clicking the U icon.

8. Click the left-alignment icon to change the alignment from right to left.

9. Now type in the ID number, *1093*.

Hands On:
Changing Frame Attributes

You've eliminated the underline attribute, but now you've lost the effect of a rule separating the quote number from the date information. You could use the drawing tools to create a free-floating rule between these two items. But it is less work in the long run to format the text frame with a $\frac{1}{4}$ -point border at its base.

If you draw a rule instead of formatting it with the text frame, you must be careful to align it with the edges of the text frame. In contrast, a border always matches the size of the text frame. Also, if you move the frame, you might unintentionally leave a drawn rule behind because it is a separate object. But a border automatically travels with the text frame. To create a border along the bottom of the selected text frame, follow these steps:

1. With the text frame selected, open the Layout menu. Choose Border.

2. When the Border dialog box appears, click the bottom of the sample frame.

   The border attributes that you designate will now appear only on the bottom of the frame, as indicated by the two arrows pointing to the base of the frame.

Helping Hand: Task Switching in Microsoft Windows

Typing in the numbers as they appear in Figure 3-2 provides excellent practice for filling in text frames. However, if you completed this quote sheet in a real business environment, you would be responsible for calculating the totals.

The true power of Windows becomes apparent when you realize that you can invoke the Windows Calculator to complete the math operations for this sample quote sheet. (Hint: You can find the icon for the Calculator in the Accessories program group.)

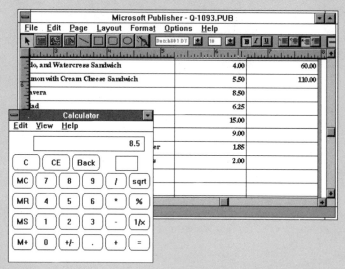

By arranging the two programs on the screen, you can easily switch between them.

3. Instead of choosing one of the standard point sizes, create a custom border width. Click the custom width text box and replace the proposed 10-pt value with 0.25 pt.

4. Leave the color Black.

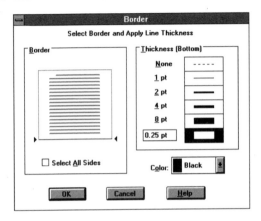

5. Click OK.

   The text will now appear to be floating above a rule.

   Take the time to fill out the rest of the form. You can copy the sample text as it appears in Figure 3-2. As you enter the copy, feel free to experiment by changing any or all of the text and frame formatting options.

   After you finish entering your text, save and print the document.

6. Open the File menu. Because you are working with an untitled document, choosing either Save or Save As opens the Save As dialog box. (If the file had been saved previously the Save command would store the file using the current name and overwrite any previous version of the file stored on disk. The Save As command would allow you to store the file with a new filename and preserve the previous version with the old filename.)

7. Complete the dialog box by typing in an appropriate filename.

   Q-1093 is a handy moniker for the file. It names the type of document (Q for quote) and also gives the actual ID number.

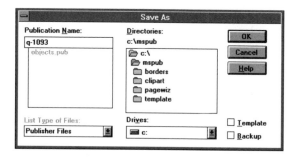

8. Open the File menu once again, and choose Print.

9. Accept the defaults by clicking OK.

What's Next?

In this chapter, you created a template using the magic of PageWizard technology. Hopefully, you now are comfortable enough with the skills learned here to create and modify other simple publications on your own.

In Chapter 4, you will employ another PageWizard to generate a more sophisticated document — a two-page newsletter. You'll learn how to import text files, manipulate artwork, and copy and paste objects within a Microsoft Publisher document.

THE POWER OF PAGEWIZARDS

Newsletters are far and away the most common desktop publishing project. The internal publications of large corporations, professional and technical journals, and simple church or community news bulletins are quite different from one another, and yet they are all newsletters.

Small businesses can increase sales by distributing newsletters that alert customers to new products and services. Newsletters are also a great way to provide background information and instruction to potential buyers. For example, our fictitious business — Epicurean Delights — can use a newsletter to distribute useful recipes and provide interesting food-related anecdotes as well as to promote specialty-food products. The premier issue of *The Epicurean,* (the official newsletter of our gourmet food store) will focus on the store's newest venture — a line of organically grown fresh herbs.

In this chapter you will again invoke a PageWizard to create a new publication. This time, though, you'll respond to different questions and watch as the PageWizard generates a newsletter design that includes sample pictures and formatted text frames.

In the course of creating the newsletter with a PageWizard you'll have a chance to examine different design options. After the PageWizard has done its work, you'll learn how to import both text and pictures into the waiting frames. To fine-tune your publication you'll learn how to edit text, scale pictures, and modify the layout.

The Newsletter PageWizard

In Chapter 3, you learned that Microsoft Publisher offers six PageWizards.

Two of these — the Three-Fold Brochure PageWizard, and the Newsletter PageWizard — can help you create a customer-oriented publication. Let's consider both to see which one best suits the needs of Epicurean Delights.

On one hand, the Three-Fold Brochure PageWizard generates a single-sheet publication that folds like a letter and contains a mailing label. Epicurean Delights doesn't plan to spend money on a mass mailing and therefore doesn't need a mailer format for its brochure.

On the other hand, the newsletter format is valuable precisely because it doesn't look like an advertisement. Newsletters increase sales, but they do so with a soft sell. In addition the newsletter format provides great design flexibility. For example, the Newsletter PageWizard lets you decide how many pages to include in your publication. It also lets you choose the number and width of the text columns. So by choosing a two-page, two-column design you can easily accommodate the three stories that constitute the first issue of *The Epicurean*. One short feature announces the availability of fresh herbs. Another short piece entertains readers with interesting herbal trivia. A final, longer story describes the fresh herbs currently on sale in the Produce Department and includes a recipe as well.

The copy for the newsletter is already written, but newsletters consist of more than words. This is where the PageWizard makes its dramatic entrance. The Newsletter PageWizard can create newsletters that include the publication name, department headings (or kickers), headlines, volume numbers and dates, artwork, captions, a table of contents, and assorted rules and graphic accents.

In the following exercise, the Newsletter PageWizard does all the hard work. You only need to answer several straightforward questions presented via dialog boxes. You should feel comfortable working with the Newsletter PageWizard dialog boxes because they use the same format — text boxes, check boxes, and option buttons — as do the other dialog boxes you have used, including the PageWizard dialog boxes you saw in Chapter 3.

Hands On:
Composing a Newsletter

1. If you don't already have Windows up and running, start it now. Open Publisher by double-clicking the icon. (If you are already in Publisher, open the File menu and choose Create New Publication.)

2. When the Start Up dialog box appears, click the PageWizard icon if it is not already selected. Then highlight the Newsletter option, and click OK.

   Take a moment to read the Newsletter PageWizard's opening screen. Reacquaint yourself with the direction buttons at the bottom of the dialog box. These buttons let you move forward and backward through the PageWizard program so you can return to previous dialog boxes to review or change your answers.

3. Remember that you must click Next to advance through the screens. Click Next to proceed.

   The screen that appears requires you to choose one of three design schemes: Classic, Modern, or Jazzy. Experiment by choosing each option in turn. Look carefully at the preview. You will see that the differences among these three options are purely stylistic. The arrangement of objects on the page remains the same, but the typestyles and border treatments change.

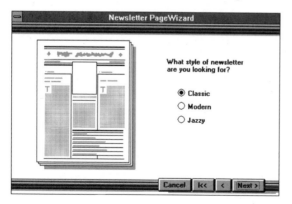

When you worked with the Business Forms PageWizard in Chapter 3, you discovered that the traditional style used thin rules and a serif typeface. The Classic-style newsletter uses the same design treatment. The Modern design scheme features a bolder look, with a sans-serif typeface, heavier boxes surrounding the text, and drop shadows. Flamboyant borders distinguish the Jazzy newsletter by emphasizing a playful arrangement of rectangles on the page.

4. For your newsletter, choose Classic, and then click Next to proceed to the next screen.

   The next screen lets you choose the number of columns you want in your layout. You can specify up to four columns. To see the different column arrangements, click each column option button in turn.

   The width of each column in your publication affects both text formatting and information density, so it's important to understand the advantages and disadvantages of each. One-column pages are too dense to read unless you use a large type size and add extra space (or leading) between lines of text. Two-column pages have wide column widths that let you choose from a number of different type sizes and styles. Publisher's two-column layout also gives you great flexibility when you position illustrations and other visual elements. Three-column grids use narrow columns that let you set copy in a fairly small type size, so you can increase information density without sacrificing legibility. The four-column layout proves that adding more columns does not necessarily mean that you can accommodate more words. Extremely narrow column widths force you to use a small type size. And using a small type size forces you to add extra spacing between the lines of copy to increase legibility.

5. Choose the two-column design.

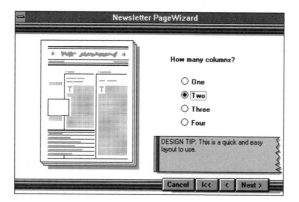

Here the PageWizard has created a very flexible two-column design that is actually based on a five-column grid. Column 1 is left open to hold accent materials, such as pictures. Columns 2 and 3 combine to create one text block. Columns 4 and 5 combine to form the second text block.

Click Next.

6. The next screen asks you to type the name of your newsletter. Type:

   The Epicurean

   As you type, the sample, highlighted text is deleted automatically. Proceed to the next screen.

7. Accept the Yes option to tell the PageWizard that you want to print on both sides of your paper. Click Next.

   Choosing to print on both sides of the paper causes odd-numbered and even-numbered pages to have different formats. Think of your pages as having inside and outside edges, rather than left and right edges — like the facing pages in a book.

8. A text box lets you type the number of pages you want in the newsletter. Type *2,* and then click Next.

   Until you gain experience with newsletter design, you might find it difficult to predict the size of your publication. Don't worry. If you miscalculate the number of pages you will need for your newsletter, it's simple to add or delete pages later.

9. Newsletters can contain many different elements. The current screen lets you decide whether or not to include four elements. For example, the sample newsletter is very short and so does not require a Table of Contents. Refer to the following table to complete this screen. Remember that inserting an X in the check box includes an item (Yes) and removing an X excludes an item (No).

Table of Contents	No
Fancy first letters	No
Date	Yes
Volume and Issue	Yes

10. Continue to the next screen. Choose English from the list of 11 languages. Click Next.

    At this point, the PageWizard is ready to create the newsletter, but you may want to backtrack through the dialog boxes first to review or change your answers. To review your answers, click the left-pointing arrows that run along the bottom of the window.

11. To accept all your responses, you'll click Create It — but don't do so yet. First read the following section to learn how you can watch the PageWizard at work.

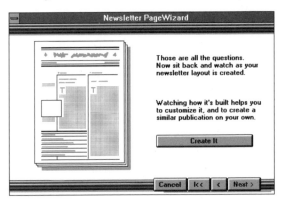

Watching the PageWizard at Work

You might be tempted to take a coffee break while the PageWizard creates the newsletter design. But if you are willing to invest a few minutes, you can take advantage of the unique learning opportunity that the PageWizard offers. The PageWizard will show you the proper way to create a newsletter. It will insert pages, set up column guides, import pictures, and insert text. Remember that you can change the speed of the PageWizard by manipulating the scroll bar at the bottom of the window. Slowing the Page Wizard down will make it easier for you to follow the PageWizard's actions and will give you plenty of time to read the running commentary.

 ### Hands On:
Setting Speed Controls

1. Click Create It to start the PageWizard.

2. When the comment dialog box appears, drag the scroll box to the left.

Don't expect to learn all the nuances of desktop publishing by watching a PageWizard in action. But you can learn some important design concepts, such as how to employ layout guides and background pages.

Layout Guides

Well-designed publications rely on an underlying structure, called a grid. In Publisher, grids function as layout guides to help you draw text frames and align elements. Although the PageWizard creates only two columns of text for your newsletter, it begins the document with a five-column grid. The PageWizard reserves the first column for accent elements, such as pictures and quotes. Then the PageWizard draws two text frames — one to occupy the space defined by columns 2 and 3, and one to occupy the space defined by columns 3 and 4. Note that even when you employ layout guides, you must still draw a text frame to insert copy into a document.

Background Pages

Multiple-page documents contain organizational devices — such as page numbers, footers or headers, logos, and border treatments — that appear on every page or on every odd or even page. (If you had chosen not to print on both sides of the paper in the last exercise, the odd and even pages would have the same layout and share the same Background page.) If you watch the PageWizard at work you will see that it wisely places these elements on Publisher's Background pages.

The Background pages contain any text or design elements that will appear on every odd or even page in your publication. In contrast, the Foreground page contains text and design elements that are specific to an individual page. You work on a Background page and a Foreground page separately, but when you view or print a page, Publisher combines the Background pages and Foreground pages to complete the layout.

The following illustration shows the relationship between Background and Foreground pages. Think of the foreground as a transparent surface. The text and graphics that you place on the foreground float on the clear overlay. The text and graphics that you place on the background show through the clear overlay.

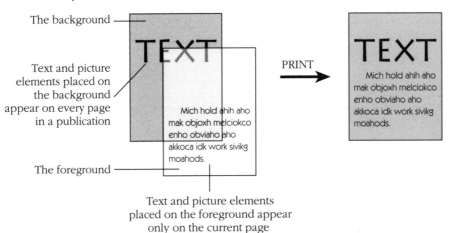

The background

Text and picture elements placed on the background appear on every page in a publication

The foreground

Text and picture elements placed on the foreground appear only on the current page

While the PageWizard works on a Background page, the Background Page icons replace the page controls in the lower left corner of the screen, as shown in the following illustration. In addition, the PageWizard dialog box comments on the fact that a Background page is being used.

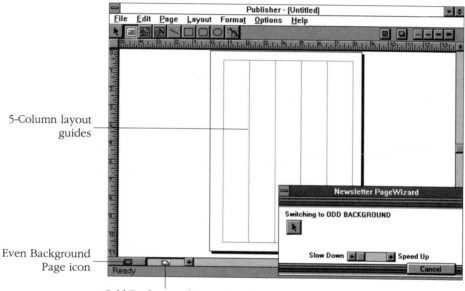

5-Column layout guides

Even Background Page icon

Odd Background Page icon

A final screen alerts you when the PageWizard has finished composing the newsletter. Click OK to complete the PageWizard.

Analyzing the Design

You have already explored the mechanics of creating a newsletter. In this section, you'll have an opportunity to analyze the newsletter with an eye toward a few basic design principles that apply to all newsletters.

Take a good look at your newsletter. You can get an on-screen preview of the printed page by using the Options menu to hide the layout guides and object boundaries. But remember to redisplay the layout guides and boundaries before proceeding with the exercises.

Although *The Epicurean* is a fairly simple newsletter, it contains a number of elements common to all newsletters. The PageWizard lets you choose whether or not to include certain elements, such as the volume number and the date. Other elements, like the logo and headlines, are so essential to newsletters that the PageWizard automatically includes them. The PageWizard inserted the following elements, which are shown in Figure 4-1 on the next page, when you created the newsletter:

Logo. The logo is the largest element on the first page. It identifies the newsletter and uses a distinctive typestyle to impart a unique personality to the publication.

Volume number, date, page number, and running head. It's important to include identifying information, such as volume number and page numbers, in your publication. Notice how this information is easy to find and yet is always tucked out of the way so that it doesn't distract readers from the main body of the text.

Rules. Rules separate and organize the page into distinct areas. The double rules on page 1 separate the logo and identifying information from the stories. On page 2, the same device separates the header and page number from the editorial copy. Vertical rules define columns of text, and horizontal rules highlight the beginning of each story.

Kickers. Kickers appear above each headline. They identify columns that appear in every issue or announce the topics of the stories that follow. Kickers allow readers to skim through long publications to find their favorite columnists or quickly identify story content.

Helping Hand: Saving the Publication

Nothing is more frustrating than losing hours of work because you failed to save your file while you worked on it. Though this reminder will appear only once, you should save your work frequently. Remember to use an appropriate filename, such as HERBS.PUB. For detailed instructions, see "Saving a Document" in Chapter 2.

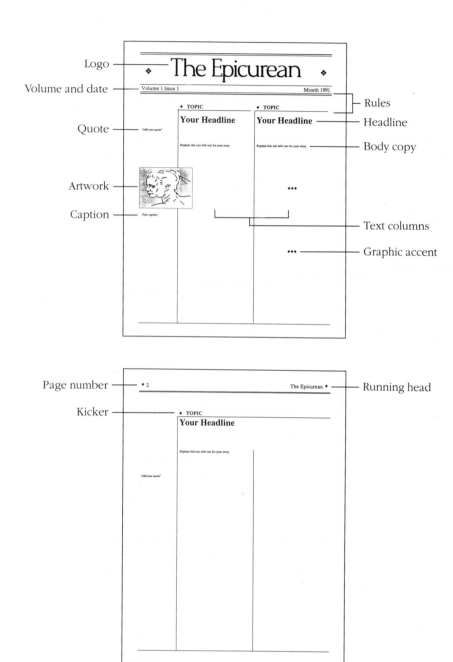

Figure 4-1.
The Epicurean *newsletter*.

Headlines. The headlines in the sample newsletter use a type size that doesn't overwhelm the narrow column width. The serif typeface works well with the Classic design scheme.

Body copy. Sample text for the body copy indicates the starting position of each text frame. When you analyze a design, it is often easier to think of body copy as a single large rectangular shape (indicated by the text frame) rather than as lines of text.

Artwork. Artwork should support the text in the newsletter. In *The Epicurean,* the picture energizes the design by slightly overlapping the text frame.

Quotes and captions. The quotes and captions are set in italics to add visual interest and texture to the page. But they are set in the same typeface as body copy. A good rule of thumb is to limit the number of typefaces in any publication to two. Use boldfacing, italics, and different point sizes for contrast.

Graphic accents. Never use graphic accents indiscriminately. Graphic accents should work with the newsletter's structure and content. The Newsletter PageWizard provides a graphic accent in the form of three linked diamonds. Later in this chapter, you will use this design element to visually separate paragraphs.

Helping Hand: Checking the Type Specifications

The typefaces in your document may not match the sample illustrations in this chapter. The PageWizard can use only the typefaces installed on your particular computer and printer. To find out which font the PageWizard used for a particular piece of text, click the text frame or highlight the text. The Toolbar displays the typeface, point size, and formatting options of the selected text.

For more information about fonts, see Appendix C, "Printing with Microsoft Publisher." For more information about Bitstream Facelift, see Appendix A, "Installing Microsoft Publisher."

Content Versus Design

Beginning desktop publishers often assume that text takes precedence over design — meaning that the design should change to accommodate the words. But to create a successful design, you must sometimes edit your copy to fit the format.

In the following exercises, you'll learn that superior newsletters result from a give-and-take relationship between design and content. So in addition to importing a picture, you will learn how to resize the image to make it work with the layout. And in addition to entering or importing text, you will edit the words to force a story to fit on the page. Finally, you'll learn how to modify the layout itself in order to accommodate important text or pictures.

Getting the Picture

When the PageWizard created the newsletter, it imported a piece of sample art. Now you need to replace the dummy illustration with one more suited to the contents of your newsletter.

Finding the right illustration for any publication is no easy task. To find appropriate clip art, you must often cast your net as widely as possible and then let the available images inspire you. For example, the premier issue of *The Epicurean* is about herbs and edible flowers. So the illustration you will see on the following pages shows a nasturtium — an edible flower for sale at Epicurean Delights. The picture is part of a commercially available clip-art library of floral images from Totem Graphics — proving that clip art is available on almost any subject.

Although the nasturtium picture isn't available to you in Microsoft Publisher, you can complete the exercises in this chapter by using the clip-art image of irises supplied with the program. So instead of edible nasturtiums, your newsletter will contain a picture of inedible irises.

 ***Hands On:***
Importing a Picture

1. Select the picture frame on page 1 of *The Epicurean*.

   You'll know that the picture frame is selected when eight handles appear around it.

2. Open the File menu and choose Import Picture.

   The Import Picture dialog box appears. You should feel comfortable with this dialog box because it is similar to other dialog boxes you've already used. The Drives and Directories list boxes allow you to search your hard disk, network, or floppy disks to locate the file you want to import.

3. If you are using the clip art supplied with Publisher, switch to the CLIPART directory to see the list of available picture files.

   Publisher can import graphics files in a variety of formats. The file format is identified by a three-letter extension at the end of the filename. For the moment you will import a file with a CGM (Computer Graphics Metafile) extension. All the clip-art files that come with Publisher are CGM files. Publisher also imports EPS, TIFF, WMF, BMP, and PCX files. For a more thorough discussion of graphics file formats, refer to Chapter 9, "Picture Perfect."

4. Highlight the name of the file you want to import. For example, FLWRIRIS.CGM in the CLIPART directory is a picture of irises.

5. Click the Preview button to take an advance look at the file. The Preview feature lets you look at the contents of the picture file before you import it into the newsletter. Preview is especially useful when you need to choose an image from a clip-art collection that contains unfamiliar filenames.

Helping Hand: Selecting Objects

If the Import Picture command appears grayed out (and therefore unavailable), you have not properly selected a picture frame. Publisher requires you to select an object before you perform an action on it.

Click outside the menu to close it, and then click the sample picture so the eight selection handles appear. Then choose the Import Picture command from the File menu again.

For more detailed instructions on selecting objects, see Chapter 2, "Microsoft Publisher Basics."

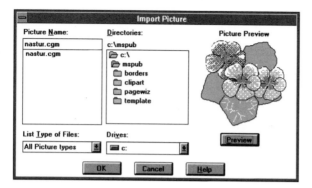

6. Click OK to import the artwork into the picture frame.

   The picture frame already contains an image, so Publisher displays
   a dialog box that asks whether you want to remove the existing picture and paste a new picture into the selected frame.

7. Click OK to delete the old picture and insert the new picture.

   Publisher assumes that you want the artwork to fit into the picture
   frame and will distort the picture slightly to make it fit. To correct
   this problem, you could grab one of the frame handles with the
   mouse and drag it to resize the picture by eye. Or you could use a
   menu command to return the selected picture to its original size
   and shape.

8. Make sure the nasturtium (or iris) picture is still selected, and then
   open the Format menu.

9. Choose the Scale Picture command. (Remember that the ellipsis following the command means a dialog box will appear.)

   If you click the Original Size check box in the Scale Picture dialog
   box, the artwork will return to its original size and shape. One
   word of warning about CGM files: in all likelihood, the original size
   will be too large for your publication.

   Instead of using the Original Size check box, you can use the Scale
   Height text box and the Scale Width text box to restore the original

proportions of the picture and, at the same time, scale it to the right size. If you enter the same values in both text boxes, the picture will not be distorted.

10. Type *25* in both the Scale Height and Scale Width text boxes, and then choose OK. This will scale the picture at 25 percent of its original size.

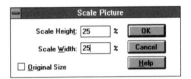

Entering Text

When the PageWizard created this newsletter, it inserted dummy text into all the text frames. You will now use two different methods to replace the dummy copy with real kickers and headlines.

When you work with small text blocks, such as headlines, kickers, and captions, the most efficient way to change the copy is simply to type it in. But for longer text blocks, as you'll learn later in this chapter, you can create the text in a word processor and then use the Import Text command to bring the word processing files into the publication.

 ### Hands On:
Typing Text

If you completed the exercises in Chapter 3, you should be an expert at entering text. Refer back to Chapter 3 if you need a refresher.

1. On page 1, select the text frame for the first kicker (below the volume and issue numbers) that contains the text "TOPIC."

2. Press F9 to toggle to Actual Size view (if you are not already in that view).

3. Highlight the dummy copy, and replace it with the following text, using all caps:

NEWS

Helping Hand: WordArt

When the PageWizard designs the headlines for your newsletter, it tries
to use one of the typefaces currently installed on your system. If your
system does not have a typeface that the PageWizard can scale to an
appropriate point size, the PageWizard will create the headline using
Publisher's WordArt tool.

To see if Publisher used text or WordArt to create your headlines, click a
headline to select the frame. If the Toolbar shows the font and point
size, your headlines are text. If you do not see this information, the headlines are WordArt.

If the PageWizard used WordArt to create your headlines, you must use
the WordArt tool to replace the sample headline text with your own
headline text. Here's how to do it:

1. Double-click the frame that contains the headline to invoke the
   WordArt dialog box.

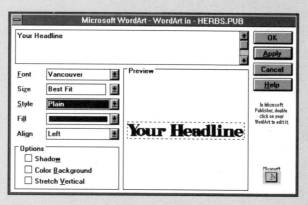

2. Type your headline in the text box at the top of the window.

3. For our example, leave all the settings as they are. Click OK to place
   the new headline in the newsletter.

For more information about using Publisher's WordArt, see Chapter 7,
"Designing with Type."

4. Select the text frame that contains the first headline. It is located immediately below the NEWS kicker that you just typed. Highlight the dummy headline text, and type the following text in its place:

   `An Herb for All Seasons` .

   You may want to press Enter after the word "for" to create lines of even length. If the PageWizard used WordArt to create your headlines, you must use the WordArt tool to change the text. (See the sidebar on page 111 for more information.)

5. Repeat step 3 to replace the date with *June 1992,* the kicker in the second column with *Trivia,* and the headline in the second column with *Of Gods, Men, and Herbs.*

6. Switch to page 2 of the newsletter by clicking the right arrow at the lower left corner of the screen.

7. On page 2, replace the kicker with the text *The Produce Department,* and the headline with *Herbs: Fresh from Our Store to Your Kitchen.*

You might discover that the headline doesn't fit into the text frame. To fix this problem, you must make the text frame larger.

8. Open the Options menu and make sure that Snap to Guides is activated. (A check mark appears if the snap mode is active.)

9. With the text frame selected, drag the center handle on the right until all the text appears.

   With Snap to Guides turned on, you should have no trouble aligning the text-frame boundary to the layout guide that separates the third and fourth columns of the underlying grid. Whenever you resize or reposition elements in your newsletter, use the underlying grid to maintain the integrity of the design.

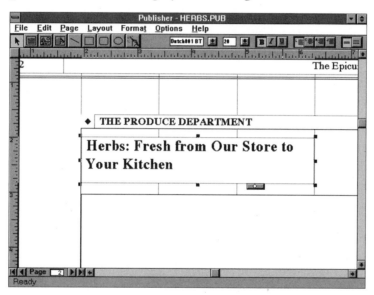

Resizing a Text Frame Versus Resizing Text

Whether you resize a text frame or a picture frame, you start by selecting the frame. Then you drag a handle to increase or decrease the size of the box. In both cases, you can hold down the Shift key while dragging the handle to maintain the proportion (or aspect ratio) of the box.

However, when you resize a picture frame, the image it contains changes size
to fit the new frame. In contrast, when you resize a text frame, the type it
contains does not change size. The type size and style assigned to the copy
determines the space it takes up in a text frame. Enlarging the text frame
merely allows you to fit more text into it. Shrinking a text frame reduces the
amount of text you can fit.

As you gain experience with Publisher, you will learn the different rules gov-
erning text and text frames. For now, keep in mind the following:

- To place text on a page in Publisher, you must either create or select a text
  frame first.

- To change the size and appearance of your type, you must assign a
  typestyle to the copy. Publisher lets you modify typeface, point size, and
  text attributes such as boldfacing and italics. You can also assign spacing
  attributes to text in order to control indents, line spacing, and column
  alignments.

- You can resize, reshape, and move text frames. You can also assign formatting options — including fill patterns, fancy borders, and drop-shadow effects to text frames.

Importing Text

Until now, you have typed short pieces of copy, such as headlines, directly
into the text frames. You will find, however, that it is more efficient to import
the body copy from a word processing program. As you work through the
various exercises in this book, you will discover that you can format your
text — with font, point size, and paragraph spacing — from within your
word processor. However, for this exercise you will create and import three
unformatted text files. If you want your text to match the samples in this chapter, create the files using the text shown in Figure 4-2 on the next page. Save
the first article as HERBS.WPS, the second as GODS.WPS, and the third as
PRODUCE.WPS.

The following exercises refer to Microsoft Works for Windows 2.0 as the
word processing program. Publisher can import text files from other word
processing programs, including Microsoft Word, WordPerfect, WordStar, and

The Epicurean

Volume 1 Issue 1   June 1992

◆ NEWS

An Herb for All Seasons

If you are like most people you have a kitchen shelf filled with spices you never use. The jars are open, but the contents have never been sampled. You probably have good excuses for your culinary mis-

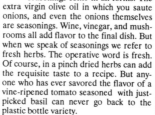

Nasturtium, see page 2.

conduct. Perhaps you bought Parsley, Sage, Rosemary, and Thyme for the poetry of it all, and then never had the time to research recipes. Or an unsuccessful foray into Chinese cooking convinced you never to use Star Anise again.

Whatever your past experiences, the time has come to rehabilitate your palate. The first step of course is to realize that seasonings come in all forms. The extra virgin olive oil in which you saute onions, and even the onions themselves are seasonings. Wine, vinegar, and mushrooms all add flavor to the final dish. But when we speak of seasonings we refer to fresh herbs. The operative word is fresh. Of course, in a pinch dried herbs can add the requisite taste to a recipe. But anyone who has ever savored the flavor of a vine-ripened tomato seasoned with just-picked basil can never go back to the plastic bottle variety.

Finding fresh herbs in the heart of Chicago is easier than it's ever been, if you are willing to live with a limited selection. Green grocers carry the basics like Parsley, Dill, and Basil. But when it comes to searching out the more unusual seasonings, such as Borage, Lovage or Fenugreek, consider Epicurean Delights your backyard herb garden.

◆ TRIVIA

Of Gods, Men, and Herbs

The history and myth of herbs is more than entertaining--it's downright instructive. These stories can help us to appreciate the role these small plants have played in society through the ages and around the world.

◆◆◆

For example, Bay leaf is a well known seasoning for bouquet garni in stews, soups, and sauces. But did you know that the very same leaf, Laurus nobilis, graced the head of Apollo's disciples in the form of a Laurel wreath? Apollo's priestess would ingest Bay leaves before reading the oracle of Delphi. Not surprisingly Bay, like other herbs, can have a narcotic, trance-inducing effect in large doses.

◆◆◆

Thyme was a standard addition to the bath water of Roman soldiers. The name itself, which is derived from the Greek *thymon*, means courage. One wonders if these ancient soldiers who conquered the world would have been as stalwart without the noble leaf.

◆◆◆

Skirret was originally cultivated by the Chinese for its flavorful root. Easy propagation made it a favorite of peasant vegetable gardens. Adventurous merchants who traded in the Orient brought the plant to Rome. In fact Skirret was so valuable it was accepted by the Emperor Tiberius as tribute.

Figure 4-2.
The final newsletter includes elements generated automatically by the PageWizard and modifications to the elements made by you.

Figure 4-2. *continued*

◆ THE PRODUCE DEPARTMENT

Herbs: Fresh from Our Store to Your Kitchen

Chicory

In Medieval times Chicory, or Cichorium intybus, was grown in floral clocks because it's bright blue flowers open at the same time everyday and close precisely five hours later.

You can add the young leaves, which are pleasantly bitter, to salads. In addition you can roast and grind the root to produce a totally natural coffee substitute. An infusion of the root, using water as the base, will produce a mildly diuretic tonic.

Fennel

Foeniculum vulgare has been cultivated for hundreds of years. Little wonder, since every part of the plant is edible; the bulb root, the spidery leaves, and the tiny seeds. You can use the seeds to flavor breads and sauces. The leaf and young stems are ideal seasonings for oily fishes and game meats, such as blue fish, venison, and wild hare.

In the United States bulb fennel, or Florentine fennel (Finnocchio) is increasingly popular as a salad. A celery-like texture, and a fresh licorice taste has made this root vegetable a favorite of today's nouvelle cuisine chefs.

Lemon balm

You may scoff at the idea of an herbal tea as a cure for melancholy. But Melissa officinalis, or Lemon balm is still used today in aroma therapy–an admittedly arcane branch of herbal medicine.

There are too many culinary uses of Lemon balm to list here. Suffice to say that almost anything can benefit from its bright lemony taste, including salads, fish sauces, mayonnaise, and jellies.

Nasturtium

Only in recent times has Nasturtium, or Tropaeolum minus, been considered a purely ornamental plant. Persians nibbled the nasturtium petals as early as 400 B.C. But today's open-minded cooks are rediscovering the slightly peppery taste that this edible flower can add to salads.

Smallage/Wild Celery

The Shakers introduced Smallage, or Apium graveolens, to the Americas. By doing so they carried this traditional herb, which enjoyed great favor in the ancient Greco-Roman world, to the new world.

The seed, when ground finely, can be used as a salt-substitute. Boiling the seeds instead makes a tea that is reputed to calm nervousness. Add the leaves to soups, curries, and pickles. The dried leaves of the Smallage plan have a stronger flavor than cultivated celery.

Sorrel

There are two varieties of Sorrel that each boast distinctively sharp tastes. We prefer French Sorrel, or Rumex acetosa, because it's milder flavor is better suited to classic dishes such as Sorrel Soup.

However, the Sorrel leaf can be cooked like spinach as long as you remember to change the cooking water once to reduce the acidity. Served as a vegetable Sorrel makes an especially fine accompaniment to beef.

Sorrel Soup
This variation of a classic soup is both low in fat and refreshingly tasty.

1 lb. sorrel
4 tbs. walnut oil
3 cups chicken broth
1 cup yogurt
salt and freshly ground pepper to taste

Wash the sorrel thoroughly and remove tough stems. Cut the leaves into thin strips. Heat the walnut oil in a deep saucepan. Saute the leaves for five minutes, or until just wilted. Add the chicken broth and simmer for five minutes over low heat.
Cool the soup, and then puree the mixture. Fold the yogurt into the soup mixture, and return to the refrigerator for at least an hour to allow the flavors to mellow. Garnish with a sorrel leaf and serve cold.

Windows Write. If you use a word processor not mentioned here, be sure to save the file in ASCII (plain text) format. Publisher can also import plain text files.

Hands On:
Importing Text

1. Click the left arrow near the page-number display at the bottom of the screen to return to page 1 of the newsletter.

2. Select the first text frame for body copy. Remember that you can't perform any action on a text frame, including importing text, unless you select the frame first.

3. Highlight the sample text, and then erase it by using the Del key. Press F9 to switch back to Full Page view.

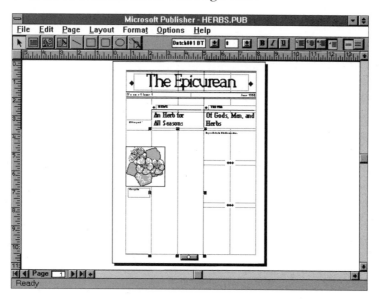

4. Open the File menu. Choose Import Text.

5. Use the Directories list box to switch to the directory containing the files you want to import.

6. Open the Type of Files list box, and select Works for Windows 2.0 (or the name of the word processing program you used).

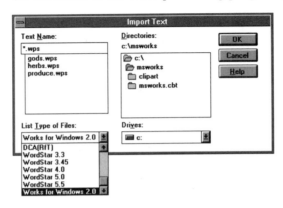

Helping Hand: Text-Frame Buttons

Publisher gives you clues about the status of the text in a text frame. A button that appears at the bottom of selected text frames indicates one of three conditions:

- If the button contains a diamond, all of the text is displayed.

- If the button contains an ellipsis, some of the text is not displayed and is temporarily stored as overflow.

- If the button contains three arrows, the text continues in another text frame.

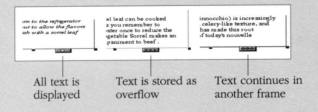

All text is displayed   Text is stored as overflow   Text continues in another frame

If you select Works for Windows 2.0, Publisher's import function automatically looks for files with a WPS extension. However, you can search through all your files by replacing the extension in the Text Name box with an asterisk (*).

7. The first file you will import is HERBS.WPS. Highlight the filename and click OK.

   Before Publisher imports the text, it displays a message box that tells you the text will not completely fit into the text frame. Publisher asks whether you want to autoflow the text. This function automatically flows the text that doesn't fit in the text frame into other text frames in the document.

8. Respond to the dialog box by choosing No so the text won't flow to any other text frames. (You will use autoflow in a later chapter.)

   Publisher imports the text file into the frame. The typestyle automatically reverts to 12-point Times Roman.

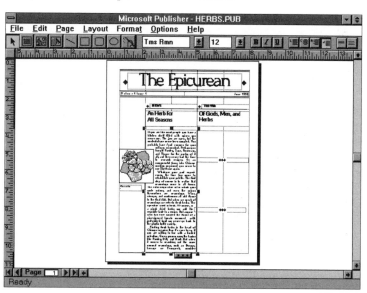

Notice that the copy automatically flows around the picture. Publisher always wraps text around picture frames and other text frames. In addition, the text frame hasn't changed in size, so some of the copy is not visible. Although you can't see the copy, it is still attached to this text frame. If you enlarge the text frame, you will reveal all the overflow copy.

To import the remaining two stories, repeat steps 2 through 7. Import the file GODS.WPS into the second text frame on page 1. Then import the file PRODUCE.WPS into the first text frame on page 2. Remember to select the proper text frame before you attempt to import the story.

Copy Fitting

In real life, text seldom fits perfectly into a frame on the first try. In the following simulation, you will learn to adjust both the text and the design to achieve a perfect fit. This process, called copy fitting, involves more art than science because there is usually no single easy fix — only trial and error.

In the following exercises, you'll employ four methods to fit your imported copy to the newsletter's layout: altering type specifications, modifying the layout, flowing copy to a second text frame, and editing the text.

 ### Hands On: ### Changing the Typestyle

1. Return to page 1 of the newsletter.

2. Select the text frame for the first story (HERBS.WPS). You should see eight handles surrounding the frame.

   You must highlight all the text in the text frame to change the type specification. However, at the moment you can't see (and therefore can't highlight) the text that overflows the frame. Fortunately, Publisher contains a menu command that can help.

3. Open the Edit menu and choose Highlight Story.

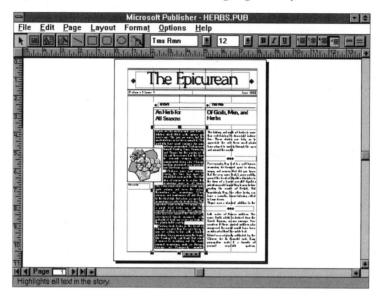

The story — including the hidden, overflow copy — is now highlighted.

4. Open the Format menu. Choose Character.

   The Character dialog box appears. The Toolbar offers many of the same commands that appear in the dialog box. However, to change several attributes at once, it is faster to use the dialog box.

5. In the dialog box, choose the Dutch typeface (or a similar serif font, such as Roman).

6. Enter *11* as the point size. (You'll need to type this in because it is not one of the preset choices.)

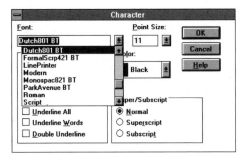

7. Click OK.

   When you return to the working screen, you will see that the story still doesn't fit into the frame. Don't jump back to the character dialog box to reduce the point size: you can make more subtle adjustments to copy-fit the text.

8. With the text still highlighted, open the Format menu and choose Indents and Spacing.

9. Change the First Line Indent to 0.17 inch. This starts each paragraph with an automatic indent.

10. In the text box for Space Between Lines, type *12 pt*. You can adjust the space between lines (also called leading) in 1-point increments. Leading plays an important role in document design because it affects both copy fitting and legibility.

    By changing the leading, you save 1 point (or $\frac{1}{72}$ of an inch) between each line of text. That may not sound like much, but the cumulative effect will be dramatic.

11. Choose Justified alignment.

    Justified text aligns along both the left and right margins. This alignment lets you fit more words on each line if you use it in conjunction with hyphenation.

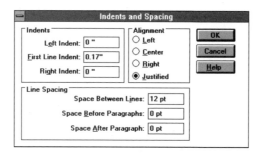

12. Click OK to return to the working screen.

13. Open the Options menu and select Hyphenate.

    If you check the confirm option in the Hyphenate dialog box, Publisher presents you with each possible hyphenation. Click Yes to accept the suggested hyphenation, or click No to leave the word unhyphenated.

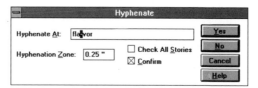

    The text now fits in the text frame because the text is set in a smaller size and because words have been hyphenated at the right margin. The text frame button changes from an ellipsis to a diamond, which means that there is no more overflow text.

    Next you'll repeat these steps to format the copy in the second text frame. You should be able to find all the dialog boxes you need by using the Format menu commands.

14. Use the Highlight Story command on the Edit menu to highlight all the text in the second text frame.

15. In the Character dialog box, choose 11-point Dutch (or another serif font, such as Roman).

16. In the Indents and Spacing dialog box, choose Justified text, a First Line Indent of 0.17 inch, and Line Spacing of 12 points.

Modifying the Layout

Turn your attention to page 2 of the newsletter. You've imported one story that fills the first column. You've also typed in a kicker and a headline. Next you will add a recipe that features one of the herbs in the newsletter.

Before you can insert a recipe, however, you must create a text frame for it or modify an existing text frame to make it work with the design. When the PageWizard created the newsletter it inserted a piece of display text for a pull quote at the far left side of the page. Although this text block is too small to contain an entire recipe, you can easily enlarge it to accommodate the text. You can also move it so that it mimics the position of the picture frame on page 1.

Remember that PageWizards create wonderful preliminary designs, but sometimes the designs need alteration to accommodate your content. The modifications you'll make to this text block will transform the quote into a sidebar. A pull quote is often picked from the actual story to pique a reader's interest. In contrast, sidebars focus the reader's attention on ancillary information without disrupting the flow of the main story.

Hands On:
Resizing and Repositioning Text Frames

1. Select the text frame containing the quote on the far left side of the page.

2. Resize the text frame by dragging the handles so that it measures 2 ½ inches wide by 3 ¾ inches deep.

3. Position the text frame so that it overlaps the adjacent text frame containing the main story by 1 inch.

4. Press F9 to switch to Actual Size. Highlight the sample text and use the drop-down list box on the Toolbar to change the point size to 10.

5. Type the following:

```
Sorrel Soup

This variation on a classic soup is both low in fat and
refreshingly tasty.

1 lb. sorrel

4 tbs. walnut oil

3 cups chicken broth

1 cup yogurt

salt and freshly ground pepper to taste

Wash the sorrel thoroughly and remove tough stems. Cut the
leaves into thin strips. Heat the walnut oil in a deep sauce-
pan. Saute the leaves for five minutes, or until just wilted.
Add the chicken broth and simmer the soup for five minutes over
low heat.

Cool the soup, and then puree the mixture. Fold the yogurt into
the soup mixture, and return it to the refrigerator for at
least an hour to allow the flavors to mellow. Garnish with a
sorrel leaf and serve cold.
```

Notice that the text took on the same typeface and formatting attributes as the highlighted copy, even though the highlighted copy was deleted. The sidebar is almost complete, but there is a minor problem. When you deselect the text frame, you will see a rule passing through the text. You can hide the rule and complete the sidebar by changing the stacking order of the objects on screen.

Publisher layers the objects on the screen. Currently, the rule is layered on top of the text box for the sidebar. You can complete the sidebar by changing the stacking order of the objects to conceal the rule underneath the sidebar box.

6. Be sure that the sidebar is still selected. Open the Layout menu and choose Bring to Front.

The sidebar text frame moves to the top of the stack, hiding the rule.

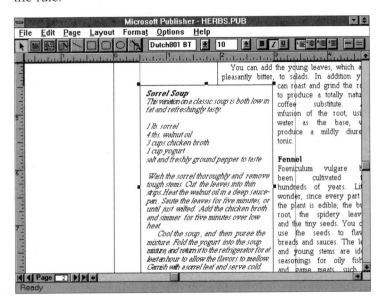

You can separate the sidebar text from the rest of the page by placing a rule around the text frame. Instead of drawing four individual rules or using the Rectangle tool to draw a box around the frame, you can assign a border rule to the text frame itself. In this way, if you resize òr move the text frame, the rules also resize or move because they are a part of the frame.

7. Be sure the text frame is still selected. Open the Layout menu and choose Border. (Be sure you choose Border and not BorderArt.)

8. When the dialog box appears, be sure that Select All Sides is checked. This command applies the same border to all four sides of the text frame.

9. Highlight the 1-point rule, leave the color Black, and click OK.

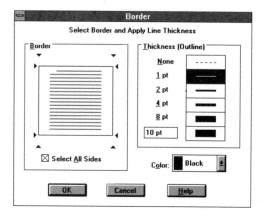

The sidebar is now complete. It mimics the layout on page 1 and lets you include a recipe in the newsletter without infringing too much on the other text frames on page 2.

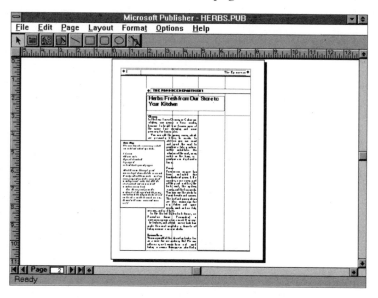

Linking Text Frames

You have not yet formatted the most important story on page 2 — the one that describes the herbs for sale in the produce department. Now you will adjust the typestyle used for the story so that it matches the typestyle used on the first page.

Hands On:
Formatting Text

1. Select the text frame.

2. In the Edit menu, choose Highlight Story.

3. Choose the Character command from the Format menu. In the dialog box, change the typestyle to 11-point Dutch (or other serif font to match the font used on page 1).

4. Choose the Indents and Spacing command from the Format menu. In the dialog box, change the paragraph style to Justified, and set 12 points of spacing between lines.

   On page 1, you used an indent of ⅙ inch to start each paragraph. In this story, you don't need to indent every paragraph. The first paragraph after a head should align flush left. By using a tab instead of a global first-line indent, you can indent only those paragraphs that need indentation. To create the same indent throughout the publication, you'll set the tab at the same measurement as you did for the paragraph indent on page 1 — 0.17 inch.

5. Choose Tabs from the Format menu. In the dialog box, type *0.17* in the text-entry box to set your tab. Click Set. Remember to click OK when you finish.

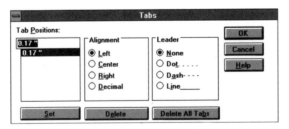

You have modified your typestyle and spacing, but the current frame still accommodates only half of the text. To fit the remaining text, you can flow the copy into another column by linking two text frames together. Linking text frames lets you control the way the stories flow in your publications. You can link frames that are adjacent to each other on the same page, as you do here. Or you can link frames on different pages, jumping stories from one page to another the way professional newspapers and magazines do.

Hands On:
Linking Text Frames

1. Be sure the first text frame is still selected and that handles appear around the text-frame boundary. Remember that when text overflows the frame, Publisher displays an ellipsis in the text-frame button.

2. To view the text frame button more clearly, move the I-beam near the bottom of the frame. Press the F9 key to switch to Actual Size view.

3. You can now easily locate the text-frame button. Click it.

   The pointer turns into a cup overflowing with text.

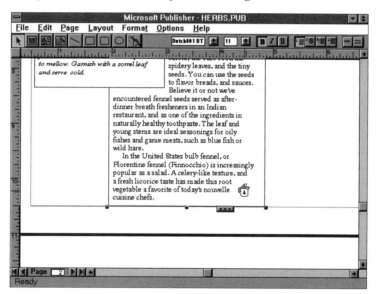

4. Toggle back to Full Page view by pressing F9 again.

5. Move the cup pointer to the empty text frame.

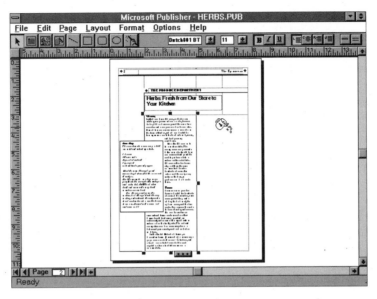

Notice how the pointer changes. The cup tips, letting you know that if you click this text frame, the copy will flow into the frame.

6. Click within the text frame.

The text flows from column 1 into column 2.

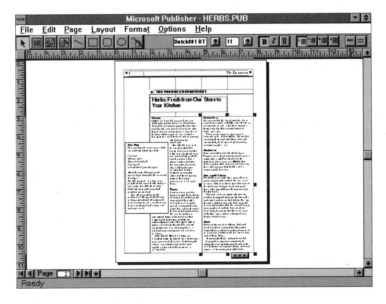

But, as the text button indicates, column 2 still has overflow material. (The final newsletter in Figure 4-2 had already been edited, so if you copied the text from that figure, your column 2 will not have overflow material. Follow the next example, however, to learn about copy fitting.)

Hands On:
Editing Text

As you have learned, you can sometimes copy-fit text by modifying your typestyle. You can also flow extra copy across text frames. But sometimes, you also need to edit your text to make it fit your design.

1. Place the I-beam at the bottom of the second column. Press F9 to toggle to Actual Size view.

2. Place the pointer over the middle handle at the bottom of the frame. You can now use the resize pointer to pull the frame down to reveal the extra text, which is only two lines long. Read the copy in the frame, and identify two lines that you can cut.

   You can easily cut the highlighted text shown in the following illustration without altering the meaning of the sentence.

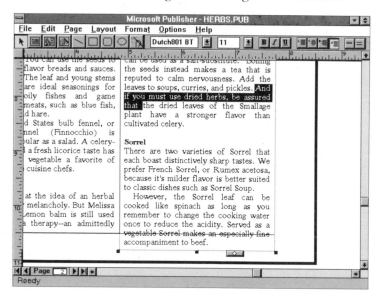

3. Highlight the text to cut, and press the Del key. Add a capital letter to the new beginning of the sentence.

4. Resize the text frame box so that the bottom rests just above the rule at the bottom of the page.

Fine-Tuning the Publication

Before you print *The Epicurean,* scrutinize it carefully. You'll find some surprises. Although the publication is almost complete, you still must tie up some loose ends.

For example, although you had the foresight to set up a tab indent for the story on page 2, you haven't inserted the tabs. Also, to add impact you might want to boldface the name of each herb in the running copy.

Hands On:
Fine-Tuning the Design

1. Zoom in to the first entry in the main story. Remember to move the I-beam to the top of the text frame. Press F9.

2. Highlight the word *Chicory.*

3. Click the B icon on the Toolbar to make the highlighted text bold.

4. Move the insertion point to the beginning of the second paragraph ("You can add the . . .").

5. Press the Tab key to insert an indent of ⅙ inch.

   Complete page 2 by adding tabs where needed and boldfacing the subheads throughout the story.

   Now give page 1 some careful attention.

6. Return to page 1 by clicking the left arrow near the page-number display at the bottom of the screen.

   When you worked on page 1 before, you didn't write a caption for the artwork. The PageWizard also created a text frame for a quote, which you don't need.

7. Select the text frame for the caption.

8. Highlight the dummy text and type

   `Nasturtium, see page 2.`

   The caption appears in 8-point Dutch italic typestyle (or similar font).

9. To delete the extra text frame for the dummy quote, select the text frame.

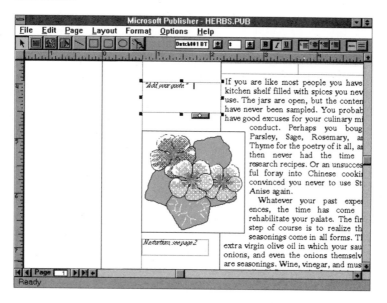

10. In the Edit menu, choose Delete Text Frame.

    The text frame and the text within it disappears. (The Cut Text Frame command moves the text frame to the Clipboard, but the Delete Text Frame command cuts the entire frame without saving it in the Clipboard.) You can also delete a text frame by using the keyboard shortcut Ctrl-Del. (Pressing Del by itself merely erases one letter of text within the text frame.)

    On page 1, notice that the story "Of Gods, Men, and Herbs" consists of short, self-contained anecdotes. In addition, this part of the page contains elements that function as graphic accents (the three diamonds).

In the next step, you'll use the graphic accents to separate paragraphs. In this way, the graphic accents can serve both a design and an editorial function.

A close examination of the graphic accent reveals that it is not a single object but is actually composed of a blank rectangle and a small picture (three diamonds). You'll want to move both objects at once, so you will select the two objects as a group.

11. Draw a selection box around the items you want to move. To do so, place the pointer on a free area of the page (try the right margin area). Drag the pointer downward and to the left to create a box around the two items.

The selection box includes only those elements it surrounds completely. Be sure that the selection box completely encompasses the rectangle and the three diamonds. Don't worry if your selection box slightly overlaps a text frame. Unless you completely surround the text frame, it will not be part of the selection group.

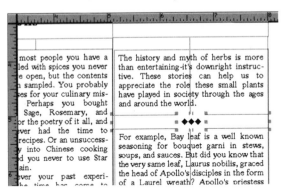

Now that you have selected both objects, you can copy, paste, and move them together in the same way you would move a single object.

12. When you position the pointer over the group, it turns into the move pointer. Now you can drag the objects to a new location. Place the objects between the first and second paragraphs.

It may take a little practice to get the copy to break at exactly the right point. Publisher leaves a margin around the graphic elements. As a result, the amount of text that is displaced is larger than the size of the frame. Experiment with positioning. Each time you move the graphic element, Publisher shows you exactly how the text will flow.

13. Repeat steps 11 and 12 to select the other graphic accent and move it between the second and third paragraphs.

14. With the two elements still selected as a group, open the Edit menu and choose Copy Object(s). As you learned in Chapter 1, the Copy command places a duplicate of the selected elements in the Clipboard.

15. Use the scroll bars to move to the last two paragraphs.

16. From the Edit menu, choose Paste Object(s) to insert the copy of the graphic elements residing in the Clipboard back into Publisher. Then position the grouped objects between the two paragraphs.

    The graphic elements now serve an editorial purpose. They separate individual entries in this running copy.

The final newsletter illustrates how well you've learned to manipulate both PageWizards and Publisher. You've not only used the PageWizard to create a preliminary document, but you've used the program's formatting options and design tools to modify the design to fit your needs.

Hands On: Ending the Work Session

You can now save and print the newsletter.

1. Open the File menu. Choose Save. Publisher updates the HERBS.PUB file you saved earlier in this chapter.

2. Open the File menu and choose Print.

3. Accept the defaults and click OK.

    Publisher prints the publication to the default printer.

What's Next?

In this chapter, you created a complex document. Although the PageWizard did most of the preliminary work, you learned that a successful publication requires your attention and creativity. You imported picture and text files, assigned typestyles, and modified the layout. Hopefully, you also learned newsletter design principles that will help you to create your own PageWizard newsletters.

Section II takes you in a different direction. You will begin to design projects from scratch, although PageWizard technology will always be available from the Toolbar. Each chapter, and its associated project, focuses on specific Microsoft Publisher design tools. The next chapter, for example, deals extensively with Publisher's layout tools.

Section II

DO-IT-YOURSELF DESIGN

Chapter 5

PLANNING A PUBLICATION

In the previous chapters, you used PageWizards to produce two documents for Epicurean Delights — a customized business form and a two-page newsletter. The staff at Epicurean Delights was so impressed with the results that they all jumped on the PageWizard bandwagon. Now they use PageWizards for a wide variety of purposes — to produce invitations to catered events, to design calendars outlining the cooking class schedule, and even to make paper airplanes for the fun of it.

Elizabeth Jarmen, the owner of the store, was especially happy with the newsletter because it successfully enticed customers to try the fresh herbs for sale in the Produce Department. She discovered that pictures especially help sales. Many people bought nasturtium blossoms because they were intrigued by the illustration in the newsletter. In fact, the newsletter created such a demand for edible flowers that Elizabeth has embarked on a new mail-order venture with her local grower. Epicurean Delights will now ship edible flowers as refrigerated produce, in seed form for gourmet gardeners, and as blooming potted plants to customers throughout the United States. So she needs a mail-order catalog.

Although Elizabeth uses PageWizard technology almost every day, it won't help her for this project because Microsoft Publisher doesn't provide a Page-Wizard that produces catalogs. A quick check of the TEMPLATE directory reveals that, although Publisher offers ready-made designs for both a catalog and a price list, neither design meets Elizabeth's needs. Elizabeth wants to produce a small, elegant mailing piece of no more than 8 or 12 pages that will fit (along with other literature about the store) into a standard letter-sized envelope. To accomplish this goal, she will have to begin the design process from scratch.

In this chapter, you will produce an effective, low-cost mail-order catalog for Epicurean Delight's edible flowers. You will learn that designing this catalog includes determining the page size, choosing the typeface, and positioning pictures — all without help from Publisher's PageWizard technology and without using a template design. In the process, you will get hands-on experience working with Publisher's page borders, layout guides, and frame attributes.

To produce this catalog, you will employ Publisher's background page and take advantage of the program's ability to generate additional pages with text and picture frames in place.

Planning Ahead

When planning a publication, you need to think ahead and consider all the factors that affect your design options. As you will discover, the layout process entails more than simply drawing text and picture frames on a page. You must plan your design to accommodate factors such as the size of your mailing envelope and the weight of your paper stock, both of which can dramatically affect costs.

For example, if you want to produce a self-mailer, you'll need to use heavy cover stock to protect the contents of the catalog or magazine. And your design must also accommodate a mailing label and postage. If you decide to mail your publication in an envelope, visit a stationery store and jot down the sizes of standard envelopes. Ordering custom envelopes for an oddly sized publication can be very expensive.

Elizabeth Jarmen has already decided to send out her catalogs in standard, number 10 business envelopes, which measure 9 ½ inches by 4 ⅛ inches. Ideally, her publication should be slightly smaller so she can easily slip it into the envelopes.

Another physical factor that must be considered is the paper size: Microsoft Publisher distinguishes between the paper's measurements and the final trimmed size of your publication. Obviously, you can make your pages smaller than standard 8 ½-inch by 11-inch sheets of paper. In fact, Publisher can automatically add crop marks to the corners of the printout to help you know where to trim the excess paper. However, Publisher will not allow you to specify a page size larger than your paper size.

In the following exercise, you'll choose a paper size and orientation. You'll also specify a trim size for your publication pages.

Hands On:
Paper Size Versus Page Size

1. Open Windows and click the Publisher icon.

2. Click the Blank Page button in the Start Up dialog box.

3. Click OK to move to Publisher's work area.

   The standard 8 ½-inch by 11-inch page appears on the screen. Before you change the page size, check the paper size. Keep in mind that the currently installed printer limits your paper-size options. To check paper-size options, you must open the Print Setup dialog box.

4. Open the File menu and choose Print Setup.

   The Print Setup dialog box lets you choose a specific printer for each publication. In the illustration on the next page, you can see that, although Windows was set up to use a PostScript printer as the default printer, this publication will be designed for the HP LaserJet instead. A drop-down list box tells you which paper sizes you can use with the currently selected printer.

Helping Hand: The Work Area

If you want your own screen to match the illustrations in this chapter, set up your work area as follows by using commands from the Options menu:

- Turn on Snap to Guides.

- Show Object boundaries.

- Configure the Settings dialog box to use inches as the unit of measure, to display Publisher's Helpful Pointers, and to have typing replace the selection. (See Chapter 2, "Microsoft Publisher Basics," and Chapter 3, "Desktop Publishing Wizardry," for more information about these menu items.)

5. In the Print Setup dialog box, choose the printer you will be using, Portrait orientation, and Letter 8 ½ x 11 inch paper.

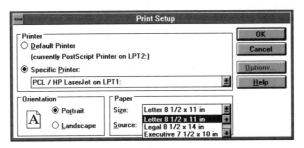

6. Click OK to return to the working screen.

   Publisher assumes that if your paper size is 8 ½ inches by 11 inches, your page size will also be 8 ½ inches by 11 inches. To change this, you must access the Page Setup dialog box.

7. Open the Page menu and choose Page Setup.

   The Page Setup dialog box allows you to specify the page size that you want by typing measurements into the appropriate text boxes. The dialog box also offers layout options for standard formats such as business cards and greeting cards.

   The Layout Option selections automatically choose the correct page size for you and, in some cases, affect the way that your publication prints. For example, if you choose Side-Fold Greeting Card, Publisher prints four pages on a single sheet of paper, and two of the pages print upside down. This "imposition," which is the technical word for the arrangement of several pages on a larger sheet of paper, ensures that the four pages of the greeting card appear right side up and in the correct order when you fold the sheet to make your card.

   To create the Epicurean Delights mail-order catalog, you'll use the Book layout option.

8. In the Layout Option section, select Book.

   Notice how the Preview section at the right now displays two pages on a single sheet of paper. Publisher assumes that you want to use the whole sheet, so it made the page size 4 ¼ inches by 11 inches. Unfortunately, this size won't fit into our 9 ½-inch by 4 ⅛-inch envelope. The following instructions will help you set up a workable page size.

9. Press the Tab key to move to the Page Size Width text box. Type *3.5*.

   Don't worry about indicating the unit of measure. Publisher assumes you mean inches.

10. Press Tab to move to the Page Size Height text box. Type *8.5*. Press Tab again.

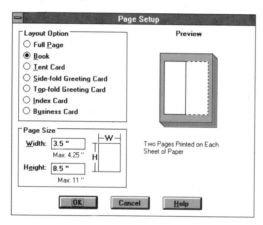

Notice how the preview changes. The gray area now indicates the part of the page you must trim away in order to achieve your specified page size.

The current layout offers several advantages:

☐ Once folded, a catalog measuring 3.5 inches by 8.5 inches will easily fit into a number 10 (letter-sized) envelope.

☐ The Book layout prints two pages on each sheet of paper in a way that will let you easily assemble the catalog.

☐ The page size you designated gives Publisher enough room to include crop marks in the unused area around the page.

11. Click OK to return to the work area.

Creating Consistency Among Pages

Good designers know that visual variety works only when supported by a consistent underlying structure. In longer documents, you can repeat elements on each page to provide visual consistency. The following list describes the design elements that are commonly used to create a consistent layout:

- Margins establish page boundaries that you should not violate.

- Headers clearly identify the publication. In this case, the header contains the name of the store.

- Footers usually contain a page number (or folio) to help readers locate information easily. Footers can also provide volume or date information.

- Kickers, or category headings, help divide long publications into manageable sections. In this catalog, a kicker separates the section on edible flowers from the sections on gardening and cookbooks.

Many beginning designers, eager to start working with text and pictures, ignore these unifying elements when they begin a publication. In the following exercise, you will avoid this common pitfall by using Microsoft Publisher's Layout menu and Page menu to develop an underlying design structure. The unifying elements will include page borders, headers, kickers, and footers and will repeat on all the pages in your publication. Let's start by creating consistent page borders.

Hands On:
Layout Guides

1. Open the Layout menu and choose Layout Guides.

   The Layout Guides dialog box appears. This dialog box lets you customize your pages in a number of ways. You can set up nonprinting layout guides for columns and rows or mirror your design to create left-hand and right-hand pages. You will return to this dialog box several times while creating your sample catalog. For the moment, let's concentrate on the page margin settings.

As the preview shows, there isn't much room on the page to place text or pictures because Publisher uses a default margin of 1 inch on all four sides of the page.

If you reduce the 1-inch default margin, you will see how page margins function as a structural element within the design.

2. Highlight the measurement for the left margin (using either the mouse or the Tab key). Type a new measurement of *0.25.*

3. Repeat for the right, top, and bottom settings.

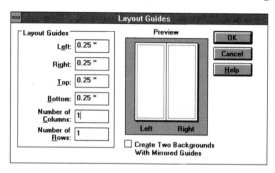

As you proceed through each text box, notice how the preview changes to reflect the new margin settings.

4. Click OK to return to the work area.

When you return to the screen, you'll see the new, narrower margins, which appear as dotted red lines. Margins have both an aesthetic and a practical purpose. Aesthetically, the margin creates white space that makes the page easier to read; practically, the page margin provides a safety area so that when you trim the final printed page, you won't accidentally cut away any of the copy or pictures.

Working in the Background

In Chapter 4, you saw that Publisher can overlay Background and Foreground pages. The elements placed on the background automatically appear on each page. Because the header and footer information will appear on almost every page of your document, it makes sense to place these elements on the Background page.

Hands On:
Placing Objects on the Background

1. Open the Page Menu and choose Go to Background.

   As you gain experience with Publisher, you'll switch between the Background and Foreground pages without a second thought. You can use the keyboard shortcut Ctrl-M to quickly alternate between the two pages.

   At the moment, you might be a little confused because the Background page looks identical to the Foreground page: empty. However, look carefully at the lower left corner of the screen. Publisher identifies this as the Background page by replacing the page number display with an icon that represents the background.

   You work with Background pages in the same way you work with Foreground pages. You must draw text frames to add text to the page, and you must draw picture frames to add artwork.

2. Click the Text Frame tool to activate it.

3. Bring the crossbar pointer to the page area and drag the mouse to draw a text frame along the top of the page. The edges of the frame should abut the top and side page margins. The text frame should measure 3 inches wide by ¾ inch deep.

   If you turned on Snap to Guides in the beginning of this chapter, you should feel the pointer snap to the margin guidelines as you draw the text frame. Using Snap to Guides in conjunction with nonprinting layout guides lets you work with precision, even in Full Page view.

4. With the text frame still selected, press F9 to switch to Actual Size view.

   Now that you have a close-up view of the text frame, you could plunge in and type some copy. But first change the default typestyle, which is currently 10-point Times Roman.

5. Use the Toolbar options to assign the following typestyle to the selected text frame: 12-point Dutch (or some other serif typeface, like Palatino), center-aligned.

6. Choose Indents and Spacing from the Format menu to change the space between lines of text (leading) to 20 points. Be sure that you type the new line-spacing measurement, exactly as it appears here, in the Space Between Lines text box. If you omit the "pt" — which designates points — Publisher will add 20 lines of space.

   `20 pt`

   Choose OK.

7. Now type the following text. (Remember to press Enter after typing the first line.)

   `Epicurean Delights`

   `Edible Flowers`

   You could have created the same effect by drawing two smaller text frames — one for each line of text — and then manually centering them. However, it is much more efficient to create a text frame that aligns automatically to the page margins and then use Publisher's formatting to center the text perfectly.

   To ensure that the reader sees these two items as separate text phrases, you will draw a rule between them. And to add just the slightest bit of visual interest to the header, you will increase the line weight from the default 1-point width.

Helping Hand: Creating Regular Shapes

You can use the Shift key in conjunction with Publisher's drawing tools to create regular geometric shapes. For example, if you hold down the Shift key while you create a rule, it will be constrained to form a perfect horizontal or vertical line. Likewise, if you hold down the Shift key while you draw a rectangle, it will be constrained to form a square. And if you hold down the Shift key while you draw an oval, it will be constrained to form a circle.

8. Click the Line tool on the Toolbar.

9. Set the starting point by bringing the crossbar pointer to the left side of the text frame and centering it vertically between the two lines of text. Then hold down the Shift key while you drag the crossbar until it aligns with the right side of the text frame.

10. With the rule selected, change the line width by selecting the button on the Toolbar that displays the icon of a 2-point rule. (It's the third from the right.)

Your header is now complete.

Now let's complete the Background page by creating the footer.

11. Using the scroll box, move to the bottom of the page.

Although all the copy in the footer will appear to be on one line, you must create two different text frames because one phrase will align on the right, and the other will align on the left.

12. Click the Text Frame icon on the Toolbar.

13. Bring the crossbar pointer to the lower right corner of the page, and draw a box that measures ¾ inch wide by ⅜ inch deep.

14. With the text frame selected, use the Toolbar options to change the typestyle to 8-point Dutch. Set the alignment to right-aligned.

15. Type *Page*. Be sure to type one space after the *e*.

You don't need to manually type a page number on each Foreground page because Publisher has an automatic page-numbering command. Be sure that the pointer still appears after the word *Page*.

16. Open the Page menu and choose Insert Page Numbers.

    A small number sign (#) appears on the Background page. Publisher will automatically replace this symbol with the correct page number on each page in your document.

    Now create a text frame for the date of the publication. Rather than repeating steps 12 through 15, you can duplicate the text frame that you just created, replace the copy, and change one formatting attribute.

17. With the text frame containing the page number still selected, open the Edit menu, and choose Copy Text Frame.

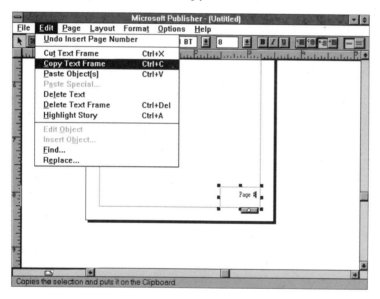

18. Open the Edit menu once more and choose Paste Object(s).

    Publisher places a copy of the text frame and the text it contains in the center of the screen.

19. Move the copy of the text frame to the lower left corner.

20. With the new text frame selected, change the alignment from right to left by clicking the left-alignment icon on the Toolbar.

21. Highlight the copy and replace it by typing *Spring 1992*.

22. Finally, draw a 2-point rule above the text at the 7 ⅞ -inch mark on the vertical ruler. The rule should span the page from border to border. Remember that you can change the line width by using the icons on the Toolbar and you can constrain the line to be horizontal by holding down the Shift key.

If you look through any magazine or book, you'll notice that page numbers are usually positioned on the outside borders to make them easier to find. Right-hand page numbers appear on the right, and left-hand page numbers appear on the left. An option in the Layout Guides dialog box lets you achieve this effect by creating mirrored Background pages. The following exercise will show you how Publisher's mirrored backgrounds work.

Hands On:
Creating Mirrored Backgrounds

1. Press F9 to zoom out and view the entire page.

2. Open the Layout menu and choose Layout Guides.

   You used this dialog box previously to set up page margins, so it should look familiar to you.

3. To create mirrored guides, click the Create Two Backgrounds with Mirrored Guides check box located under Preview.

   Notice that the layout guide labels change from Left and Right to Inside and Outside — the appropriate labels for mirrored guides.

4. Click OK.

   When you return to the background screen, you'll see two Background Page icons — one left, and one right.

5. Move to the left Background page by clicking the icon on the left.

   The left Background page contains the same elements as the right Background page except that the text frames for the page number and date are reversed. Although Publisher created a mirror image of the right background, it didn't change the text formatting instructions. Notice that the page number is still right-aligned even though it is located on the left-page border, and the date information is incorrectly left-aligned, so you need to make corrections.

6. Select the text frame containing the page-number marker. Click the left-alignment icon on the Toolbar.

7. Select the text frame containing the date. Click the right-alignment icon on the Toolbar.

As this exercise has demonstrated, to use the Mirrored Guides option effectively you must first position your objects on the Background page. If you had invoked the Mirrored Guides option before drawing your text frames, Publisher could not have copied any objects to the left-hand page. It isn't enough to know which command to use; you must also know when to use it.

Knowing *when* to use a command is also important when you design Foreground pages. For example, once you develop a layout for a single page, you can automatically duplicate the same arrangement of text and picture frames on new pages as you add them to your publication.

In the following section, you will concentrate on the first page of the catalog. After you finalize the layout, you will add a few new pages to your publication, using the first page as a model.

The Design Process

Designing a publication is rarely a logical, linear process. Even professional art directors must revise and fine-tune their layout. Fortunately, Microsoft Publisher makes it easy for you to modify your layouts, which lets you experiment with different design solutions.

Before you begin a design, make a list of the elements that should appear in the publication. For example, each page of your sample catalog will include a text block describing the featured flower; a picture of the flower; and ordering information, including an item number and a price.

Beginning designers often have trouble arranging layouts because they focus on concrete objects rather than abstract shapes. They think of an illustration as a picture of a flower rather than as another rectangle on the page. You might find it easier to begin your design using geometric shapes filled with different tints and patterns rather than actual text and pictures.

Take a look at Figure 5-1, which presents a very rough version of the sample layout. Notice how the shapes and differing gray densities create a pattern for your eyes to follow. Text and pictures work in exactly the same way. The darkest rectangle represents a picture, the large light gray rectangle represents a text frame. And the striped rectangle at the bottom of the page mimics the pattern created by the price-list information. Forget that text blocks consist of words. Forget that picture frames contain images. Start to see these elements as shapes and patterns.

The small page size of your sample publication restricts the layout to a single column of text. But when you design your own publications, you can create a series of sketches using different column widths and arrangements. The tinted

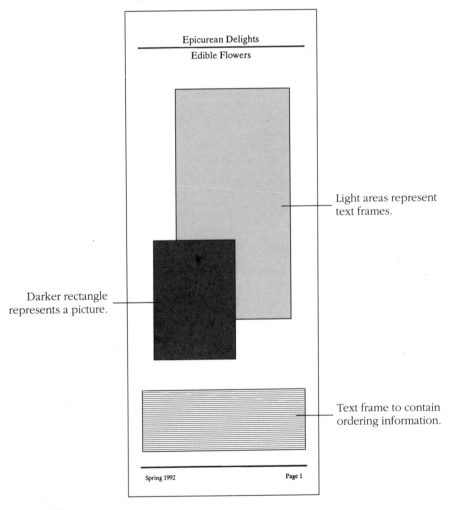

Figure 5-1.
The beginning design process.

rectangles really do approximate the relationship of text to graphics. To prove it, take a look at Figure 5-2 on the next page, which shows the same arrangement of elements using type and a real illustration.

This is an acceptable design, but it does have one major flaw: the illustration is the only area of visual interest. You can create a sense of balance by introducing a design element for each of the two text blocks.

In the final design, shown in Figure 5-3 on page 155, the primary text block is emphasized not by a large heading — which would compete with the illustration — but by a fancy first letter (also called a drop cap) created using a PageWizard. A header, filled with a light gray tint, adds some needed weight to the price information.

Publisher lets you quickly and easily modify your layouts so that you get past the trial-and-error stage and reach success speedily. With Publisher, it isn't necessary to know beforehand that a fancy first letter would be a better device than a headline. You can easily try both options and compare them.

Using the Layout Tools

In the following exercises, you will duplicate the layout shown in Figure 5-3. You will *not* produce a final catalog — your sample document will contain only four pages. You won't worry about including a response coupon or an order form, but you will learn how to use Publisher's powerful layout tools to create a publication with several pages.

You have already opened the Layout Guides dialog box twice — to set page margins and then to create mirrored guides. In the next exercise, you will use the same dialog box to set up nonprinting column guides.

Publisher lets you display guides for up to 256 columns and 256 rows. If you have a color monitor, you'll notice that layout guides appear on screen as light blue lines. Although layout guides appear on screen and can be used to align objects, they never print on the page.

You can increase the power of Publisher's layout guides by working in Snap to Guides mode. As you draw or move objects, the pointer literally jumps to align with a guide. When you use guides in this way, you can work with great precision, even without using rulers.

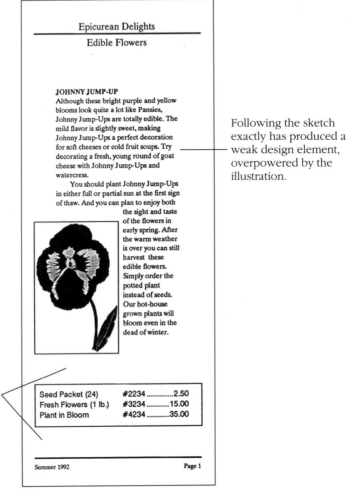

Epicurean Delights

Edible Flowers

JOHNNY JUMP-UP
Although these bright purple and yellow
blooms look quite a lot like Pansies,
Johnny Jump-Ups are totally edible. The
mild flavor is slightly sweet, making
Johnny Jump-Ups a perfect decoration
for soft cheeses or cold fruit soups. Try
decorating a fresh, young round of goat
cheese with Johnny Jump-Ups and
watercress.
    You should plant Johnny Jump-Ups
in either full or partial sun at the first sign
of thaw. And you can plan to enjoy both
                          the sight and taste
                          of the flowers in
                          early spring. After
                          the warm weather
                          is over you can still
                          harvest these
                          edible flowers.
                          Simply order the
                          potted plant
                          instead of seeds.
                          Our hot-house
                          grown plants will
                          bloom even in the
                          dead of winter.

Seed Packet (24)   #2234 ....2.50
Fresh Flowers (1 lb.) #3234 ....15.00
Plant in Bloom   #4234 ....35.00

Summer 1992   Page 1

Following the sketch
exactly has produced a
weak design element,
overpowered by the
illustration.

Elements floating
in white space
don't create a
cohesive design.

Figure 5-2.
The preliminary design with text and art in position.

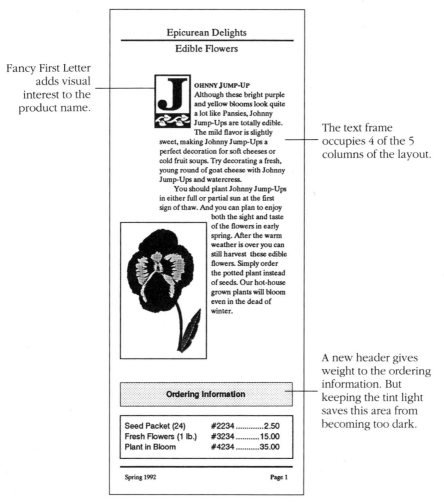

Fancy First Letter adds visual interest to the product name.

The text frame occupies 4 of the 5 columns of the layout.

A new header gives weight to the ordering information. But keeping the tint light saves this area from becoming too dark.

Figure 5-3.
Adding decorative elements to text helps create a balanced design.

Start the design process by setting up a five-column, one-row grid. This grid will serve as the underlying structure for your text frames.

Hands On:
Establishing a Grid

1. Open the Page menu, and choose Go to Foreground.

2. Open the Layout menu, and choose Layout Guides.

3. In the Number of Columns text box, enter *5*.

4. Click OK.

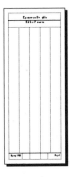

Five columns now appear within the page margins. Follow the next few steps to draw and format three text frames. As you draw, note how the pointer snaps to the guides. But also be aware that frames do not need to span the grid completely. For example, the first text frame that you create will span four of the five column guides.

5. Select the Text Frame tool and draw a box that starts 1 ¼ inches from the top of the page and ends 5 ¼ inches from the top of the page. The box should fill columns 2, 3, 4, and 5 of the underlying grid.

   Don't worry about formatting this text frame — you'll format it after you import the text.

6. Select the Text Frame tool and draw a second box near the bottom of the page just above the footer. The text frame should span all five columns and measure ¾ inch deep.

Because you will type directly into this text frame, you can save yourself some work and apply a typestyle now.

7. Apply the following (or similar) sans-serif typestyle to the second text frame by choosing the appropriate items from the Toolbar: 10-point Swiss, left-aligned, single-spaced.

   In addition to assigning a typestyle, you can also choose a border for this frame and set up default tab stops (to align prices and item numbers).

8. With the text frame selected, open the Format menu, and then choose Tabs.

9. When the Tabs dialog box appears, enter two tab stops using the measurements from the following table. Remember to click the Set button to include each new tab setting in the list box. After you enter both tab settings, click OK.

Position	Alignment	Leader
1.5	Left	None
2.5	Decimal	Dot

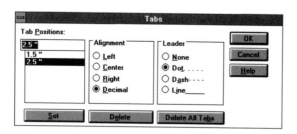

10. With the text frame still selected, open the Layout menu and choose Border.

11. When the appropriate dialog box appears, apply a 1-point rule to all four sides of the text frame. Leave the color black. Click OK.

12. Draw a third text frame that will contain the kicker, "Ordering Information." It should measure ⅜ inch deep and span all five columns. Position the frame ⅛ inch above the bottom text frame.

13. With the text frame selected, apply the following typestyle by choosing the options from the Toolbar: 10-point Swiss, bold, center-aligned, single-spaced.

14. Open the Layout menu and choose Border.

15. When the dialog box appears, apply a 1-point rule to all four sides of the text frame. Leave the color black.

16. Open the Layout menu and choose Shading.

17. When the Shading dialog box appears, select a dot pattern. Leave the foreground color black and the background color white to apply a light gray tint to the text frame. Click OK. The Preview pattern in the following dialog box was selected from the third row, center column of the Style palette.

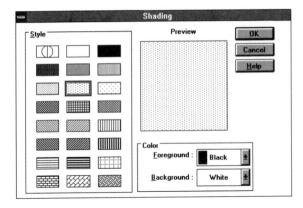

Although the Snap to Guides option makes it easy to create and align objects, sometimes you'll want even more flexibility. For example, the final layout requires that the picture span 2 ½ columns of the underlying grid. In order to avoid fighting the magnet-like pull of the guides, you'll turn Snap to Guides off temporarily.

18. Open the Options menu, and choose Snap to Ruler Marks.

This automatically turns Snap to Guides off and lets you draw in ¹⁄₁₆-inch increments, which is the size of the divisions on Publisher's ruler in Actual Size view.

19. Click the Picture Frame tool and draw a frame that starts 3 ¾ inches from the top of the page and aligns with the left page margin. The frame should end at the 6-inch mark on the vertical ruler and the 1 ¾-inch mark on the horizontal ruler.

20. To turn Snap to Guides back on, open the Options menu and choose it.

At this point, you have nearly finalized your design. The following illustration shows the various elements of the design in place. You may be tempted to duplicate this design for the rest of the pages in your publication. However, you should resist the temptation until you give this design a trial run — by importing text and artwork and printing the page.

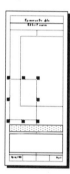

Hands On:
Filling in the Frames

1. With the picture frame selected, open the File menu and choose Import Picture.

   Note that the sample catalog pages reproduced in this chapter use illustrations that exactly match the content of the text. The pictures that you see of Johnny-jump-ups, nasturtium, and sweet violet are all part of a commercially available clip-art library from Totem Graphics. Although these particular pictures won't be available to you, you can complete the exercises in this chapter by using clip art that is supplied with Publisher — such as the image of irises (FLWRIRIS.CGM).

2. Use the Directories and Drives list boxes to locate the picture file you want to import, such as FLWRIRIS.CGM.

3. You can use the Preview option to look at the picture before you import it.

4. Click OK.

   Now that the picture is in place, you can turn your attention to the text elements.

5. Select the gray-tinted box and type *Ordering Information.*

6. Select the bottom text frame and type the following copy, using the tab settings you created previously to align the columns:

Seed Packet (24)	#2234	2.50
Fresh Flowers (1 lb.)	#3234	15.00
Plant in Bloom	#4234	35.00

   As you learned in Chapter 4, you can usually create large text blocks more efficiently by using a word processing program and then importing the text into Publisher.

   If you use Microsoft Works for Windows (or another Windows-based word processor), you can create all the text for the catalog in one file and then import only the paragraphs you need by copying to and pasting from the Clipboard. The illustration at the top of the next page shows both Publisher and Works open on the Desktop.

Helping Hand: Aspect Ratio

A picture's aspect ratio is the relationship between its height and width. If the picture of the flower looks squashed either vertically or horizontally, the aspect ratio needs adjustment. Use the Scale Picture command on the Format menu to adjust the shape of the picture frame.

(For more information, see Chapter 4, "The Power of PageWizards.")

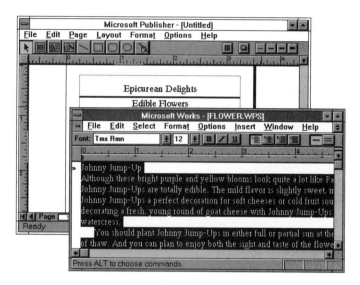

7. In Works, highlight the text concerning Johnny-jump-ups.

8. Open the Edit menu, and choose Copy.

9. Make Publisher the active program by clicking on the Publisher window or by using the Task List Manager. Select the main text frame.

10. Open the Edit menu, and choose Paste Text.

11. Highlight all the text for the body copy, and choose the following formats from the Toolbar: 9-point Dutch, left-aligned, single-spaced. Note that the drop-down box on the Toolbar lists 8 point and 10 point as options. To set this text in 9-point type, simply type the point size in the text box and press Enter.

The PageWizard Returns

In this chapter, you have designed a publication from scratch. However, even when you create your own designs, you will find Publisher's PageWizard technology useful. For example, the completed design includes a fancy first letter. Instead of creating a fancy first letter from scratch, you can use a PageWizard.

Hands On:
A Fancy First Letter

1. Click the PageWizard icon to select it.

2. Using the crossbar pointer, draw a box to contain the fancy first letter. Start the box flush with the top of the text frame. The box should be approximately $7/8$ of an inch deep and should span the second column guide.

   As soon as you finish drawing the frame, the PageWizard dialog box appears.

3. In the list box, highlight the Fancy First Letter PageWizard and click OK.

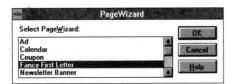

   In order to duplicate the fancy first letter that appears in Figure 5-3 follow these steps to respond to the PageWizard dialog boxes.

4. Choose the Bottom Border design.

5. Choose the Vine pattern for the background.

6. Type *J* for the initial cap.

7. Click Create It to put the PageWizard to work.

   When the drop cap appears in position, you'll notice that you now have a new and fancier letter *J* in addition to the original letter *J*. You now need to set the rest of the name in a heavier type to match the style of the drop cap. But first delete the extra letter.

8. Select the text frame that contains the body copy, and use the I-beam pointer to position the text-insertion point at the very beginning of the copy.

9. Using the delete key, remove the extra letter *J*.

10. Now, using the I-beam pointer, highlight the rest of the flower's name.

11. Open the Format menu, and choose Character.

12. When the dialog box appears on screen, click Bold and Small Capitals in the Style list box, and then choose OK.

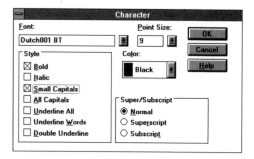

You have now finalized the design. It should match the page shown in Figure 5-3.

13. To be sure, print a copy of your design by opening the File menu and choosing Print.

14. When the dialog box appears, accept the default settings, and click OK.

Building on the Foundation

If the printout meets with your approval, you are ready to add additional pages to the publication. Microsoft Publisher can automatically duplicate the layout of text and picture frames you just created on every new page you add.

Hands On:
Inserting Pages and Duplicating Objects

1. Open the Page menu and choose Insert Pages.

   The Insert Pages dialog box appears. It lets you insert blank pages, automatically create text frames, or duplicate the layout of a specific page.

2. Add two more pages to the document by typing *2* in the Number of new pages text box.

3. Select After Current Page.

4. In the Options list box, choose Duplicate All Objects On The Page. Notice that Publisher displays the number of the page that it will copy.

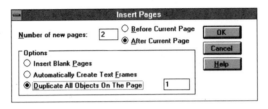

5. Click OK.

When you return to the screen, you'll find that you now have three pages in your document, all with identically positioned text and picture frames. Unfortunately, Publisher does not duplicate the content of the frames or the frames' default type specifications. You'll have to reapply the Dutch and Swiss typestyles to the appropriate text frames. However, Publisher does maintain other frame attributes — so your line widths, alignment options, margin settings, and even tab stops were duplicated along with the frames.

You can now move through your document and complete the entries for nasturtium and sweet violet. Use the procedures you've learned to bring text and pictures into the waiting frames.

Use the final document, shown in Figure 5-4, as a reference. This figure contains all the text you'll need for the sample catalog.

In addition, Figure 5-4 shows you how you sometimes must change a design to accommodate a different illustration or a facing page. For example, on page 3 the picture element is square — not rectangular — and it has been moved to the outside of the page to mirror page 2. However, both page 2 and page 3 still conform to the underlying grid — the text blocks occupy four of the five underlying columns, and the bottoms of the picture frames line up with one another.

Epicurean Delights

Edible Flowers

S WEET VIOLET
A nosegay of Viola odorata is a gift of sweet affection. The purple blooms are, quite appropriately, a symbol of Venus. The Romans fermented crushed flowers to make a sweet wine, but modern-day cooks use crystallized blossoms as an edible decoration for desserts. Herbalists infuse the flowers, and use the tonic to cure headaches and insomnia.

Because it is difficult to grow this plant from seed, Epicurean Delights offers seedlings which can be transplanted to an outdoor site in early spring. Once rooted however, these hardy perennials will return to bloom year after year.

Epicurean Delights

Gourmet Gardening

Ordering Information

Seedlings (24)	#2236	............7.00
Fresh Flowers (1 lb.)	#3236	...........15.00
Plant in Bloom	#4236	...........35.00

Page 4   Spring 1992

Spring 1992

Figure 5-4.
The final printout of the Epicurean Delights Gourmet Gardening catalog.

Figure 5-4. *continued*

Epicurean Delights

Edible Flowers

JOHNNY JUMP-UP
Although these bright purple and yellow blooms look quite a lot like Pansies, Johnny Jump-Ups are totally edible.
The mild flavor is slightly sweet, making Johnny Jump-Ups a perfect decoration for soft cheeses or cold fruit soups. Try decorating a fresh, young round of goat cheese with Johnny Jump-Ups and watercress.
You should plant Johnny Jump-Ups in either full or partial sun at the first sign of thaw. And you can plan to enjoy both the sight and taste of the flowers in early spring. After the warm weather is over you can still harvest these edible flowers. Simply order the potted plant instead of seeds. Our hot-house grown plants will bloom even in the dead of winter.

Ordering Information		
Seed Packet (24)	#2234	2.50
Fresh Flowers (1 lb.)	#3234	15.00
Plant in Bloom	#4234	35.00

Epicurean Delights

Edible Flowers

NASTURTIUM
Only in recent times has Nasturtium, or Tropaeolum minus, been considered a purely ornamental plant.
Persians nibbled Nasturtium petals as early as 400 B.C. Nasturtiums reached their peak of popularity in the kitchens of 17th Century Europe. The flowers, stems, and young leaves of this plant are edible. The flavor is peppery, and has a marked similarity to watercress. Indeed, Nasturtium's tangy, slightly hot taste has made it a favorite salad ingredient of today's Nouvelle-cuisine chefs.
You should plant Nasturtium in full sun, waiting for spring to overtake the last frost. The plants will begin to bloom in summer, but you can expect the harvest to last through the fall. You can keep picked flowers fresh for several days by floating them in a bowl of water stored in the refrigerator.

Ordering Information		
Seed Packet (24)	#2235	2.50
Fresh Flowers (1 lb.)	#3235	15.00
Plant in Bloom	#4235	35.00

Creating Unique Pages

Microsoft Publisher contains a host of tools that let you develop a consistent design for multiple pages in a publication. However, every publication also contains pages that should be unique. For example, cover pages rarely employ certain standard elements — such as page numbers and headers — that appear in the rest of the document.

Publisher lets you turn off the background display so the design elements on it are hidden. In the following exercise, you'll use the Ignore Background command to create a design for the cover of your sample catalog.

 Hands On: ***Turning the Background Off***

1. Make sure page 1 is displayed.

2. Open the Page menu. Choose Insert Pages.

3. Instruct Publisher to add one page before the current page.

4. Choose Insert Blank Pages.

5. Click OK.

   The new page 1 displays on screen. It contains all the background elements you created previously.

6. Now open the Page Menu. Choose Ignore Background.

   This command affects only the currently displayed page. So, as you can see in Figure 5-4, page 1 no longer contains the page number, header, and footer lines, but all these elements appear on subsequent pages.

   Now that the background elements no longer display on this page, you can create a front cover design. Figure 5-4 shows a simple design that you can emulate. The following hints might help you in your endeavor:

   ☐ Use layout guides to position the elements in the logo. Set the column guides to 1 and the row guides to 5.

   ☐ Set the type in 14-point Dutch and set the initial caps in 18-point Dutch.

☐ To create the fancy rule, draw a skinny rectangle and format it with the Vines BorderArt pattern. Resize the rectangle so the top and bottom edges overlap. When you collapse a rectangle in this way, the BorderArt pattern appears as a fancy rule.

Printing

At this point, you've completed the layout process and can save and then print your publication. At the beginning of this chapter, you chose the Book layout in the Page Setup dialog box. Now you can see the results of that choice.

Microsoft Publisher will use the Book layout to print two pages of the catalog on a single sheet of paper in a *spread* as you saw in Figure 5-4. In addition, the program will automatically add trimming guidelines (crop marks). Most importantly, Publisher will arrange the spreads so that when you fold the sheets of paper you have enough room to fold it in half and create a spine.

Hands On:
Printing the Book Layout

1. Open the File menu. Choose Save.

2. Type an appropriate name in the text box, such as "Flowers." Click OK.

3. Open the File menu. Choose Print.

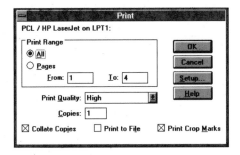

4. In the dialog box be sure Print Range is set to All and Print Quality is set to High. Check both Collate Copies and Print Crop Marks.

5. Click OK.

You can now produce the publication either by photocopying the pages on both sides of the paper or by delivering your pages (called mechanicals) to a professional printer or copy shop for inexpensive reproduction. Either way, you'll have created a four-page booklet.

What's Next?

In this chapter, you learned how to lay out a publication using Microsoft Publisher's power tools. Arranging objects on a page and formatting text provide the most creative and enjoyable parts of the design process. However, these tasks should not overshadow the importance of using layout guides or mirrored backgrounds to create consistent, professional-looking layouts.

You'll use the layout skills you learned here to create a company letterhead in the next chapter. You'll keep the design simple so that you can concentrate on Publisher's text-formatting features. By writing a straightforward business letter, you'll discover how to use Publisher's desktop publishing tools in conjunction with your favorite word processor.

Chapter 6

FOCUSING ON TYPE

When Epicurean Delights first opened several years ago, Elizabeth Jarmen used simple linen stationery that showed only the name and address of the store in plain type. But her recent experiences with Microsoft Publisher have convinced her that personalized stationery would make a better impression on clients and business associates.

In this chapter, you'll create a design for Epicurean Delights' letterhead. You could import pictures and use Publisher's drawing tools to create a complex design with artwork and fancy borders as you did in previous chapters. But instead, you'll see how far you can go using standard text in combination with Publisher's formatting features.

You already used a number of Publisher's text-formatting features in previous chapters. You chose typefaces, determined point sizes, and changed attributes such as boldface and italics. But Publisher offers other features for subtly controlling the appearance of text. These features let you adjust

- Kerning (the space between characters)
- Leading (the space between lines of text)
- Paragraph indents
- Spaces between paragraphs

When you complete the letterhead design, you'll save it as a template for Epicurean Delights' new business stationery. You'll then use that template to generate a two-page business letter.

Although Publisher provides some word processing features (including a spelling checker and a find/replace feature), it is not intended to replace a true word processing program. So instead of composing your letter in Publisher, you'll import the main body of the letter from an external word processor. Because Publisher's import filters preserve the formatting information in the file, any boldface or italics you apply when you write the letter will appear in the imported document.

The Layout Preparation

You might expect designing a letterhead to be a straightforward project requiring very little preparation. But a letterhead design takes as much forethought as a newsletter or catalog design. Before you begin any design project, you should properly configure your installed printer, work-area settings, page size, and layout guides. You'll find that all of your design projects flow more smoothly if you configure your system and layout settings.

To prepare the layout, you must first choose your page size and orientation.

Hands On:
Customizing the Work Area

1. Start Windows and click the Microsoft Publisher icon.

2. When Publisher's Start Up dialog box appears, choose Blank Page. Click OK to move to Publisher's work area.

3. Open the Options menu. Be sure Snap to Guides is turned on and Object Boundaries are displayed.

4. Choose Settings from the Options menu to display the Settings dialog box. Confirm the following settings:

    Starting page number is 1.

    Unit of measure is inches.

    Typing replaces the selected text.

    Helpful Pointers are displayed.

    Click OK to close the Settings dialog box.

    In the previous chapter, you learned that Publisher distinguishes between the paper size (determined by the paper tray of the currently installed printer) and the page size of a document. Be sure to synchronize these two settings.

5. From the File menu, choose Print Setup.

6. In the Print Setup dialog box select an appropriate printer, a paper size of Letter 8 ½ inches x 11 inches, and Portrait orientation. The examples in this chapter assume that an HP LaserJet II is installed.

7. Open the Page menu and choose Page Setup.

8. In the Page Setup dialog box, be sure that Full Page is selected. This option prints one page of the document on each sheet of paper. Also, be sure the page width is set at 8 ½ inches and page height is set at 11 inches.

   You will be able to work more efficiently and align the elements of your letterhead design more accurately if you set up margins and nonprinting guides.

9. Open the Layout menu and choose Layout Guides.

10. In the Layout Guides dialog box, set up a ½-inch margin guide on all four sides of the page. Be sure to type the dimension as .5.

11. Create a grid three columns wide by one row deep.

12. Click OK to return to the working screen.

Positioning Text Frames

Text frames are primarily used to position text blocks on the page. You can also use text frames to define several areas on the page. In your letter, you will have separate text frames for the logo treatment, the store address, and the body of the letter.

You can format text frames to influence the appearance of text in other ways as well. For example, the Frame Columns and Margins command, located on the Layout menu, lets you create margins for individual text frames. This command also lets you set up multiple columns of text within a frame by indicating the number of columns the frame should contain and the amount of space that should separate each column.

You'll work with text frame columns in the next chapter, as you continue to focus on text design. For your letterhead project, though, you'll concentrate on text-frame margins.

Because you know that you need to draw a number of text frames, use the right mouse button to select the Text Frame tool. The right mouse button keeps the text frame tool active so that you can draw multiple text frames. If you use the left mouse button, the pointer automatically switches back to the Selection tool after you draw the first text frame.

Hands On:
Drawing Multiple Text Frames

1. Using the right mouse button, click the Text Frame icon on the Toolbar.

2. Using the following table as a guide, draw five text frames. Each frame spans one or two columns of the three-column grid. With Snap to Guides turned on, each text frame will automatically align with the appropriate layout guides.

Frame	Spans columns	Begins at (on vertical ruler)	Ends at (on vertical ruler)
1	1 and 2	$\frac{7}{8}''$	$1\frac{1}{4}''$
2	1 and 2	$1\frac{1}{4}''$	$1\frac{5}{8}''$
3	3	$\frac{1}{2}''$	$1\frac{1}{4}''$
4	3	$1\frac{1}{4}''$	$1\frac{5}{8}''$
5	1, 2, and 3	$1\frac{5}{8}''$	$10\frac{1}{2}''$

Publisher automatically assigns a default frame margin of 0.08 inch to each text frame. However, to complete this letterhead design you'll need to set different margin settings for each frame. Using different settings, you'll be able to center type vertically in the logo and create wider margins for the main body of the letter. To change the margins or any other attributes of the text frames, you must first deselect the Text Frame tool.

3. Click the Selection tool on the Toolbar to deselect the Text Frame tool.

4. Select the first text frame that spans columns 1 and 2.

5. Open the Layout menu. Choose Frame Columns and Margins.

Notice that you can create only symmetrical frame margins. The left and right margins must be equal, and the top and bottom margins must be equal.

Since you have configured Publisher to use inches as the default unit of measure, the frame margin appears as 0.08 inch.

6. In the text box for Left and Right margins, type *0*.

7. In the text box for Top and Bottom margins, type *.10*.

Helping Hand: Changing the Page View

You might find it easier to create the text frames if you magnify your view of the page. You can use the F9 key to toggle to Actual Size view. But feel free to experiment with the other page views. You might find it easier to work in the 50 percent, 66 percent, or 75 percent views. As you can see in the accompanying illustration, which shows the work area at 75 percent of actual size, intermediate views allow you to see a larger portion of the page on screen and also lets you identify the ruler divisions more easily.

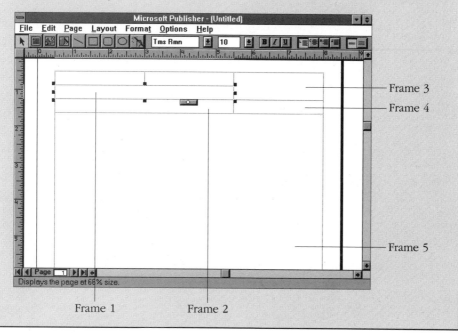

Don't bother to enter a unit of measure here. Publisher assumes you are entering the value in inches.

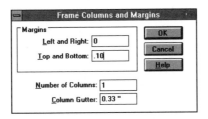

8. Click OK.

9. Repeat steps 5 through 9 to assign margins to the remaining text frames. Use the following table to enter the correct measurements in the dialog box:

Text frame	Left and right margins	Top and bottom margins
2	0	.1
3	0	.15
4	0	.09
5	.5	.5

Notice that you entered measurements that at first glance might seem minuscule. But keep in mind that type is measured in points, not inches. An inch equals approximately 72 points, so a measurement of 0.1 inch (or 7.2 points) is significant when you are designing with 12-point or even 30-point type.

You can also specify measurements in picas or points instead of inches. Publisher lets you enter measurements into dialog boxes in inches, centimeters, picas, or points — regardless of the unit of measurement you chose when you set up your publication. Simply type the abbreviation for the units you want to use after the number: *in* for inches, *cm* for centimeters, *pt* for points, or *pi* for picas. For instance, if you type *7 pt* in the Frame Column and Margins dialog box as a top margin, Publisher converts the measurement to the closest inch equivalent — 0.1 inch.

The Look of Words

Now that you have arranged your text containers — or frames — you can begin to design the letterhead. Microsoft Publisher's type-handling tools let you change the appearance of text to create visually interesting, and professional-quality designs.

In previous chapters, you learned how to change the appearance of text easily by using the Toolbar. By simply clicking buttons, you changed the typeface, point size, and alignment of highlighted text.

Publisher offers you more sophisticated control over the appearance of your text via the commands found on the Format menu. The Format menu options let you change several text attributes simultaneously and also give you access to options not found on the Toolbar. For example, you can use the Character command to change the color of text or to change lowercase text to all capitals. You can also use the Spacing Between Characters command to change letterspacing or the Indents and Spacing command to change line spacing. These commands let you enhance legibility, copy-fit text, and create special design effects.

Scalable Typefaces

To get the best results from Publisher's text formatting features, you should use scalable typefaces. Unlike bitmapped fonts, which are created at specific point sizes, scalable typefaces are created as an outline of each letter. Therefore, Publisher can generate any size type — from .5 through 500 points — from the outline without any loss of quality.

Scalable fonts are available from many sources. Some printers, such as Post-Script printers and the HP LaserJet III, have built-in scalable fonts. You can also use a Windows-based type-manager program to access scalable fonts.

The exercises in this book rely almost exclusively on fonts generated by one type-utility program: Bitstream FaceLift for Windows. FaceLift makes its scalable fonts available to any laser, ink-jet, or dot-matrix printer installed in the Windows Control Panel. Bitstream Facelift offers seven high-quality typefaces, including Dutch and Swiss (the Bitstream versions of Times Roman and Helvetica).

To explore the way type works in the context of a document, you'll develop the letterhead design in two sections. In the first section you'll design a logo for the store's name and address. This will let you explore the issues surrounding display type. The second section covers the basics of body copy, including how to retain formatting when you import word processing files.

Display Type

You might think display type means big headlines and fancy logos, but display type actually refers to any text that piques the reader's interest or organizes a document. So display type includes more than headlines and logos. Elements such as pull quotes, captions, subheads, kickers, and even page numbers all qualify. Your sample letter includes three kinds of display type: the logo treatment of the store's name, the store's address, and a page number.

Choosing a Display Typeface

One of the often-repeated rules of design states that sans-serif typefaces are more suitable for display text than serif typefaces. And it is true that the simple outlines of sans-serif typefaces (like Swiss) are suited to bold treatments. At large point sizes, the serifs (or curved endings) of typefaces like Dutch can become overly decorative and distracting.

However, there are no hard and fast rules. Successful display types sometimes trade off a little legibility for added flair or feeling. You might think it strange

Helping Hand: Font Substitution

If you do not have a type-manager program or a printer with built-in scalable fonts, you can still complete this exercise. Windows 3 contains three scalable fonts: Modern, Roman, and Script. But be warned, when you use these fonts, your screen display may not always match your printout. Only programs like Bitstream Facelift can provide a screen image of your text that will always match the printout. For more information about font technology and a comparison of scalable and bit-mapped fonts, see Appendix C, "Printing with Microsoft Publisher."

to refer to the feeling elicited by a typeface. But typefaces can be formal or casual, can project an aggressive company image or an avant-garde attitude. In fact, to find the right typeface, you might need to buy additional fonts.

Take a moment to look at the following sample text. Examine the way the store name looks set in three typefaces: Dutch, Bitstream Cooper Black, and Park Avenue. (All three come with Bitstream FaceLift for Windows.)

Epicurean Delights

Epicurean Delights

Epicurean Delights

The Bitstream Cooper Black typeface (in the center) is perfect for an informal document, like a party announcement or a school newspaper, and the Park Avenue typeface looks perfect for an old-fashioned wedding invitation. But neither of these two typefaces will work for the Epicurean Delights letterhead. The Dutch typeface — which is more elegant than Cooper Black and more businesslike than Park Avenue — offers a better solution.

You can make the logo design even more interesting by adding a contrasting, yet complementary, typeface. By using the Dutch and Swiss typefaces together in your design, you can put a slight avant-garde spin on the logo.

The printout of the logo design, shown in Figure 6-1 on the next page, clearly demonstrates the best use of serif and sans-serif type. The simple, strong lines of the sans-serif type remain legible even when printed as white letters against a black background. In contrast, the graceful curves of the serif type show up best against a pure white or light gray background.

Now that you've analyzed the design, you will learn which tools to use in order to create it. Since you already have the text frames in position, you can go ahead and create the type.

100 South Riverside Plaza Chicago IL 60606

Tel. 312-999-9999/Fax 312-222-2222/Orders 800-999-9999

EPICUREAN

D E L I G H T S

Figure 6-1.
The Epicurean Delights logo treatment.

Hands On:
Creating a Logo

1. Select the text frame at the upper right corner of the screen (text frame 3), and type *Epicurean* in uppercase and lowercase letters.

2. Highlight the text. Choose Character from the Format menu. In the Character dialog box, set the typestyle as 30-point Dutch bold, and format it as small capitals.

3. Click OK to accept these specifications.

4. With the text still selected, choose Indents and Spacing from the Format menu. In the dialog box, choose Center alignment. In the Space Between Lines text box, type *31 pt.*

   Remember to include the "pt" abbreviation so that Publisher uses points instead of line spaces.

   Note that the spacing between lines is only 1 point larger than the size of the type. This tight line spacing lets Publisher fit large text into a relatively small text frame. If you had left the default setting of 1 space, Publisher would have displayed an alert box saying that it could not fit the type into the frame.

5. Click OK to return to the working screen.

6. To add a light gray tint to the text frame, open the Layout menu and choose Shading.

7. When the Shading dialog box appears, select a light gray tone in the Style section. Click OK.

   To create the second part of the logo, you'll first assign the black fill and assign a default typestyle to the text frame. Then you'll type the copy.

8. Select the next text frame in the right column (text frame 4).

9. Open the Layout menu. Choose Shading.

10. When the Shading dialog box appears, select the solid black option from the Style section. Click OK.

11. With the text frame still selected, open the Format menu and choose Character.

12. When the Character dialog box appears, set the typestyle as 12-point Swiss bold, and format it as all capitals.

13. To change the color of the text from black to white, open the Color drop-down list box and select White. Click OK.

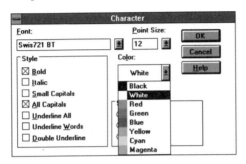

When you return to the working screen, you'll see a black box.

14. Open the Format menu again and choose Indents and Spacing.

15. In the dialog box choose Center alignment. In the Space Between Lines text box type *13 pt*. Click OK. A white insertion point appears in the black frame.

16. Type *Delights*. You can type the word using either uppercase or lowercase letters.

    Note that Publisher ignores the shading while you type. In this case, you won't see the characters you type because you're typing white characters on a white background. After the frame is deselected, Publisher displays the shading again, and the text becomes visible. When you see the type, it will appear in the default typestyle, which is all capitals.

    To finalize the design, you'll use Publisher's kerning command (Spacing Between Characters) to spread the letters evenly across the entire text frame.

17. Select all but the last letter in the word "Delights." (The Helping Hand below explains why including the last letter would space out the letters incorrectly.)

18. With the text selected, open the Format menu. Choose Spacing Between Characters.

19. When the dialog box appears, select Move Letters Apart, and change the spacing from the default of 3 pt to 13 pt. Click OK.

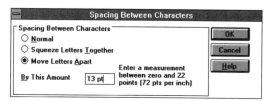

As you have seen, Publisher's ability to control the spacing between characters lets you turn plain text into dramatic graphic elements. You can also use kerning to increase text legibility.

Often you must remove letterspacing to increase the legibility of headline text. Some letter pairs create gaps that become especially noticeable at large point sizes. By highlighting individual letters in a headline, you can use the Spacing Between Characters dialog box to remove up to 9.75 points of space between characters.

Helping Hand: Inter-Character Spacing

When you use the Spacing Between Characters command, Publisher does not actually adjust the space between characters; it adjusts the space following characters. For example, to move the letters D and E in "Delights" closer together, you need select only the D.

Keep this in mind when you use character spacing to spread text for a design effect. Select all the letters you want to spread — except the last letter. If you highlight the last letter, Publisher will add extra spacing after it, and the type will be incorrectly centered in the text frame.

However, it is sometimes necessary to add letterspace to improve the legibility of small type or body copy. In the following exercise, you'll adjust character spacing to complete the letterhead design.

Hands On:
Improving Legibility

It usually makes sense to use a small, compact typestyle for presenting address and telephone information, especially when the information contains many numbers — such as toll-free telephone numbers, fax numbers, and nine-digit zip codes. Unfortunately, small type is harder to read. You can make the small type in your document easier to read by adding letterspacing. Try it now.

1. Select the top text frame in the left column (text frame 1). Format it as 10-point Swiss, left-aligned.

2. Open the Format menu. Choose Indents and Spacing.

3. When the dialog box appears, type *11 pt* in the Space Between Lines text box. Click OK.

4. Now type the following text on one line:

    `100 South Riverside Plaza Chicago IL 60606`

5. Select the text.

6. Open the Format menu. Choose Spacing Between Characters.

7. When the dialog box appears, type *0.5 pt* in the text box. Click OK.

    Even though you have added only 0.0069 inch (or ½ point) of space between characters, this small adjustment will make the text easier to read.

8. To format the various telephone numbers, select the second text frame (text frame 2) and repeat steps 1 through 7. But instead of the store's address, enter the following information:

    `Tel. 312-999-9999/Fax 312-222-2222/Orders 800-999-9999`

You can now complete the logo by adding a rule that spans the width of the page. The rule serves a purely decorative purpose. It ties the various elements of the letterhead together as a cohesive unit, both by connecting the left and right sides of the page and by providing a transitional gray shade between the two tinted text frames in the right column.

Hands On:
Graphic Accents

1. Select the Line tool.

2. Position the crossbar pointer at the 1 ¼-inches mark on the vertical ruler. Draw a line that extends across the three columns of the lay-out grid. Remember: To make the line perfectly horizontal, hold down the Shift key while you draw it.

   In previous exercises, you used the Toolbar to apply quick formats to rules. In this case, you'll use the Line dialog box (invoked from the Layout menu) to access Publisher's full range of formatting options for rules.

3. With the rule selected, open the Layout menu. Choose the Line command.

   In the Line dialog box you can change the weight of the line, either by selecting one of the four preformatted sizes or by specifying a custom size anywhere from ¼ point to 127 points. You can also assign one of eight colors or automatically add arrow endings.

   Publisher doesn't offer gray tints for objects such as lines, rectangles, and ellipses. However, Windows automatically interprets colors other than black and white as shades of gray when you print on a black-and-white printer. Yellow, for example, is interpreted as a light gray, and cyan is interpreted as a middle-tone gray. The shades of gray that your printer produces depend on its ability to print gray tones.

4. In the Line dialog box, highlight the entry *10 pt.* Type *6 pt* in this text box to create a custom line.

5. Open the Color drop-down list box to reveal the choices.

6. Select Cyan.

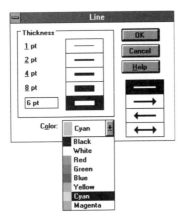

7. Click OK to return to the working screen.

Organizing a Document with Display Type

Display type can help organize long documents. In a complex report, you might use several kinds of display type, including subheads, figure references, and captions. In this simple letterhead, you will organize the document using page numbers.

In Publisher, you add automatic page numbers to a document by placing the page-number symbol on the Background page. Because the page number is on the background, it will appear on every page of your document. Business letters usually omit the page number from the first page. You'll use the Ignore Background command from the Page menu to hide the page number for the first page of the two-page letter.

Hands On:
Adding Background Elements

1. On the Page Menu choose Go to Background.

2. Select the Line tool on the Toolbar and draw a rule that spans the width of all three columns. Position the line at 1 ¼ inches on the vertical ruler so it matches the rule on the first page.

3. With the line selected, open the Layout menu. Choose the Line command.

4. Assign a custom width of 6 points and select Cyan from the Color
   list box.

5. Draw a text frame in the far right column, above the rule, beginning at 1 inch on the vertical rule and ending at 1 ¼ inches.

6. Type the word *Page* with a space after it.

7. Open the Page menu. Choose Insert Page Numbers. Publisher will
   insert the correct page number on the page.

8. Highlight the text and format it as 10-point Swiss, right-aligned.

9. Open the Page menu. Choose Go to Foreground.

10. Open the Page menu. Choose Insert Pages.

11. Accept the default settings in the dialog box to insert one blank
    page after the current page. Click OK. The second page should be
    displayed. The elements on the Background page should appear at
    the top of the page.

12. Draw a text frame that begins at 1 ⅝ inches and ends at 10 ½
    inches on the vertical ruler. The frame should span all three
    columns.

13. With the large text frame selected, open the Layout menu and
    choose Frame Columns and Margins.

14. In the dialog box, create margins of 0.5 inch on all four sides to du-
    plicate the format on page 1. Click OK.

15. Return to the first page. Open the Page Menu, and choose Ignore
    Background. This will prevent the page number on your Back-
    ground page from overlapping the logo design.

You now have a functional letterhead design. Next you'll print a copy of the
current document to review your work. Then you'll save the file as a template
so you can easily reuse the design.

 Hands On:
Printing and Saving the Letterhead Template

1. Open the File menu and choose Print.

2. Accept the program defaults. Choose OK.

If the two-page design meets your approval, save it as a template.

3. Open the File menu, and choose Save As.

4. When the Save As dialog box appears, activate the Template option by clicking the check box in the lower right corner.

5. Enter an appropriate filename in the text box. For this example, the name LETTER will not duplicate any filenames already stored in the MSPUB\TEMPLATE directory.

   To take advantage of the template you just saved, you must start a new publication.

6. Open the File menu, and choose Create New Publication.

7. When the Start Up dialog box appears, choose Templates.

8. Use the scroll bar to find the LETTER template. Highlight the filename, and click OK.

   When you open a template, Publisher opens an untitled copy of the publication. The original template file isn't opened or changed, so you can use it over and over again.

Body Copy

Body copy is the heart and soul of any publication — whether the document is a brief letter or a complex newsletter. And yet, body copy is neglected more than any other design element.

In the next few exercises, you will give the body copy in your letter the attention it deserves. You'll learn how to choose the best typeface for your project and how to control the density of text on your pages. Finally, you'll learn how Publisher's word processing filters let you import text with the formatting intact.

Choosing a Typeface

When you choose a typeface for body copy, you must consider legibility first. Documents with hard-to-read type can drive readers away.

Designers frequently use serif typefaces (like Dutch) for body copy. The decorative strokes, or serifs, at the end of each vertical or horizontal stroke help readers group words together. In addition, serif typefaces vary thin and thick strokes more than their sans-serif counterparts. The visual variety in each letter can prevent fatigue when reading long passages.

Should you completely avoid sans-serif typefaces? No, but you should use them with discretion. Restrict your use of sans-serif type to short or moderate-sized text blocks. And remember: extra white space increases legibility. Be sure to adjust the spacing between lines of copy and between characters, if necessary.

Whatever typeface you ultimately choose, be sure that it is a typeface designed for text, rather than for display purposes. Take a look at the sample paragraphs in the following illustration. Only the Dutch and Swiss typefaces are appropriate for the main body of the letter. An entire page set in 12-point Cooper Black, which is a display face, would overwhelm the eye because of the strong contrast between the bold letters and the white paper.

Even though Epicurean Delights occupies a rather small storefront, we do have experience catering events for up to 500 people. Over the years we have developed a cadre of professional cooks, stylists, waiters, and bartenders. And I feel confident that we could cater any business or celebratory occasion for you.

Even though Epicurean Delights occupies a rather small storefront, we do have experience catering events for up to 500 people. Over the years we have developed a cadre of professional cooks, stylists, waiters, and bartenders. And I feel confident that we could cater any business or celebratory occasion for you.

Even though Epicurean Delights occupies a rather small storefront, we do have experience catering events for up to 500 people. Over the years we have developed a cadre of professional cooks, stylists, waiters, and bartenders. And I feel confident that we could cater any business or celebratory occasion for you.

These three paragraphs illustrate one other important point about body copy. Although all three type samples are the same point size and have the same leading and column measure, they occupy very different amounts of space. The paragraph requires five lines of copy when set in the Dutch typeface and seven lines of copy in Cooper Black.

You can dramatically affect the number of words that fit on a line or the density of words on the page simply by choosing a different typeface. When you choose a typeface for your publication, keep these factors in mind:

- *Weight* — The weight of a font refers to the thickness of the strokes that form the letters, which can be light or heavy. Cooper Black is a good example of a heavy typeface. "Black" is often used to designate a type weight that is heavier than boldfacing.

- *Width* — Some typeface families contain fonts that are condensed or expanded. The letters in a condensed font are narrower, so you can fit more text on a line, and the letters in an expanded font are wider. You can usually tell whether a typeface is condensed or expanded by its name. For example, Helvetica Condensed is the condensed form of the Helvetica typeface.

- *X-Height* — X-height refers to the height of the lowercase letters in a font. In a typeface with a large x-height (like Swiss), the lowercase letters are almost as tall as the capital letters. In a typeface with a small x-height (like Dutch), the lowercase letters are much shorter in relation to the capital letters. Because the width of a font is usually proportional to its height, a typeface with a large x-height occupies more space on a line than a typeface with a small x-height.

When you need to fit a large amount of text into a few pages, choose a typeface with a shorter x-height. When you need highly legible type at small point sizes choose a typeface with a tall x-height.

For your sample letter, you'll use the Dutch typeface, which is a highly legible serif typeface. Because you will use a single, wide column for the text, you can choose from a range of type sizes. Any size from 10 to 14 points would be acceptable. The basic rule is that the wider the column you use, the larger the type size you need. For a fairly dense page, choose 11-point type. Experiment with different type sizes on your own, and you'll find that very small type on a wide column is difficult to read.

Integrating Imported Text

The body copy that you'll use in the next exercise was created using the word processor in Works for Windows. The text was formatted in Microsoft Works and assigned the following typestyle: 11-point Dutch, single-spaced. In addition, individual words were boldfaced or italicized for added emphasis. When you import a Works file, Publisher retains the existing typeface and the bold and italic formatting instead of changing it to Publisher's default typestyle of 10-point Times Roman. Notice in the following illustration that the text formatting operations in Microsoft Works are almost the same as those in Publisher. Both products are part of the Microsoft Solution Series and have similar command structures.

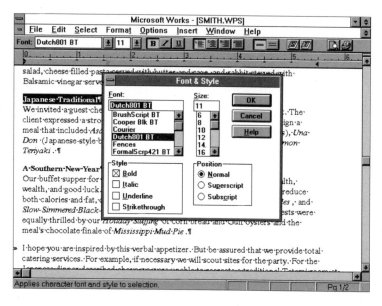

Using Figure 6-2, shown on the following page, as a guide, type in the text of your sample letter using your word processor. Be sure to copy the boldface and italic formatting, but don't worry about the paragraph formatting — you'll take care of that in Publisher. Save the file. Next, you'll import the file and integrate it into your letter template via a word processing filter.

EPICUREAN

D E L I G H T S

100 South Riverside Plaza Chicago IL 60606

Tel. 312-999-9999/Fax 312-222-2222/Orders 800-999-9999

April 24, 1992

Mr. Harry Smithson
Smithson Public Relations, Inc.
200 South Riverside Plaza
Chicago, IL 60606

Dear Mr. Smithson,

I was so pleased to get your call today. In these busy times it is unusual for someone to call with a compliment on a job well done. Michael Alonso, who heads our catering department, actually has quite a lot of fun coming up with new sandwich ideas for your monthly staff meetings. And though you might consider a monthly lunch for 30 people a small job, we truly appreciate the business.

Of course, I was even more pleased by the prospect of handling some of the larger catered events sponsored by your public relations firm. From our brief conversation it would appear that you are in need of a versatile caterer who can supply both food and panache for parties of all sizes.

Even though Epicurean Delights occupies a rather small storefront, we do have experience catering events for up to 500 people. Over the years we have developed a cadre of professional cooks, stylists, waiters, and bartenders. And I feel confident that we could cater any business or celebratory occasion for you.

The brief descriptions below might give you a better idea of the scope of our talent.

A Tuscan Evening
This Northern Italian menu is as far removed from spaghetti and meatballs as you can get. We prepared a sit down dinner for 82 people that included *Funghi alla Griglia, Insalata di Finnochio, Agnelotti con Burro e Salvia*, and *Coniglio con Polenta*. The English translation follows: grilled Portobello mushrooms, Florentine fennel salad, cheese-filled pasta served with butter and sage, and rabbit stewed with Balsamic vinegar served over a custard corn mush.

Japanese Traditional
We invited a guest chef to prepare this authentic meal for a group of eight. The client expressed a strong preference for seafood. Our response was to design a meal that included *Asari Jiru* (a Miso soup served with fresh Pacific clams), *Una Don* (Japanese-style barbecued eel), *Somen Buckwheat Noodles*, and *Salmon Teriyaki*.

A Southern New Year
Our buffet supper for 300 people included foods that are said to bring health, wealth, and good luck. Though we took a few liberties with the recipes to reduce both calories and fat, our *Honey-Glazed Ham, Braised Cabbage and Apples*, and *Slow-Simmered Black-Eyed Peas* were a huge success with the crowd. Guests were equally thrilled by our *Holiday Stuffing* of corn bread and Gulf oysters and the meal's chocolate finale of *Mississippi Mud Pie*.

Figure 6-2.
Final printout.

I hope you are inspired by this verbal appetizer. But be assured that we provide total catering services. For example, if necessary we will scout sites for the party. For the Japanese dinner described above we were unable to recreate a traditional Tatami room at the client's office. But we did manage to rent space at a local cultural institution that has many fine examples of Japanese art. In addition we can develop menus that meet special dietary restrictions, and can even supply printed invitations and menus.

If you'll forgive the obvious pun, I am a strong believer in bread cast upon the waters. I hope your good experiences with Epicurean Delights will encourage you to use our catering services in the future.

Sincerely,

Elizabeth Jarmen
Proprietor

Hands On:
Word Processing Filters

1. Select the largest text frame (text frame 5) on page 1 of the letter.

2. Open the File menu. Choose Import Text.

3. When the Import Text dialog box appears, open the List Type of Files drop-down list box. Choose Works for Windows 2.0 or the word processor you used.

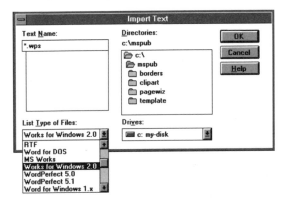

Helping Hand: Other Word Processing Filters

If you use a word processor other than the one in Works for Windows, you can still complete this exercise. Publisher also has filters for other popular word processors. Publisher can read the native file formats of the following word processors:

- Microsoft Word (for both Windows and DOS)

- Microsoft Works (for both Windows and DOS)

- WordPerfect

- Windows Write

- WordStar

Publisher can also import files stored in industry standard file formats: DCA (RFT), RTF, and Plain Text (ASCII).

4. Use the Drives list box and the Directories list box to locate the correct file.

5. Click OK to import the file.

   Publisher informs you that the file will not fit in the text frame and asks whether you would like to autoflow the text throughout the document.

6. Click Yes.

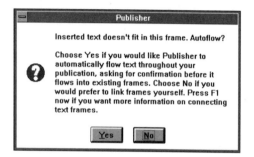

Publisher imports the text file into page 1. It then switches to page 2 and asks if the text should be flowed into the empty frame. Click Yes. The remainder of the copy flows into the waiting text frame. Notice that the copy has your original formatting, including the Dutch typeface, a type size of 11 points, and attributes such as boldface and italics.

Take a moment to examine the sample letter in Figure 6-2. Notice the restrained use of boldface and italics. Bold formatting accents the subheads within the body of the letter and provides some internal organization. Italics set off the recipe names. Italics should indicate titles (whether of a book or a recipe), or add an inflection (such as irony) to a word within a paragraph. Italics should never take the place of bold formatting.

You should rarely (if ever) use an underline. This formatting attribute is a holdover from typewriter days — when underlining was the only way to add emphasis. Underlined text is difficult to read because the underline interferes with the descenders on letters such as *p* and *g*. You can usually replace underlined text with italicized text. If you want a line effect, use rules instead of underlines.

Fine-Tuning Paragraph Styles

To fine-tune the appearance of a long text block, you can use the paragraph controls found in the Indents and Spacing dialog box. You used this dialog box in previous projects to alter the space between lines and to change the alignment of text blocks. In the next exercise, you will see how the paragraph formatting options can affect word density.

Publisher, like word processing programs, lets you adjust the space before and after paragraphs as well as the space within paragraphs (leading). Increasing the leading of a text block often improves legibility. Decreasing the leading (even by a small increment such as a ¼ or ½ point) can help you to copy-fit text.

You should get into the habit of using the Indents and Spacing dialog box to add extra space before and after paragraphs. You'll be rewarded with paragraphs that seem clearly separated and yet still related to one another. Don't insert a blank line to add space — doing so causes ugly gaps of white.

Hands On:
Paragraph Formatting

You will first adjust the spacing between lines and paragraphs in your letter to a setting more sophisticated than Publisher's default of one space.

1. Select the text frame on page 1. Choose Highlight Story from the Edit menu. This highlights all the text in the story, even if the story spans multiple pages.

2. Open the Format menu. Choose Indents and Spacing.

3. When the dialog box appears, type *12.5 pt* in the Space Between Lines text box.

   Notice that you can indicate fractions of a point by using decimals.

4. Now type *10 pt* in the Space After Paragraph text box.

5. Click OK to return to the working screen.

   When you review the letter on screen, you will discover that you need to edit the paragraph spacing. Publisher added 10 points of space after every paragraph. Unfortunately, this also added 10 unnecessary points of space after each bold heading. To correct the paragraph spacing for these headings, you must follow a simple but tedious procedure.

6. Select the heading that reads, "A Tuscan Evening."

7. Choose Indents and Spacing from the Format menu. In the dialog box, change the Space After Paragraph attribute to 0 (zero).

8. Click OK.

9. Repeat steps 6 and 7 for the other headings ("Japanese Traditional," and "A Southern New Year").

You can use Publisher's indents in a straightforward manner to mark the beginning of each paragraph. Or you can specify negative measurements to create special effects such as hanging indents. For your sample letter, you will use the left and right indents to set off several special paragraphs from the main text block.

10. Highlight the three paragraphs and three headings that describe Epicurean Delights' catering successes. ("A Tuscan Evening," "Japanese Traditional," and "A Southern New Year" are the three headings.)

11. Open the Format menu. Choose Indents and Spacing.

12. When the dialog box appears on screen, enter a left and right indent of 0.5 inch each.

13. Switch the alignment option from Left to Justified.

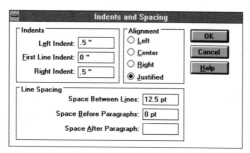

Take a moment to examine this illustration. You will notice that one entry box remains blank. The currently highlighted text actually contains two formats for the Space After Paragraph option. The bold headings are set with no space after a carriage return, and the text is set with a 10-point space after a carriage return. Publisher alerts you to this conflict in the paragraph formats by leaving the Space After Paragraph option blank.

As long as you do not enter a new, overriding measurement, Publisher will maintain both paragraph formats. This feature lets you change one aspect of a complex typestyle or paragraph format for paragraphs that might not have all their attributes set the same way. In this case, you can change the indents without affecting the space between paragraphs.

14. Click OK.

When you return to the working screen, you will immediately see the effects of the modified paragraph format. The indented and justified paragraphs have extra emphasis.

Hands On:
The Publisher Spelling Checker

Whenever you format or edit a document, there's a chance that you'll introduce errors. It's a good idea to run Publisher's built-in spelling checker as a final review of your publication.

Publisher's 100,000-word dictionary catches most misspellings. It also finds repeated words. You can add new words that you frequently use (and misspell) to the dictionary.

1. Place the I-beam at the top of the text frame, before the date line.

2. Open the Options menu. Choose Check Spelling.

   The Spelling dialog box appears and questions every possible misspelling in turn. If the program recognizes a word as a possible misspelling, it will offer alternative spellings.

   Publisher shows its best guess for the correct spelling in the Change To box and other possible spellings in the Suggestions list. If you do not want the choice in the Change To box, either type a new word or select another word from the list box.

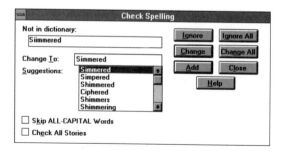

3. In this example, the correct spelling of the word "Simmered" appears in the Change To box. To accept the correct spelling, you click the Change button at the right side of the dialog box.

When Publisher finishes checking your copy, you can check other text frames (whether single or linked) or exit the spelling checker.

4. Click No to return to the working screen.

With these final corrections made, you can print the document and save it to a file.

What's Next?

You can apply the skills you learned in this chapter to every project you undertake. You now have the expertise to make Microsoft Publisher's type and paragraph formats work for you. This means that you can take ordinary text and transform it into a design device that is as much a picture as it is words. You can also use text formats as copy-fitting tools to increase the density of words on a page.

Believe it or not, you have not yet explored all of Publisher's text-handling capabilities. In the next chapter, you will use many of the commands you used in this chapter to create a multi-column advertisement. In addition, you'll break loose and create typographic special effects using Publisher's WordArt program.

Chapter 7

DESIGNING WITH TYPE

In the last chapter, you designed stationery for Epicurean Delights. In the process, you learned that when handled properly, type can function as the primary design element in a layout. Logos, headlines, and fancy first letters can all energize your layouts. Other type-design elements — such as tables, pull quotes, and coupons — can also add contrast and visual interest.

Now a new project at Epicurean Delights provides the perfect opportunity to explore the power of designing with type. As a way to use downtime in her catering kitchen, Elizabeth Jarmen has decided to offer cooking classes at Epicurean Delights. She wants to create a flyer promoting the classes. Microsoft Publisher provides her with the perfect tools for the project — WordArt, a self-contained utility that you access from the Toolbar, and PageWizards.

As you work through the exercises in this chapter, you'll use both the Word-Art tool and PageWizard technology to create a dynamic, all-type layout.

Types of Type

To create the cooking class flyer, you will work with two kinds of typefaces. You will create the body copy using Microsoft Publisher's standard typefaces in standard text frames. And you will create the display copy using special typefaces that are part of the WordArt program.

You cannot use WordArt typefaces in Publisher's text frames. Likewise, you cannot use WordArt to manipulate the typefaces that you use in Publisher text frames. Publisher treats the type that appears in text frames differently from the type that appears in WordArt frames.

WordArt frames and text frames each have advantages and limitations. Text frames are superior for handling large blocks of type. You've seen how text-frame controls — such as leading and inter-character spacing — can increase legibility and even generate a few special effects. However, text frames pose problems if you want to create complex designs with type. For example, Publisher automatically wraps text around layered objects, such as picture frames, WordArt frames, and other text frames, which makes it difficult to stagger type or overlap letters in a design. Furthermore, unless you have a color printer, the type in text frames prints only in black or white — no shades of gray are available.

WordArt typefaces do not have these limitations. You can overlap and stack WordArt frames to create complex type designs without generating awkward text wraps. In addition, you can assign one of 16 colors to WordArt text and print colors as shades of gray on black-and-white printers. Also, WordArt's style and alignment options let you easily create special effects. Best of all, WordArt provides 19 display typefaces, ranging from classy fonts to playful alphabets.

Choosing a WordArt Typeface

A typeface is more than the letters of the alphabet — it projects a mood. A restrained, conventional-looking typeface lets readers know that your message is serious. A font that looks like it's straight out of a comic book is probably a good choice for an informal party invitation.

When you design a logo or a headline, spend the time to find a typeface that enhances your message. Because this process is more of an art than a science, WordArt lets you preview the font choices, making it easy for you to experiment until you find the right typeface.

The illustration on the next page shows how typeface choice can support your message. Notice how the words and the typeface look like they were designed for each other. The Snohomish font (which is a WordArt typeface) looks like it was lifted from an embroidered sampler in your grandmother's kitchen. Its rounded, handcrafted script letters provide a perfect visual for a headline about home cooking. In contrast, the Touchet typeface provides a high-tech look for space-age text.

The relationship between typeface design and headline content isn't always so obvious. For example, in your sample headline, shown in Figure 7-1 on the next page, the word "Flavor" is set in an elegantly thin typeface called Langley. The thin typeface subtly supports the basic premise of the advertisement: low-fat food can be flavorful.

The rest of the display type was set in Bellingham, which provides visual contrast to the main phrase. If all three words appeared in the Langley typeface, the headline design wouldn't be as strong or as interesting.

This headline design takes full advantage of the functions that the WordArt tool offers. For example, WordArt lets you stretch the already slim Langley typeface vertically to create an even thinner silhouette. WordArt also produced the light gray color and the drop-shadow effect in the Bellingham font. And WordArt made it easy to align the word "Workshop" with the word above it on both the left and the right.

Finally, WordArt provided two formatting options to create the banner that cuts across the corner of the page — an option that automatically slants the type at a 45-degree angle and another that adds a colored background. These features let you highlight text at the top of your page without competing with the other headline text.

To learn about these formatting options, you should get to work with the WordArt tool. You'll now recreate the headline design that dominates the layout of the flyer. In fact, the headline is so important that it occupies a third of the page.

Figure 7-1.
The completed headline.

Hands On:
Working with WordArt

1. Open Publisher.

2. When the Start Up dialog appears, click the Blank Page icon. Then click OK.

3. When Publisher appears on screen, assign the following parameters:

   In the Page Setup dialog box (accessed from the Page menu), set the Layout option to Full Page, and set the Page Size to 8 ½ inches wide by 11 inches high.

   In the Layout Guides dialog box (accessed from the Layout menu), create 1-inch margin guides on all four sides of the page. In addition, set up the page with 6 columns and 3 rows.

   In the Options menu, turn on Snap to Guides.

4. Use the Rectangle tool to create a box that aligns with the page margins.

5. Format the rectangle with a transparent fill and a 2-point rule. This creates a black-ruled border around your page design.

Helping Hand: Flexible Layout Guides

You will find it easier to complete this advertisement if you take the time to create a flexible grid.

The headline in this sample flyer spans one-third of the vertical dimension of the page. So you'll find it easier to position if you divide the page into three rows using nonprinting guides.

The headline spans two-thirds of the width of the page. However, it is centered on the page. If you do a few simple calculations you'll see that in order to center the headline you must leave one-sixth of the page free on the left and right of the text. To position the headline horizontally, use a six-column grid. The headline will span columns 2, 3, 4, and 5.

6. Click the WordArt icon in the Toolbar.

7. Draw a WordArt frame that begins at 1 ½ inches on the vertical ruler, ends at 3 inches on the vertical ruler, and spans columns 2, 3, and 4.

Your screen should look like the one in the following illustration. Notice that the WordArt frame looks like other frames you have created in Publisher, with eight selection handles appearing around its periphery.

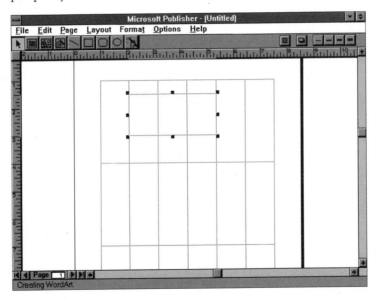

Immediately after you draw the WordArt frame, the WordArt window appears. You can't type text directly into a WordArt frame, so you must use the WordArt window to enter text and apply special effects. As you can see in the illustration on the next page, you type your copy in a special text box at the top of the WordArt window.

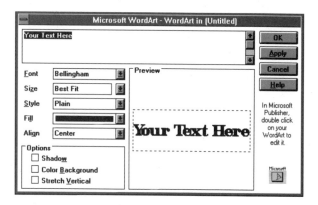

8. Replace the sample text with the word *FLAVOR* (all in capital letters).

   Don't press the Enter key when you finish typing. Pressing Enter would add a line break and a blank line to the WordArt frame.

   You can format the text using the Font, Size, Style, Fill, and Align options. To view the available choices within each category, open the associated list box by clicking its downward-pointing arrow.

9. Open the Font drop-down list box, and select Langley.

10. Leave the Size as Best Fit, the Style as Plain, the Fill as black, and the alignment as Center.

11. Turn on the Stretch Vertical option.

12. Click OK to return to the working screen.

Helping Hand: Previewing Special Effects

The WordArt window contains a preview that shows you how your selections for font, size, style, fill, and alignment will look.

As you work in WordArt, you could use the mouse to open a drop-down list and click to select a single option. However, if you open the drop-down list and then use the Up and Down arrow keys, you can cycle through the options without closing the list. As you move through the options you can see the effect of each because the Preview is updated to show you the change.

WordArt Frames

You can assign margins, fill patterns, borders, and drop shadows to WordArt frames just as you can to text frames and picture frames. However, in many ways WordArt frames are hybrids, combining aspects of both text frames and picture frames. For example, if you assign a point size to WordArt type, the WordArt frame functions like a text frame. Remember that resizing a text frame allows you to see more words or fewer words but does not change the size of the type. The same is true of the WordArt frame.

However, if you choose the Best Fit option, the WordArt frame functions like a picture frame even though it contains text. When you choose Best Fit (as you did in the previous exercise), the type changes size to fit the frame as you resize it.

By using the Best Fit option, you can draw a frame that works with your design. WordArt does the hard work to figure out the correct point size.

You can also assign a horizontal or vertical stretch to type created with WordArt. If you use the Fit Horizontally alignment or Stretch Vertical option, you can distort the outline of the letters to condense or expand them by resizing the WordArt frame. These stretch factors can help you to create special effects and to align words with precision. You will now stretch the first word in your sample headline.

 Hands On:
Resizing WordArt via Frames

1. Select the frame surrounding the word "Flavor."

2. Open the Page menu, and choose Actual Size view.

3. Choose Frame Margins from the Layout menu. Assign a margin of 0.17 inch to both the top and bottom of the frame. Leave the left and right margins set at 0. Choose OK.

4. Use the resize pointer to drag the right middle frame handle to the right until it reaches the next column guide. The frame should now fill columns 2, 3, 4, and 5.

5. Use the resize pointer to drag the bottom middle handle downward to the $3\frac{7}{16}$-inch mark on the vertical ruler.

Publisher treats the text inside the frame like a picture. Not only does the type become larger, but it stretches vertically to fit the size of the frame.

Resizing text by manipulating the WordArt frame is an easy way to align words with one another precisely. In the exercise below, you'll use the Fit Horizontally option to make the word "Workshop" exactly as wide as the word "Flavor." Even though the words are of unequal lengths and are set in different typefaces, you can align them by resizing the WordArt frame.

Hands On:
Aligning WordArt Elements

1. Click the WordArt icon on the Toolbar.

2. Draw a WordArt frame that follows the layout guides. It should span columns 2, 3, 4, and 5 horizontally. The top of the new frame should abut the bottom of the WordArt frame that contains the word "Flavor." It should extend downward to the guideline between rows 1 and 2.

3. When the WordArt dialog box appears, type *WORKSHOP* in the text box.

4. Assign the following attributes to the text:

   Leave Bellingham as the font.

   Assign a size of 36 points.

   Leave the style as Plain.

   Change the fill to yellow.

   Choose the Fit Horizontally alignment option.

5. In the Options box, turn on the Shadow attribute.

6. Click Apply to preview the effect.

7. Click OK to return to the working screen.

Because you used the Fit Horizontally option, each letter has stretched to fill the entire width of the WordArt frame. As a result, the word "Workshop" is exactly as wide as the word "Flavor" above it.

Helping Hand: Printing Shades of Gray

Publisher's WordArt program lets you assign one of 16 colors to each text phrase. If you use a color printer, Publisher reproduces the hues you assign as closely as possible. If you print on a black-and-white printer, Publisher converts the color assignment to a shade of gray which is a good way to extend the range of gray tones for WordArt elements. As you can see in the following illustration, yellow actually prints as a light shade of gray on an HP LaserJet printer.

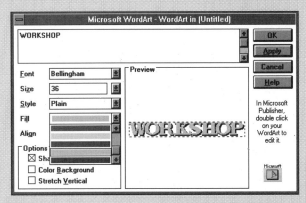

However, changing the color of WordArt elements is a little tricky. The color that you assign to text automatically determines the colors that WordArt uses for the Shadow and Color Background options. For example, yellow text always has a black shadow and a medium gray background. This combination works well because there is enough contrast among the colors to keep the type legible, even when you output to a black-and-white printer. On the other hand, red type, which prints as black on a laser printer, becomes barely readable with the Shadow and Background options turned on.

Before you finalize any design, you should print samples to see how each color, or its equivalent shade of gray, reproduces on your printer.

You can configure WordArt to maintain text at a specific point size by turning off the Best Fit, Stretch Vertical, and Fit Horizontally options. In fact, WordArt can actually resize a frame to accommodate text set at a specific point size. In the following exercise, you'll learn about some uses for this WordArt feature.

Hands On:
Specifying Point Sizes in WordArt

1. On the Toolbar, click the WordArt icon.

2. Draw a WordArt frame that starts at 1 ¼ inches on the vertical ruler, ends at 1 ½ inches on the vertical ruler, and spans columns 3 and 4.

3. When the WordArt dialog box appears, type *THE.*

4. Assign the following attributes:

    Leave Bellingham as the font.

    Assign a size of 24 points.

    Leave the style as Plain.

    Change the fill to yellow.

    Leave the alignment as Center.

5. In the Options section, turn on Shadow.

6. Click OK.

    WordArt presents a message box telling you that your text is too large to fit into the current WordArt frame. You can enlarge the frame automatically, or you can return to WordArt to change the point size.

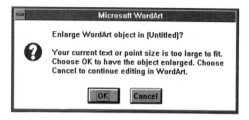

7. Click OK to enlarge the frame.

WordArt's Special Effects

You can add drama to a headline or logo by using one of the ten WordArt Style options. For example, you can rotate type so that it reads vertically or at a 45-degree angle. You can reverse text both horizontally and vertically by clicking the Upside Down option. The Arch effect lets you wrap text along a curve, and the Button option positions three lines of copy in a circle — one along the top, one along the bottom, and one through the middle.

When you choose one of these Style options, WordArt applies the effect based upon the dimensions of your frame and the point size of your type. You'll see this principle in action in the next exercise, where you'll create a banner that slants across the corner of the advertisement.

Hands On:
Choosing a Style

1. Switch back to Full Page view.

2. Click the WordArt icon on the Toolbar. Draw a WordArt frame that measures approximately 2 ½ inches square near the upper right corner of the page. The exact position of the frame isn't important because you'll need to reposition the element after you rotate it.

3. When the WordArt dialog box appears on screen, type *Special Offer.*

4. Assign the following attributes:

    Leave the typeface as Bellingham.

    Assign a size of 24 points.

    Select the Slant Down (More) option from the Style drop-down list box.

    Change the fill color to white.

    Leave the alignment as Center.

5. Under Options, click the Color Background check box to turn it on.

    The Preview is certainly interesting, but the view of the banner isolated from the rest of the design isn't really much help. Good news: You can move the WordArt window around on screen while it is active. To see the banner in relation to the larger design, simply move the dialog box out of the way.

6. Use the mouse to drag the title bar of the WordArt window until you can see the upper right corner of the advertisement.

7. Click the Apply button to apply your modifications to the banner without closing the WordArt dialog box.

   When you use the Apply button, your changes appear on the page, but the WordArt dialog box remains open. In the following illustration it's obvious that the type is too large for the corner of the ad because the banner obscures part of the main headline.

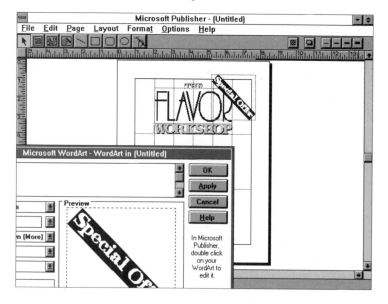

To solve this problem, set the text in a smaller point size. You can make the smaller sized text bolder by changing it to all uppercase letters.

8. Move the WordArt dialog box back into view.

9. Retype the phrase in all capital letters: *SPECIAL OFFER*.

10. Change the point size to 14.

11. Click OK to return to the working screen.

12. Resize and reposition the WordArt frame until the black stripe of the banner overlaps the page margins.

Helping Hand: Overlapping Frames

When you position the banner in the upper right corner, you'll notice that the edges of the banner clumsily overlap the 2-point border.

You can trim the edges of the banner so that they align with the advertisement's black border by drawing white rectangles that hide the overlap.

The following illustration shows you a selected rectangle extending over the right edge of the page. The rectangle was formatted with no border and an opaque white fill. Because the page is also white, the white rectangle effectively erases the overlapped edges of the banner.

For more information about how to layer objects to "erase" portions of an element, see Chapter 8, "Accent on Graphics."

The Limitations of WordArt

Now that you've experienced the advantages of WordArt's special effects, you should be warned about a few of its limitations. All of WordArt's style effects have preset parameters. This means that you can turn them on and off, but you can't adjust them. For many of the Style options, such as Top to Bottom vertical orientation, the preset parameters don't cause problems.

However, several of the Style options demand careful planning if you want to avoid awkward designs. For example, to use the Button effect successfully, you need three lines of copy. If you type one line, WordArt automatically repeats the line three times. If you type two lines, WordArt repeats the second line twice. Similarly, the Arch Up and Arch Down effects, which wrap text along a curve, look best when you draw a large frame and type a long phrase. If you use the Arch effect with small frames or single-word headlines, you'll force WordArt to distort the letters beyond recognition.

One final caveat. WordArt typefaces are scalable up to a size of 846 points — which is larger than a sheet of letter-sized paper. In some cases, however, resizing the type degrades the image. At certain point sizes — especially if you rotated the type — the curve segments that make up each letter become irregular because they are scaled disproportionately. You'll have to experiment with point size, formatting options, and typefaces to find the right combination for the best-looking text.

PageWizards and WordArt

You have seen how easy it is to access and use WordArt, but there is an even easier way to take advantage of WordArt functions: by using a PageWizard. You already used Microsoft Publisher's PageWizards in Chapters 3 and 4 to create entire publications. You can also use PageWizards to add partial page elements to your publications, such as advertisements, newsletter nameplates, calendars, fancy first letters, coupons, and tables. As you can see in Figure 7-2 on the next page, the final design for this flyer includes a reply coupon. To create the coupon, you will use a PageWizard. And in turn, the PageWizard will use WordArt.

THE FLAVOR WORKSHOP

SPECIAL OFFER

Flavor not Fat
Epicurean Delights is proud to present The Flavor Workshop, a series of cooking classes dedicated to the idea that healthy, natural food can also be delicious.

Our classes are based upon sound theories of nutrition, but we are first and foremost good cooks. So while we do consciously try to reduce the amount of butter and cream in our cooking, we substitute flavorful seasonings (like garlic and wine) instead.

Course Curriculum
We begin each lesson with a brief 15-minute lecture on an important food-related topic, such as the benefits of Omega fatty-acids in salmon.

Of course the most amount of time is spent actually cooking the meal. You'll learn how to use fresh salsas and reduction sauces to intensify the flavor of the food you prepare. Our recipes rely on cooking techniques like poaching and steaming which retain moisture while reducing calories. And because our recipes have been streamlined for the home chef, you can easily cook these meals for your own family.

The finale of each class is a veritable feast where you and your fellow students eat the meal you've just learned to cook.

Flexible Hours
To accommodate your busy schedule, we offer our cooking classes on six weekday evenings or three weekend afternoons. The $125 fee covers the entire cost of the 12-hour class, including groceries. And if you enroll before Labor Day, you can receive a free $25.00 gift certificate from Epicurean Delights gourmet food shop.

Come, join Elizabeth Jarmen,

professional chefs, and nutritionists for a culinary adventure that begins in our kitchen, and ends in your home.

Tuesdays: Oct. 6-Nov. 17
6:30- 8:30 p.m.
6 classes
Saturdays: Oct. 10 - 24
2:00-6:00 p.m.
3 classes
Fill out the coupon below or call our toll free number:

800-999-9999

Epicurean Delights
100 South Riverside Plaza
Chicago Illinois 60606

Yes, Enroll Me!

☐ I mailed my check for $125.00 to Epicurean Delights, 100 South Riverside Plaza, Chicago IL 60606 before Labor Day to qualify for my free $25.00 gift certificate.

Name _____   ☐ Tuesday Evenings
Address _____   ☐ Saturday Afternoons

_____   ☐ Payment Enclosed
Tel. _____   ☐ Bill Me

All classes are subject to a minimum enrollment of 10 students.

Figure 7-2.
The completed advertisement includes a fancy headline, body copy, and a reply coupon.

A reply coupon normally occupies only a portion of a page. So when you use a PageWizard to create a coupon (or any other partial page element), you must first draw a frame to define the area.

After you draw the frame, the PageWizard takes over the design process. Of course, you must respond to a few dialog boxes. These ask general questions that let you choose the design style you want and let you include or exclude certain elements. The PageWizard does all the hard work, including aligning multiple text frames, figuring out the correct point size for copy, and using WordArt to create display type. You will now use Publisher's PageWizard technology to create the coupon in your sample advertisement.

Hands On:
A PageWizard Coupon

1. In the Options menu, turn off Snap to Guides.

2. Click the PageWizard icon on the Toolbar.

3. Draw a frame that measures approximately 4 inches wide by 2¾ inches deep. The frame should occupy the bottom row and span columns 3, 4, 5, and 6.

   Although it seems strange, be sure to draw the frame so that it does *not* align precisely with the layout guides. (That's the reason you turned Snap to Guides off.) If you draw this frame flush against column 2 and flush with the page border on the right, you will create two layout problems. First, you will create an awkward text wrap for the body copy that you'll add to the frame. Second, you will obscure the 2-point rule that surrounds the entire advertisement.

4. When the dialog box listing all of the available PageWizards appears, choose Coupon. Click OK.

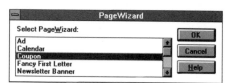

If you have worked through the exercises in Chapters 3 and 4, you will have no trouble responding to the PageWizard dialog boxes. The few questions that they ask let you determine the general appearance of your coupon.

5. Use the following list to respond to the PageWizard dialog boxes:

> Choose the Classic design style.
>
> Indicate that Yes, the coupon will be mailed back.
>
> Position the check boxes at the right.
>
> Select Coupon cutout as the BorderArt pattern.
>
> Click Create It to put the PageWizard to work.

The following illustration reproduces the coupon exactly as the PageWizard creates it. Notice that the PageWizard assembles the coupon from a number of objects, including text frames, WordArt elements, and pictures.

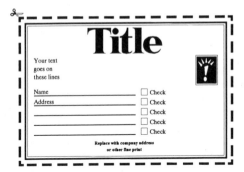

To customize the coupon, you must use Publisher's standard tools. For example, use the text editing functions to replace the dummy text with the copy shown in Figure 7-2. Also, the final design does not contain a picture. To remove the dummy picture, first select it, and then either choose Delete Picture Frame from the Edit menu or press the Del key.

In order to edit the sample title, which was created with WordArt, you must return to the WordArt window. To edit an existing WordArt element, you access WordArt by double-clicking on the frame.

Hands On:
Editing WordArt Elements

1. Double-click the WordArt frame that contains the word "Title."

   The WordArt dialog box appears. The text box contains the sample text from the frame. The WordArt window also displays the current formatting attributes for font, size, style, fill, and alignment.

2. Replace the text in the text frame with

   `Yes, Enroll Me!`

3. Change the formatting attributes to match the following:

   The font is Bellingham.

   The size is 14 points. (Since this point size is not an option in the drop-down list, type it in.)

   The style remains Plain.

   The Fill remains Black.

   The alignment remains Center.

   Turn off the Stretch Vertical option.

4. Click OK to return to the coupon.

5. Complete the coupon design by replacing all the sample text with the copy in Figure 7-2.

Notice that the PageWizard used WordArt only to generate display type for the title. The PageWizard employed Publisher's conventional text frames for the body copy. In general, WordArt works best for short phrases set in large point sizes: in other words, for display type. When you need to create larger blocks of copy or set text in small point sizes, you should use Publisher's conventional text frames and scalable fonts.

Standard Text Frames

There are several reasons why you should not use WordArt for long blocks of copy. You cannot import text from a file stored on disk into the WordArt window. WordArt also makes it difficult to work with multiple lines of copy because it cannot adjust line spacing. And it forces you to break lines with hard carriage returns (using the Enter key).

Helping Hand: Word Processing File Formats

The body copy that you'll use in this exercise was created using the word processor in Works for Windows. Using Works for Windows, you can format the type as 10-point Dutch. When you import the text into a Publisher document the formatting is preserved.

However, you can also complete this exercise using another word processor. Copy the text (as shown in Figure 7-2) and save it to a file. Name the file AD, followed by the appropriate three-letter extension. Then use Publisher's Import Text command to bring the text into your document. Publisher can read the native file formats of Microsoft Word, Microsoft Works, WordPerfect, Windows Write, or WordStar. Publisher can also import text stored in industry-standard formats, such as ASCII (Plain text), DCA (RFT), or RTF.

On the other hand, when you use standard fonts and text frames, you can use Microsoft Publisher's typographic controls to increase legibility by adjusting the space between characters, the space between lines, and the paragraph indents. In addition, placing text in a text frame lets you wrap text around other design elements, such as picture frames, text frames, and WordArt frames. The next exercise demonstrates how you can use these controls to organize and enhance the body copy in your flyer.

Hands On:
Importing and Formatting Body Copy

1. Select the Text Frame tool from the Toolbar.

2. Draw a text frame that spans all six columns and the bottom two rows. (The text frame will completely cover the coupon.)

3. With the text frame selected, choose Frame Columns and Margins from the Layout menu. In the dialog box, type the values shown in the following illustration:

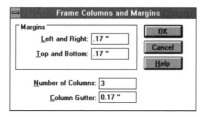

Click OK.

You can now import a long text file into this frame. Publisher arranges the copy in three columns of equal widths.

4. With the text frame selected, open the File menu. Click Import Text.

5. When the Import Text dialog box appears, click List Type of Files, and choose Works for Windows 2.0 (or the appropriate format for your word processor).

6. Use the Drives and Directories list boxes to locate the file that was saved with the filename AD.WPS.

7. Click OK to import the file.

When Publisher imports the text into the waiting frame, it arranges it in three columns. You can use character and paragraph formatting to further enhance and organize the copy.

8. Highlight the body copy. If you did not use Works for Windows to format the text, format it now as 10-point Dutch.

9. Use the Indents and Spacing command to tighten the leading from one line space to 11 points. Align the text at the left.

10. Highlight each paragraph individually. Use the Indents and Spacing dialog box to format a first-line indent. Paragraphs that follow a subhead should start flush left. Indent subsequent paragraphs 0.17 inch.

11. Highlight each subhead and format the text as 10-point Swiss bold.

12. Highlight each subhead again. Open the Indents and Spacing dialog box, and add 6 points of space above each section.

    When you finish, look at the change in the subheads. The bold-facing gives them a little extra weight but doesn't create a conflict with the main headline treatment. And using only 6 points of space instead of a blank line separates the sections without disrupting the smooth flow of the copy.

13. Toll-free numbers deserve special treatment because they encourage potential customers to respond to your advertisement even if the response coupon has been clipped. Separate the toll-free number from the surrounding text with carriage returns (the Enter key). Then increase the point size to 16 and the line spacing to 18 points.

14. With the toll-free number still highlighted, use the Toolbar options to center and boldface the text.

15. Next, use the Indents and Spacing command to create a hanging indent for the class schedules. Set the right indent at 0.25 inch, the left indent at 0.75 inch, and the first line indent at –0.75 inch.

    You've made the schedule of classes more noticeable not by making the text darker, but by adding white space. White space is an important design tool too often neglected by beginning designers.

16. When you finish formatting the text, click anywhere outside of the page to deselect the text frame.

    As you can see in the illustration on the next page, the text frame immediately covers the coupon and the body copy flows over the coupon area.

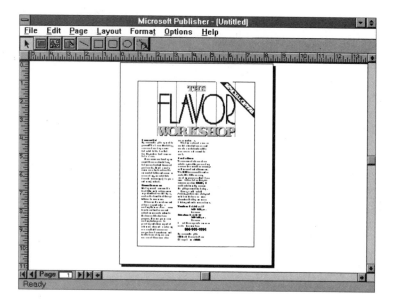

Publisher wraps text around objects placed on top of the text frame; it does *not* wrap text around objects placed beneath the text frame.

At the moment, the coupon is beneath the text frame that contains the body copy. To wrap the body copy around the coupon, you need to change the stacking order.

17. Select the text frame that contains the body copy.

18. Open the Layout menu and choose Send to Back.

When you change the stacking order, the text wraps correctly around the periphery of the coupon.

Pay special attention to the way Publisher creates the automatic text wrap. The program uses the information stored in the Frame Margins and Columns dialog box to determine how large a margin to leave between the text and the objects the text encounters (such as the coupon). In this case, Publisher offsets the text from the coupon by 0.17 inch.

You have now finished designing the sample advertisement. Save the file with an appropriate name, such as AD.PUB. Then print the publication, which should match Figure 7-2.

What's Next?

In this chapter, you concentrated on Microsoft Publisher's type-handling capabilities. You discovered that WordArt is a flexible tool for creating special effects in display type. Although WordArt does not replace the typographic controls associated with Publisher's text frames, it offers an easy way to add drama to an all-type layout.

Now that you are an expert with type, you can begin to learn about pictures. In the next chapter, you'll create a sample publication that takes full advantage of Publisher's internal drawing tools. You will create a simple picture using the program's four tools: Rectangle, Ellipse, Rounded Rectangle, and Line. And you will enhance the simple picture by using formatting options such as Shading and BorderArt.

Chapter 8

ACCENT ON GRAPHICS

At Epicurean Delights, the staff now uses Microsoft Publisher to create business forms and to design sophisticated letterheads and informative newsletters. They even use Publisher to enhance catered events with desktop published menus and invitations.

In this chapter, you will create a simple menu for one of Epicurean Delights' current catering jobs. The design itself is simple. It lists a heading for each of the four courses and two menu items under each heading.

Because this menu contains a minimal amount of text, the graphical elements of the design take on added importance. When you add graphics to a publication, you have two options. You can import a picture — such as a scanned photograph, a data-driven chart, or a line drawing — from an external source. Or you can create artwork using Publisher's internal drawing tools and formatting options.

Importing pictures from external applications can give you access to sophisticated images. But if you don't own other graphics programs, or if you don't have the time to learn a graphics application, you can create images using Publisher's convenient, built-in tools instead. You need to know only how to draw a box and how to format the appearance of objects to create simple drawings.

With Publisher's tools, you can create schematic drawings, such as flow charts; symbols, such as stop signs; and decorative elements, such as borders. You can enhance your drawings using Publisher's formatting options for line weights, fill patterns, and border designs. The exercises in this chapter prove that Publisher's formatting options frequently provide more power than the drawing tools themselves.

This chapter focuses on Publisher's drawing features. But for many documents, you'll want to use a combination of internally and externally generated images. In fact, you will discover that you can use many of Publisher's formatting options and graphical accents to enhance pictures imported from other sources.

Publisher's internal drawing tools can help you to avoid one mistake made by novice designers: using inappropriate clip art. You could probably find a clichéd clip-art image for your sample Italian food menu. But instead, you'll use Publisher's internal tools to create a more appropriate and creative design. You will draw a stylized medieval tapestry design, complete with tassel accents, as a background for your text. Figure 8-1, on pages 227 and 228, shows the menu you will create.

A Grid for Drawing

In previous chapters, you used Microsoft Publisher's layout guides to position elements on your pages. You can also use layout guides as a grid to help you create drawings with greater precision.

Publisher can handle grids with up to 256 rows and columns. So you have quite a bit of latitude when deciding what size grid to use. The most efficient grids contain units based on the smallest elements in your drawing. For example, to create a series of rectangles measuring ½ inch wide by ¼ inch deep, you should base your grid on ¼-inch increments.

Coincidentally, a ¼-inch grid is exactly what you require for the first few exercises in this chapter. The instructions that follow will help you to set up the correct page margins and layout guides.

Hands On:
Setting Up the Grid

1. Open Windows and start Publisher.

2. When Publisher's Start Up dialog box appears, select Blank Page, and click OK.

CUCINA TOSCANA

The cooking of Tuscany in Northern Italy includes simple peasant dishes from the countryside as well as elaborate recipes dating back to the Renaissance. Tonight's menu celebrates Tuscan cuisine by featuring game meats, such as quail and rabbit, "white" pasta served in a traditional butter sauce, and Tiramisu—the most popular of all Italian desserts.

Figure 8-1.
The completed menu.

Figure 8-1. *continued*

Antipasti

Warm salad of duck and Tuscan white beans
or
Grilled Portobello mushrooms, with a sauce of lemon and white wine

Primi Piatti

Stracciatella, Italian egg-drop soup
or
Agnelotti con Burro e Salvia, cheese-filled pasta with butter and sage

Secondi Piatti

Coniglio con Polenta, hunter's rabbit served over cornmeal cakes
or
Quaglia e Porcini, quail stuffed with wild mushrooms

Dolci

Tiramisu, custard made of Marscapone cheese and espresso-flavored biscuits
or
Pera in Vino, pears poached in red wine
and
Espresso, Cappuccino, or Darjeeling Tea

3. Open the Options menu. Be sure Snap to Guides is on and Object Boundaries are displayed.

4. Open the Options menu, and click Settings. Make inches the unit of measure, and turn on Typing Replaces Selection.

5. Open the Page menu, and choose Page Setup. In the dialog box, select Full Page — this prints one page of the document on each sheet of paper. Set the Page Size options to 8 ½ inches wide by 11 inches high.

6. Open the Layout menu, and choose Layout Guides to open the Layout Guides dialog box.

7. Set up a 1-inch margin around all four sides of the page.

8. Create a grid 26 columns wide by 36 rows deep. The resulting grid will look like graph paper, with ¼-inch squares.

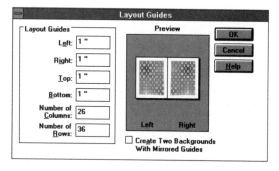

9. Click OK to return to the working screen.

Simple Geometry

Microsoft Publisher offers four drawing tools: Rectangle, Rounded Rectangle, Oval, and Line. The Toolbar contains all four tools. To create drawings with these tools, you use the same drag motion that you use to create text frames and picture frames. The tools let you draw simple geometric shapes in different sizes. To create more complex images, you must combine and overlap the four basic elements.

Constraining the Shape

You can modify the way the drawing tools work by holding down the Shift key or the Ctrl key as you draw. When you use the Shift key with drawing tools, rectangles become squares, ovals become circles, and rules automatically align along the vertical, horizontal, or diagonal axis.

When you hold down the Ctrl key as you draw, you force Publisher to create objects from the center outward. This makes it easy to center multiple elements in a radiating pattern.

You must remember to press the Shift or Ctrl key before you begin drawing and to release it only after you complete the shape. You can also use the Shift and Ctrl keys in combination. Doing so lets you create perfectly concentric circles or squares.

In the course of creating your sample menu — which consists of a title page and a second page listing menu items — you'll use both the Shift key and the Ctrl key to constrain shapes as you draw them. You will now create the largest element on page 1 — a square that serves as a background for the text.

Hands On:
Drawing a Perfect Square

1. Use the F9 key to switch to Actual Size view.

2. Choose the Rectangle tool from the Toolbar.

3. Position the crossbar pointer at the 2-inch mark on the horizontal ruler and at the $3\frac{3}{4}$-inch mark on the vertical ruler.

4. With the Shift key depressed, drag the pointer down and to the right to create a square that measures $4\frac{1}{2}$ inches by $4\frac{1}{2}$ inches. The lower right corner should be at the $6\frac{1}{2}$-inch mark on the horizontal ruler and at the $8\frac{1}{4}$-inch mark on the vertical ruler.

   Notice that no matter how you move the mouse, a square always appears on screen. Remember to keep the Shift key depressed until you complete the square and release the mouse button.

Formatting Options

You just created a simple square with a black outline. As you learned in Chapter 2, you can enhance the appearance of objects like this one by applying Publisher's formatting options. You can

- Use borders to define the edges of geometric shapes, text frames, and picture frames.

- Vary the widths of lines and borders. Publisher creates lines ranging in width from 0.25 point to 127 points.

- Add drop shadows to rectangles, ellipses, text frames, and picture frames.

- Fill objects with one of 23 shading patterns, or leave them transparent to reveal objects behind.

- Apply border designs to rectangles, picture frames, and text frames. Border-Art comes in over 100 patterns, in sizes ranging from 4 points to 127 points.

The following illustration demonstrates the power of Publisher's formatting features. This figure consists of a line, a rectangle, and a circle. The rule was enhanced with arrow line endings and a line weight of 2 points. The rectangle uses Publisher's BorderArt in place of a ruled border to create the special effect of a pinned note. And the circle was filled with a gray tint, outlined with a 1-point rule, and highlighted with a drop shadow.

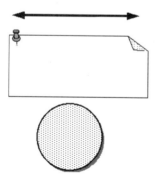

The Layout menu contains all the dialog boxes and formatting options you need to change the appearance of geometric shapes (as well as text and picture frames).

Note that the options listed on the Layout menu change as you select different objects on the Toolbar. For example, the illustration above shows how the Layout menu changes when you select a rectangle and when you select a line. The available commands let you format a rectangle with a ruled border or a fill pattern (Shading). If you select a line instead, shading is no longer an available option. Instead, a single option for line attributes (Line...) appears.

In addition to using the Layout menu, you can access many of Publisher's formatting options directly from the Toolbar. For example, four of the most frequently used line weights appear as icons on the Toolbar whenever you select a geometric shape.

Hands On:
Assigning a Format

In this exercise, you'll change the appearance of the square you drew by adding a tint and applying a ruled border. You'll use the quick formatting options located on the Toolbar.

1. With the square selected, be sure a 1-point rule (the thinnest line icon) is selected as the border.

2. Click the Shading icon. (The Shading icon looks like a rectangle filled with a diagonal line pattern.)

3. When the Shading dialog box appears, click the third pattern from the top in the right column of the Style palette. Since the Foreground color is set to Black, this pattern produces a light gray shading.

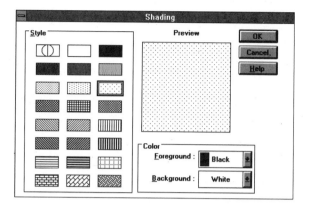

Editing Individual Objects

Although you can change the appearance of the simple geometric shapes you draw in Publisher by using formatting options, you cannot change their appearance by cutting them apart or erasing portions of them. You cannot clip a circle in half, for example, or remove part of the line around a rectangle.

However, you can manipulate geometric shapes by repositioning, resizing, or deleting them. When you create a drawing, you may want to extend it in a specific direction — horizontally to the right, for example. You can use Publisher's selection handles and helpful pointers to do so.

As you know, when you click any element in Publisher, selection handles appear around its perimeter. Geometric shapes, like rectangles and ovals, have eight selection handles. Lines have only two selection handles. You can use the selection handles to perform several resizing and positioning operations.

■ To move an object in a perfectly horizontal or vertical direction, hold down the Shift key when you use the move pointer.

■ To resize an object horizontally — either to the left or the right — use the selection handle on the side of the object, rather than at the corner. Publisher displays the resize pointer. You can move the boundary only in a horizontal direction.

- To resize an object in a vertical direction, use the selection handle on the top or bottom of the object, rather than at the corner. Publisher displays the resize pointer. You can move the boundary only in a vertical direction.

- To resize the height and width of an object simultaneously, use the corner selection handles.

- To resize an object and maintain the relationship between width and height (the aspect ratio) hold down the Shift key while you use the corner selection handle.

In the following exercise, you'll see how you can increase the power of Publisher's drawing tools by using formatting and editing functions together to create a fancy patterned line.

Hands On:
Manipulating Geometric Objects

Remember that Publisher offers different formatting options for rectangles, rounded rectangles, ovals, and lines. In order to create a line that employs a BorderArt pattern you must start with a rectangle. You can place BorderArt only in rectangles, text frames, and picture frames.

1. Select the Rectangle tool from the Toolbar.

2. Draw a rectangle with a starting point of 2 inches on the horizontal ruler and 2 inches on the vertical ruler and with an ending point of 6 ½ inches on the horizontal ruler and 3 ½ inches on the vertical ruler.

3. With the rectangle selected, open the Layout menu. Choose BorderArt.

Helping Hand: Helpful Pointers

Publisher provides special pointers that can help you to move or resize objects easily. These pointers appear when you have correctly positioned the arrow pointer over a selection handle. The shape of the pointer shows you which direction (horizontal, vertical, or diagonal) to move the mouse.

4. When the BorderArt dialog box appears, select Weaving...Braid from the Available Borders list box.

5. Click the Use Recommended Size check box to deselect it. Type *32 pt* in the Border Size text box.

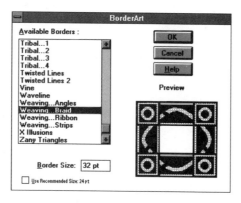

6. Click OK to return to the working screen.

   If you resize the rectangle that appears on your screen to collapse it into a line, BorderArt remains in effect and creates a formatted rule.

   You'll find it easier to complete the final step of this exercise if you first temporarily turn off Snap to Guides.

7. Open the Options menu. Click Snap to Guides to deselect this command.

8. Using the middle selection handle on the top boundary (which is hidden in the BorderArt), drag the resize pointer down until the rectangle collapses into a single line positioned at the 3 ⅓-inch mark on the vertical ruler. (If the end pieces of the BorderArt disappear, use the resize pointer to adjust the height of the rectangle until the end pieces reappear.)

9. Use the move pointer to center the rule at the 3 3/16-inch mark on the vertical ruler.

   The collapsed rectangle should now look like the illustration on the next page, which is shown in Actual Size view.

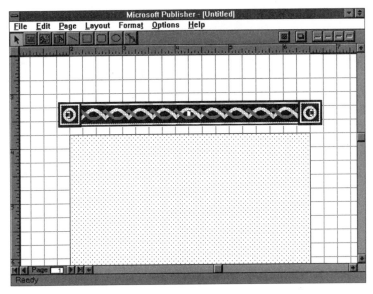

Creating Complex Shapes

In order to complete the tapestry design, you must create two kinds of complex shapes: a cutout effect for the edging and a series of concentric circles for the tassel accents.

Microsoft Publisher does not let you erase portions of geometric objects to create irregular shapes. Nor can you join elements to make a single unit. So you must create both of these effects by overlapping objects. Remember that Publisher can layer objects and change their stacking order. In the next exercises, you'll use the Bring to Front and Send to Back commands on the Layout menu to create the illusion of complex shapes.

Electronic Masking

You can create complex shapes by stacking objects of different colors. When you fill the top object with the same color as the background, you hide the object beneath it. You will use this technique, known as *masking,* to create the irregular edge of the tapestry.

In the following illustration, the cut-out is actually a small box filled with opaque white. When it prints, it will appear to be an extension of the background.

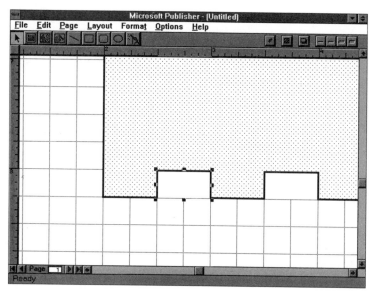

If you scrutinize the illustration, you'll discover that it uses a picture frame in-stead of a rectangle to create the cut-out effect. Unlike rectangles, which must have the same border on all four sides, picture frames and text frames can have a different border width on each side. In this case, you can omit the bor-der entirely from the bottom of the frame to create the illusion of a cut-out.

Hands On:
Electronic Cut-Outs

1. Turn on Snap to Guides in the Options menu.

2. Choose the Picture Frame tool from the Toolbar.

3. Draw a box measuring ¼ inch deep and ½ inch wide. Position it ½ inch from the left edge of the shaded square that you drew earlier. Align the bottom of the box with the bottom of the square.

4. With the picture frame still selected, open the Layout menu, and choose Shading.

5. When the dialog box appears, select the solid white pattern (the top pattern in the middle column) from the Style palette. Click OK.

6. With the picture frame selected, open the Layout menu, and choose Border to open the Border dialog box.

   Next you want to apply a 1-point rule to three sides of the picture frame.

7. Click the right side of the Border box to select it. Two small arrows appear on each end of the right side indicating that it is selected. All the other sides of the border are automatically deselected. Click the 1-point rule.

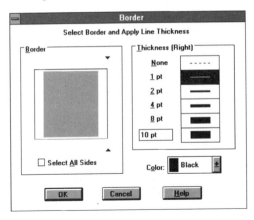

Helping Hand: Stacking Order

If you apply the solid white pattern to the picture frame and don't immediately see a cut-out effect, you probably have the picture frame layered beneath the larger gray square. Reverse the order and place the smaller rectangle on top of the larger square. With the picture frame selected, open the Layout menu, and choose Bring to Front to place the picture frame on top. You'll now see the cut-out effect.

Click the left side of the Border box. Select the 1-point rule. Click the top of the Border box, and again select the 1-point rule. Click OK.

When you return to the working screen, you'll see the cut-out effect. To complete the effect, you must copy and paste the picture frame three times.

8. With the picture frame still selected, open the Edit menu, and choose Copy Picture Frame.

   Publisher places a copy of the formatted picture frame in the Clipboard.

9. Open the Edit menu again. Choose Paste Object(s).

10. Position the duplicate picture frame (which appears in the center of the screen) ½ inch (or 2 grid units) to the right of the first picture frame.

    You don't need to copy the picture frame to the Clipboard again. A copy remains in the Clipboard until you replace it with something else.

11. Paste two more copies of the picture frame into the document. Position the copies ½ inch apart.

    The cut-out illusion works only if you align the overlapping picture frames perfectly. You'll double-check the alignment by zooming in on the appropriate area of the drawing at 200% magnification.

12. With the picture frame still selected, open the Page menu and choose the 200% command.

13. In 200% view, adjust the position of the picture frames so that the borders of the frames align perfectly with the underlying square.

    You may find it easier to view and position the frames if you temporarily turn off Snap to Guides and hide the object boundaries.

Overlapping Objects

To complete the sample drawing, you'll add circular tassels to the tapestry. The series of circles mimics the circular pattern in the BorderArt.

You will create the concentric circles by overlapping two objects. You'll use the Shift key to constrain the Oval tool so that it draws circles. In addition, you will use the Ctrl key at the same time to draw each circle from the center outward. This will let you align the circles around a common center point.

You used the Snap to Guides command previously to align elements to the grid. You can use a similar command — Snap to Ruler Marks — to draw objects with precision. You will now use this command to draw the circles using finer increments of the ruler.

Hands On:
Drawing Concentric Circles

1. Turn on Snap to Ruler Marks on the Options menu.

    This automatically turns off the Snap to Guides option.

2. Open the Page menu and switch to 200% view. If necessary, use the scroll bars to bring the bottom edge of the "tapestry" into view.

3. Select the Oval tool from the Toolbar.

4. Position the crossbar pointer $\frac{1}{4}$ inch to the right and $\frac{3}{16}$ inch below the left corner of the large square.

5. Hold down both the Shift key and the Ctrl key, and drag the crossbar to create a circle with a $\frac{3}{16}$-inch radius. The top of the circle should just touch the bottom of the large square.

Helping Hand: Formatting Attributes

You can easily format the circle by clicking the Toolbar options. The 4-point rule icon is second from the right. To invoke the Shading dialog box, click the icon that looks like a rectangle filled with diagonal lines.

6. Format the circle with a 4-point rule and light gray shading.

7. Repeat steps 3 through 5 to draw a second, smaller circle with a radius of $\frac{1}{8}$ inch.

8. Format the smaller circle with a 2-point rule and a medium gray fill.

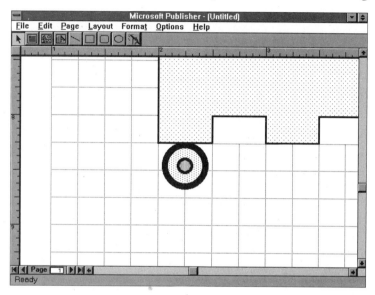

The image that results appears more complex than it really is. Because the outline rule uses a different fill from the background shading pattern, you create the illusion that the motif consists of four concentric circles, instead of two. Now that you have aligned the two circles, you can manipulate them together.

Publisher lets you select more than one element at a time. You can manipulate the group of objects the same way you manipulate single objects. You can perform cut, paste, delete, and copy operations on the group as a whole, and you can change the stacking order of the group in relation to other objects.

In the following exercise, you'll duplicate the group of two circles and then complete the drawing.

Hands On:
Group Maneuvers

1. Click the Selection tool on the Toolbar.

2. Group select the two circles using either of the following methods:

   ☐ Start on a clear area of the page to avoid accidentally selecting other objects. Drag a selection box around both circles. Be sure that you surround only the two circles and don't include any other objects — such as the white cutout picture frame — in the selection box.

   ☐ Hold down the Ctrl key as you click the larger of the two circles to select it. Keeping the Ctrl key depressed, click the smaller circle to add it to the selection group.

3. Position the group so that the circles appear attached to the bottom edge of the tapestry.

   Notice that as you move grouped objects, Publisher shows you the outline of each object. The illustration on the next page demonstrates how this can help you to position objects accurately.

4. With the two circles selected, open the Edit menu and choose Copy Object(s).

   Publisher copies the two circles to the Clipboard. When you paste a duplicate of the circles back into the document, Publisher still treats them as a group.

Helping Hand: Working with Grouped Objects

You can use the Ctrl key to add items to a selected group or to remove items from a selected group. For example, if you inadvertently include the small picture frame in the group, you can hold down the Ctrl key and click the frame to deselect it. The other elements in the group remain selected.

If you accidentally leave behind part of the group as you move it, you don't have to reposition all of the elements to recreate the group. Simply click Undo Move on the Edit menu. Use the Ctrl-click operation to add the missing elements to the group, and then move it again.

5. Open the Edit menu. Choose Paste Object(s).

6. Move the duplicates into position, ½ inch to the right of the group.

7. Repeat steps 5 and 6 three more times to complete the drawing.

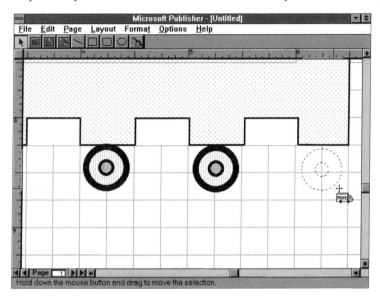

Adding Text

Now that you have finished the drawing for the title page, you can add text. You learned how to handle text in earlier chapters, so the following exercise gives only minimal instructions. If you need more information about text insertion, text formatting, or text frames, see Chapter 6, "Focusing on Type."

Before you create or position text frames, consider the issue of text wrap. Microsoft Publisher does not wrap text around internally created graphic elements, such as rules and rectangles.

However, Publisher does wrap text around picture frames and text frames. Remember that you used picture frames to create the white cutouts at the bottom of the tapestry. To avoid an awkward text wrap, you can employ one of the following techniques:

■ You can size and position the text frame so that it doesn't overlap a picture frame.

- You can create a text frame with small margins or no margins. Publisher uses the frame margin setting to determine how much space to leave between text and the object it wraps around. A small text frame margin lets you position a frame very close to text without forcing a wrap.

- You can stack a text frame on top of a picture frame. Publisher wraps text only when a picture frame is on top of a text frame.

You'll put these techniques to work in the following exercises.

Hands On: Inserting Text

1. Draw a text frame that starts at 2 ⅜ inches on the vertical ruler, ends at 3 ¼ inches on the vertical ruler, and spans the entire width of the page.

2. Open the Layout menu, and choose Frame Columns and Margins. In the dialog box, set the margins to 0 on all four sides.

3. Choose Shading from the Layout menu. In the dialog box, set the Style to Clear (the first option).

   By making the frame transparent, you can position the text close to the rule without having the edges of the frame hide any of the BorderArt pattern. If you prefer, you can choose Send to Back to layer the objects with the BorderArt on top of the text frame.

4. Choose Indents and Spacing from the Format menu. In the Indents and Spacing dialog box, set Space Between Lines to 61 pt. Assign center alignment to the text frame.

5. Type the following text:

   CUCINA TOSCANA

6. Set the initial caps in 60-point Dutch. Set the remaining letters in 36-point Dutch, all caps.

7. Draw a second text frame measuring 3 ½ inches square. Position it inside the larger gray square, ½ inch from the top and sides.

8. Open the Layout menu, choose Frame Columns and Margins, and in the dialog box, set the margins to 0 on all four sides.

9. Choose Shading from the Layout menu. In the dialog box set the Shading Style to Clear.

   The transparent fill allows the gray tint of the underlying rectangle to show through the type.

10. Choose Indents and Spacing from the Format menu. In the dialog box assign justified alignment to the text frame. Set Space Between Lines to 24 points.

11. Type the following text, and set it in 14-point Dutch.

    ```
    The cooking of Tuscany in Northern Italy includes simple
    peasant dishes from the countryside as well as elaborate
    recipes dating back to the Renaissance. Tonight's menu
    celebrates Tuscan cuisine by featuring game meats, such as
    quail and rabbit, "white" pasta served in a traditional butter
    sauce, and Tiramisu — the most popular of all Italian desserts.
    ```

Text-Frame Formatting

In the next exercise, you'll create the second page of the sample menu and in the process discover how to create more efficient drawings by formatting the text frames directly rather than by layering text frames on top of formatted rectangles. Remember that you can fill text frames with tints and patterns and assign them border rules of different widths.

Helping Hand: The Scratch Area

You can use the white area surrounding your working page as a scratch area. In the following exercise, you'll create a rectangle in the scratch area, collapse it to create a bullet, and then copy and paste the bullet into position in your document. The scratch area lets you experiment with special effects without disrupting your working page.

If you leave objects in the scratch area, they don't print because they fall outside of the page boundaries. However, they appear on screen, even when you turn to different pages in your publication. The scratch area makes it easy for you to copy elements among pages. Note that Publisher saves objects in the scratch area with the publication.

Hands On:
Integrating Text Frames into the Design

1. Open the Page Menu. Choose Insert Pages.

2. When the Insert Pages dialog box appears, choose to insert one blank page after the current page.

3. Before you type in text, change the Layout Guides. From the Layout menu, choose Layout Guides. In the dialog box, change the guides to 3 columns and 1 row.

4. Turn on Snap to Guides in the Options menu.

5. Create the first text frame, starting at 1 ¾ inches on the vertical ruler and ending at 2 ⅛ inches on the vertical ruler. The frame should span the center column.

   For the heading, you will use one of the display typefaces that comes with Bitstream Facelift — Formal Script. Using this typeface for the headings rather than for body copy guarantees that the text will remain legible.

6. Select the text frame and choose Frame Columns and Margins from the Layout menu. Set the frame margins to 0.

7. Set the typeface to 16-point Formal Script.

8. Choose Indents and Spacing from the Format menu. In the Indents and Spacings dialog box, set Space Between Lines to 22 points, and the alignment to Center.

9. Type the Italian word for appetizers: *Antipasti*.

10. With the text frame still selected, open the Layout menu and choose Border.

11. Apply a 2-point border to both the top and the bottom of the frame. Do not apply a border to the sides of the frame.

    To complete the design, you will create BorderArt "bullets" and position them on either side of the text frame.

12. Draw a rectangle approximately 3 inches wide by 2 inches deep in the scratch area. Choose BorderArt from the Layout menu, and

format the rectangle with the Weaving...Braid BorderArt pattern at 28 points.

13. Using the resize pointer, collapse the rectangle in both the horizontal and vertical directions. This creates a single point that contains only the corner motif of the original pattern. (The illustration below shows both the full-size and the collapsed rectangles.)

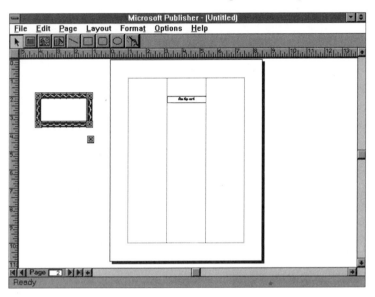

14. With the BorderArt bullet selected, open the Edit menu and choose Copy Box.

15. Open the Edit menu. Choose Paste Object(s). Position the duplicate bullet to the left of the text frame.

16. Choose Paste Object again, and position a second copy of the bullet to the right of the text frame.

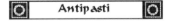

17. Create a second text frame that starts at 2 ⅛ inches on the vertical ruler, ends at 3 ¼ inches on the vertical ruler, and spans the entire page.

18. Open the Layout menu, and choose Frame Columns and Margins. In the dialog box set the text frame margins to ¼ inch (entered as .25) for all four sides.

19. Set the type in 12-point Dutch.

20. Open the Format menu, and choose Indents and Spacing. Set Space Between Lines to 15 points, and choose Center alignment.

21. Type the following copy into the frame. (Use italics for the word "or.")

    ```
    Warm salad of duck and Tuscan white beans

    or

    Grilled Portobello mushrooms, with a sauce of lemon and
    white wine
    ```

    Now that you've completed the first text frame, you can use the Clipboard to help you create the rest of the frames more easily.

22. Drag a selection box around the bullets and the two text frames to group-select the objects.

23. With the objects still selected, open the Edit menu and choose Copy Object(s).

24. Use the Paste Object(s) command on the Edit menu to paste three duplicates of this group into your document.

    When you copy a text frame to the Clipboard, one of two things happens. If the text frame is linked to one or more other text frames, Publisher duplicates all the attributes of the frame — including the size, the shape, and the attributes such as borders and margins. However, Publisher does not duplicate the text attributes.

    If you copy a text frame that is not linked to other text frames, however, Publisher copies both the text and the text formatting to the Clipboard. Therefore, when you paste the group back into the document, you can highlight the text and replace it with new copy. The new text will retain all the type specifications. Refer to Figure 8-1, on pages 227 and 228, for the rest of the menu text.

25. Place a BorderArt rule (really a collapsed rectangle) along the top and bottom of the page. (See steps 1 through 8 on pages 234–235 for reference.) Size it at 28 points, and align it with the left and right page margins.

26. Finalize the document by saving it to disk. Open the File menu, and choose Save. Use the Directories and Drives list boxes to place the file in a convenient location. Assign the file a descriptive name, such as MENU.PUB, to identify it.

Print Quality

Print the completed menu by choosing the Print command from the File menu and accepting the program defaults. Take a moment to examine the quality of the printout. You'll notice that the image created with Microsoft Publisher's internal drawing tools prints with smooth lines and balanced gray tints.

The geometric objects, borders, and BorderArt created within Publisher always print at your printer's highest resolution.

What's Next?

In this chapter, you learned how to create simple pictures using Microsoft Publisher's drawing tools. You also learned that, to create more complex pictures, you can combine multiple objects and use Publisher's extensive formatting options.

In the next chapter, you'll gather artwork from several external sources and import the images into a Publisher newsletter. You will learn how images enhance the appearance of publications and augment the contents. You will also explore Publisher's ability to format pictures, including Publisher's cropping and resizing functions. Although you will focus your attention on using and manipulating artwork, you will also use the skills you have already learned — and produce a sophisticated publication that integrates words with pictures.

Chapter 9

PICTURE PERFECT

In Chapter 4, the official Epicurean Delights newsletter, *The Epicurean,* began its life as a two-page handout. As the staff became more proficient with Microsoft Publisher, the newsletter became more sophisticated and changed its name. *Epicurean News* is now an eight-page publication that takes full advantage of Publisher's ability to integrate pictures with text.

It's simple to place pictures in Publisher documents. You have already imported pictures into sample documents such as the newsletter in Chapter 4 and the brochure in Chapter 5. In this chapter, you'll discover that pictures can be stored in a variety of file formats and you'll learn which file formats best suit your design needs. In addition, you will learn how to use Publisher's editing and formatting tools to change the appearance of imported pictures. You will create designs with visual impact by using cropping and scaling functions and by adding fancy borders to picture frames. Equally important, you'll learn how pictures and text must work together to create a cohesive, successful publication by designing two pages of a sample newsletter.

Why Use a Picture?

Before you import a picture into a publication, think about the function it will serve. Most pictures augment the text by accurately reproducing the appearance of people or things. For example, a corporate report might include a photograph of the CEO and a realistic rendering of a new product.

But pictures can also perform informational and organizational functions. Informational graphics translate hard data into pie charts and bar graphs can also represent processes and ideas in the form of flow charts and technical diagrams. For instance, an illustration that shows how to assemble a child's bike is an informational graphic.

Finally, you can use pictures to decorate and organize your publication. Small pictures can work as icons, allowing readers to easily locate the beginning of a story or helping them to recognize a regular department in a newsletter.

Of course, the same picture can perform more than one function. For example, in Figure 9-1 on the next page, you'll notice that a picture of a trout appears as an icon in the table of contents on page 1 and then again as an illustration on page 2.

People usually remember pictures more readily than they remember words. Adding illustrations to your publications — whether you add photographs, pie charts, or icons — can make your messages stick in readers' minds.

Graphics File Formats

After you decide the content of the pictures, you must determine the best file format to use. Even experienced desktop publishers become confused by the many available graphics file formats. If you learn to distinguish among the formats, you can improve the quality of the images in your publications.

You can identify a picture format by its filename extension. MS-DOS filenames usually have three-letter extensions following the period. The extension tells you the file's format. A file called PICTURE.WMF, for example, is stored in the Windows Metafile format, and a file called ARTWORK.BMP is stored in Windows Bit-Map format. Microsoft Publisher can import a wide variety of graphics file formats.

The following table lists the most common graphics file formats that Publisher can import. The industry standard format name appears in the first column. In many cases the format name was derived from a program name. For example, PCX format originally indicated a file created by PC Paintbrush and eventually became a standard file format used by many other graphics programs. The three-letter file extension for each format appears in the second column.

Computer Graphics Metafile	CGM
DrawPerfect	WPG
Encapsulated PostScript	EPS
Micrografx Designer	DRW
PC Paintbrush	PCX
Tagged Image Format	TIF
Windows Bit Map	BMP
Windows Metafile	WMF

E PICUREA N
N e w s

September 1992
Vol. 1, No. 1

L'Accademia: Food With a Philosophy

By Michael Alonso

A
PUBLICATION
OF
EPICUREAN DELIGHTS

R obbin Frances is a self-proclaimed Italophile. Having spent six years roaming the kitchens of Italy, the 31-year-old chef returned to New York three years ago--recipes in tow--to open L'Accademia, one of Manhattan's most successful small restaurants.

What keeps knowledgeable gourmets coming back to the three-star Accademia is Frances' commitment to using the best-tasting seafood, the most savory meat, and the freshest seasonal vegetables, many of which she buys from local farmers. Relying on producers close to home ("that means the Eastern seaboard") was a lesson she learned in Italy. "One of the reasons why meals in Italy are so special is because the ingredients are regional," says Frances. "Chefs know they're getting the freshest goods because their suppliers are also their neighbors." In one instance, white peaches from an Upstate New York farm owned by an old college acquaintance are the basis for a much-requested fruit tart; in another, crabmeat from

Maine complements organically grown asparagus and homemade flour-and-egg tagliatelle.

Frances' reliance on high-quality produce is part of a larger philosophy, one that can be summed up in three words: pure and simple. "Each ingredient in a dish should have integrity," she says. "I'm a believer in letting each flavor come through in all its vibrancy rather than in creating an elaborate disguise." Typifying this approach is her *Spaghetti ai Fiori di Zucca* (spaghetti with squash

Continued on page 5

Robbin Frances in the kitchen of her restaurant, L'Accademia.

Figure 9-1.

Pages 1 and 2 of Epicurean News. *These pages were reproduced on a Linotronic typesetter, which has a higher resolution than a laser printer.*

Figure 9-1. *continued*

EPICUREAN NEWS

Flying Fish Spotted in The Windy City

By Elizabeth Jarmen

L et's face it, Chicago is famous for stock-yards not fisheries. But times are changing. People are eating fish instead of red meat. Seafood is an important part of a heart-healthy diet, because it is low in cholesterol and fat.

We're proud that the freshest fish in Chicago can be found at Epicurean Delights. The arrival of Aquaculture, or fish farming

Nassau Grouper is native to the coastal waters of Florida.

as it is known among the professionals, has made Trout as commonly available as beef. We found a hatchery only hours away from the heart of the city. It tastes like the Trout has jumped out of the water and onto your plate!

Trout is a wonderful fish that is great when grilled whole over a mesquite flavored barbecue. The firm white flesh can also be fillet-ed and boned, and then gently poached in white wine.

The really exciting news, how-ever, is the introduction of Epicurean Delights' Flying Fish Service. Flying Fish is ordered by telephone and shipped by air to arrive the next day. It's the next best thing to catching it yourself! The quick turn-around time al-lows us to offer you Blue Catfish from Louisiana, Grouper from Florida, and Chinook Salmon from Wash-ington state.

Farm-raised Trout is now as plentiful as beef.

We're hoping that our marine harvest inspires you to try new recipes. Just think about Sea Bass poached in a Court Bouillon of winter herbs, or medallions of Salmon encased in a crispy potato jacket. Imagine succulent Grouper and aromatic vegetables steamed in a parchment envelope.

These recipes are particularly easy to try because they are available as prepared, ready-to-cook dishes from the Epicurean Delights kitchen. You just pop the fish into the oven, micro-wave, or skillet and enjoy a delicious meal ten minutes later. And though we may be preju-diced, we think our Lobster with Corn Relish and Green Onion Shrimp salads are worthy of main course status. For busy people who also care about the food they eat, fish is the ultimate high-quality fast food.

MENU

Nassau Grouper
Sealed in a parchment envelope.

Sea Bass
In Herbed Court Bouillon.

Salmon
With Basil Vinaigrette.

Farm Trout
Marinated in White Wine and Lemon.

Lobster Salad
With Corn Relish.

Shrimp Salad
With Green Onion.

Salmon
And Oriental Vegetables.

2

You don't need to memorize what each extension stands for. However, you should know how different formats function in Publisher documents. First, you need to explore some basic concepts concerning computer images.

Bit-Mapped and Vector Images

All graphic file formats fall into one of two categories: bit-mapped images or vectors. PCX, BMP, and TIF files are bit maps. Conversely CGM, WPG, EPS, WMF, and DRW files contain vector information.

Take a look at the illustration below. It shows two circles on the left and enlarged sections of each on the right. You will immediately interpret the two images on the left as circles. However, your computer doesn't see these elements as circles. In the case of a bit-mapped image (top left), the computer sees only a collection of square dots. The enlarged section of the bitmapped image (top right) lets you see the dots that compose the circle. These dots are also called pixels — an acronym for picture elements. All the dots have equal importance. In a black-and-white (or monochrome) bit-mapped image, the computer stores each pixel as one bit. The information contained in the file specifies the location (or map) of each pixel (or bit) — hence the term *bit map.*

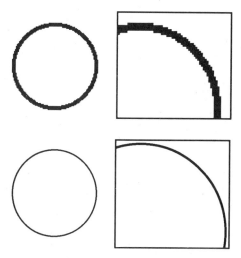

If you look at the enlargement of the vector image (bottom right), you can't detect individual dots. Vector images are composed of drawing instructions.

Your computer identifies this circle, for example, as a geometric object with a specific location, radius, line width, and fill pattern. Because your computer stores vector images as a series of instructions, you can resize vectors without losing quality. In fact, vector images — which are also called object-oriented drawings — always print at the highest resolution of which the output device is capable.

In summary, bit-mapped images consist of pixels, and vector images consist of a series of drawing instructions. Each type of image has certain advantages and disadvantages.

The Pros and Cons of Bit-Mapped Images

The black-and-white bit-mapped image in the illustration on the previous page demonstrates the biggest problem with bit-mapped images: When you enlarge a bit-mapped image, you also enlarge each pixel. As the pixels get bigger, they create a distracting staircase pattern. This effect — technically known as *aliasing* — is commonly called "the jaggies."

Resizing a bit-mapped image, either by enlarging or reducing it, can result in distortion. Therefore, when you work with black-and-white bit-mapped images, it's a good idea to keep them close to their original size and shape. Also, you should try to match the resolution of bit-mapped images to the resolution of your output device. For example, 300 dots-per-inch (dpi) laser printers produce the best quality output when black-and-white bit-mapped images also contain 300 dots per inch.

You can minimize many of the resizing problems associated with black-and-white bit-mapped images by using gray-scale or color bit-mapped images instead. Gray-scale and color bit-mapped images use intermediate shades or colors to create a gradual transition from one color to another. The color transitions — known as *antialiasing* — trick your eye into seeing smooth lines. So if you resize a gray-scale or color bit-mapped image, the quality of the picture degrades less than if you resize a black-and-white bit-mapped image. Because bit-mapped images can accommodate many colors or shades of gray, they are best suited for scanned photographs and realistic illustrations.

You can buy clip-art libraries that consist solely of bit-mapped images. These libraries contain pictures stored in a 300 dpi black-and-white format, which makes the pictures difficult to resize. You also can create bit-mapped pictures using a paint program such as Windows Paintbrush.

Desktop scanners provide the most common source of high-quality bit-mapped images. If you generate scans from original photographs, you can create digitized pictures that take up less space on your disk by trading resolution for additional colors. For example, the photograph of the chef in Figure 9-1 was scanned at only 150 dpi, but because the image contains 256 shades of gray, it prints with sufficient detail on a 300 dpi laser printer.

The Pros and Cons of Vector Images

When you import a vector image into Publisher, you can scale it or even change its proportions without a loss of quality. This lets you deliberately stretch pictures to create dramatic designs or special effects.

Because your computer stores vector images as a series of drawing instructions, they always print at your output device's highest resolution. If you print a CGM file on a dot-matrix printer, it usually prints at either 72 or 180 dpi, depending on the print head capability. On most laser printers, the same image automatically prints at 300 dpi.

Your computer also stores color information for vector images as a set of instructions. This gives vector files a superior ability to print even tints of color. But vector files do a poor job reproducing gradual color transitions, such as the shades in a photograph. For best results, use vector formats for line drawings, logos, and technical diagrams that don't use shading extensively.

In case you haven't guessed, Publisher's internal drawing tools are vector-based. In addition, Publisher's clip-art library is stored in CGM format. Most clip-art collections on the market today employ vector formats.

You can easily generate vector illustrations on your own using commercially available graphics programs. Programs like CorelDraw!, Arts & Letters Graphics Editor, and MicroGrafx Designer let you create images from scratch or modify standard clip-art images. And many programs that create charts — Harvard Graphics, Microsoft PowerPoint, and Microsoft Excel — create pie charts or histograms in vector formats.

The Pros and Cons of PostScript

Encapsulated PostScript (EPS) files can contain either vector or bit-mapped images. In either case, the information is stored in the PostScript printer language.

If you are planning a publication with numerous photographs and drawings, you should consider PostScript files for two reasons. First, PostScript laser printers do a superior job of printing complex images. The lines in vector images appear smoother, and bit-mapped images print with a wider range of gray shades.

Second, the same document file that you send to your 300-dpi PostScript laser printer will print at 1200 or 2400 dpi on your service bureau's high-end typesetting machines. So you can print accurate proofs of your publication before you send them out to a commercial printer for professional-quality reproduction. (For information on how to send a PostScript printer file to a service bureau see Appendix C, "Printing with Microsoft Publisher.")

In this chapter you'll create a newsletter that includes a variety of important pictures. In the exercises you'll use Encapsulated PostScript clip art and take advantage of the superior output quality offered by PostScript laser printers.

Note, however, that Windows is currently unable to display an EPS picture on screen. When you import an EPS file into Publisher, you will see a picture only if a bit-mapped image of the picture, called a header, was included in the file. The header contains a low-resolution representation of the image that helps you position the picture. If no header was included, the EPS file appears on your screen as a simple box with an identifying filename. The size of this bounding box indicates the dimensions of the picture contained in the EPS file.

One final caveat: you must print EPS files on a PostScript printer. If you print a publication containing an EPS image to a non-PostScript printer, Publisher reproduces the screen image — either as a low-resolution bit map or as a plain bounding box.

You can complete the exercises in this chapter even if you don't have access to a PostScript printer. Microsoft Publisher's scaling and cropping tools work on all graphics file formats. So you can use the Computer Graphics Metafile (CGM) clip-art images that are included with Publisher instead of EPS pictures and print your sample newsletter to an HP LaserJet or to a dot-matrix printer.

Flexible Layouts

If you create an underlying grid, you will find it easier to position and size pictures in your publication. To determine what size to make your grid, consider the function of your publication. For example, if you intend to create a product catalog, you might want each page to follow the same format, with photographs in the same location on every page. Such consistency of design lets readers find information quickly.

If your newsletter will incorporate pictures of varying sizes and shapes, however, you need a more flexible grid. The sample newsletter pages that you will create in this chapter use a six-column grid. This grid lets you size artwork at a number of different column measures, including widths of $\frac{1}{6}$, $\frac{1}{3}$, $\frac{1}{2}$, and $\frac{2}{3}$ of a page.

 ### Hands On:
The Underlying Grid

1. Open Publisher. Choose Blank Page in the Start Up dialog box.

2. Open the Print Setup dialog box from the File menu. Choose an appropriate printer. The examples in this chapter assume that a PostScript printer has been selected. Confirm that the Page Size is $8\frac{1}{2}$ inches by 11 inches and the Orientation is Portrait.

3. Open the Page Setup dialog box from the Page menu. Confirm that the layout view is Full Page.

4. Open the Layout Guides dialog box from the Layout menu. Create margins of 0.75 inch on all four sides of the page. Set up a grid that has six columns and one row.

Positioning Text Elements

The grid you've created will not only serve as a guide for your pictures, it will also help you to size and position the text elements in your sample newsletter. In fact, if you place text first, you will find it easier to work with the pictures intelligently. You should first lay out the logos, running headers, and headlines to block out the page design, and then import the body copy. (For more information about the elements that constitute a newsletter — such as logos, headlines, kickers, text columns, and captions — review Chapter 4, "The Power of PageWizards.")

As you place text in the newsletter, you'll notice another important aspect of working with a PostScript printer — access to PostScript fonts. Remember, your printer choice largely determines the font selection available to you.

In your PostScript-based newsletter you will use the Palatino typeface as the serif font for headlines and body copy. Use Helvetica as the sans-serif font for display type. Helvetica is very similar to the Bitstream Swiss typeface you used in previous chapters. Palatino does differ from the Bitstream Dutch font. However, if you use Bitstream fonts rather than PostScript fonts to complete this exercise, substitute a serif face like Dutch for Palatino.

To prepare your newsletter, follow the instructions in the next exercise. Use Figure 9-2 (which shows the newsletter with the text, but not the pictures, in position) as a reference.

Hands On: Designing with Text

Page 1 of your sample newsletter consists of five basic design elements: a rule that borders the page margins, a logo, the date and issue number, the table of contents, and a lead story.

1. Use the rectangle tool to draw a 2-point rule that borders the page. Position the rectangle on the left, right, and bottom guides ½ inch below the top guide. Notice in Figure 9-2 that you need approximately ½ inch of extra breathing room at the top of the page to accommodate the logo.

2. The logo is composed of three WordArt frames, a text frame, and a picture frame. It is positioned off-center — in columns 3, 4, 5, and 6 of the underlying grid. Use three WordArt frames to create the the word "Epicurean." Set the first and last letters in 72-point Ellensburg and the remaining letters in 24-point Ellensburg.

   Use a text frame, formatted in 14-point Helvetica bold, center-aligned, with a 2-point border and a shadow to create the "News" part of the logo. Complete the logo by drawing a picture frame around it. Format the picture frame with a 10-point rule at the top and a 2-point rule on the bottom and the two sides.

3. Create a small text frame in columns 1 and 2 for the date and volume number.

   Set the text in 12-point Helvetica bold, with 15 points of space between lines. Align the text flush left.

September 1992
Vol. 1, No. 1

L'Accademia: Food With a Philosophy

By Michael Alonso

**A
PUBLICATION
OF
EPICUREAN DELIGHTS**

R obbin Frances is a self-proclaimed Italophile. Having spent six years roaming the kitchens of Italy, the 31-year-old chef returned to New York three years ago--recipes in tow--to open L'Accademia, one of Manhattan's most successful small restaurants.

What keeps knowledgeable gourmets coming back to the three-star Accademia is Frances' commitment to using the best-tasting seafood, the most savory meat, and the freshest seasonal vegetables, many of which she buys from local farmers. Relying on producers close to home ("that means the Eastern seaboard") was a lesson she learned in Italy. "One of the reasons why meals in Italy are so special is because the ingredients are regional," says Frances. "Chefs know they're getting the freshest goods because their suppliers are also their neighbors." In one instance, white peaches from an Upstate New York farm owned by an old college acquaintance are the basis for a much-requested fruit tart; in another, crabmeat from Maine complements organically grown asparagus and homemade flour-and-egg tagliatelle.

Frances' reliance on high-quality produce is part of a larger philosophy, one that can be summed up in three words: pure and simple. "Each ingredient in a dish should have integrity," she says. "I'm a believer in letting each flavor come through in all its vibrancy rather than in creating an elaborate disguise." Typifying this approach is her *Spaghetti ai Fiori di Zucca* (spaghetti with squash flowers), in which traces of chopped garlic and chili pepper zip up but don't overpower the delicate yellow flowers.

What Frances doesn't procure from nearby food mongers she grows herself in an herb garden behind the restaurant, which occupies the first floor of a restored Georgian townhouse. When the windows are open in summer, even the gentlest breeze fills the dining room with the redolence of basil. It's not hard for diners to imagine they are dining in a villa somewhere on the Ligurian coast, a feeling Frances does her best to encourage.

Figure 9-2.
The text layout for Epicurean News.

Figure 9-2. *continued*

Flying Fish Spotted in The Windy City

By Elizabeth Jarmen

L et's face it, Chicago is famous for stockyards not fisheries. But times are changing. People are eating fish instead of red meat. Seafood is an important part of a heart-healthy diet, because it is low in cholesterol and fat.

We're proud that the freshest fish in Chicago can be found at Epicurean Delights. The arrival of Aquaculture, or fish farming as it is known among the profes-

sionals, has made Trout as commonly available as beef. We found a hatchery only hours away from the heart of the city. It tastes like the Trout has jumped out of the water and onto your plate!

Trout is a wonderful fish that is great when grilled whole over a mesquite flavored barbecue. The firm white flesh can also be filleted and boned, and then gently poached in white wine.

The really exciting news, however, is the introduction of Epicurean Delights' Flying Fish Service. Flying Fish is ordered by telephone and shipped by air to arrive the next day. It's the next best thing to catching it yourself! The quick turnaround time allows us to offer you Blue Catfish from Louisiana, Grouper from Florida, and Chinook Salmon from Washington state.

We're hoping that our marine harvest inspires you to try new recipes. Just think about Sea Bass poached in a Court Bouillon of winter herbs, or medallions of Salmon encased in a crispy potato jacket. Imagine succulent Grouper and aromatic vegetables steamed in a parchment envelope.

These recipes are particularly easy to try because they are

available as prepared, ready-to-cook dishes from the Epicurean Delights kitchen. You just pop the fish into the oven, microwave, or skillet and enjoy a delicious meal ten minutes later. And though we may be prejudiced, we think our Lobster with Corn Relish and Green Onion Shrimp salads are worthy of main course status. For busy people who also care about the food they eat, fish is the ultimate high-quality fast food.

MENU

Nassau Grouper
Sealed in a parchment envelope.

Sea Bass
In Herbed Court Bouillon.

Salmon
With Basil Vinaigrette.

Farm Trout
Marinated in White
Wine and Lemon.

Lobster Salad
With Corn Relish.

Shrimp Salad
With Green Onion.

Salmon
And Oriental Vegetables.

2

4. A single text frame contains the text for the table of contents.

   Format the frame with margins of 0.17 inch, a light gray tint fill, an 8-point rule at the top, and a 1-point rule on the bottom and the two sides. Notice how a narrow text width of only 1 ¾ inch gives the text frame breathing room on the left and right.

   Set the text in 12-point Helvetica, with 15 points of space between lines. Center-align the text. Use capitalization and boldfacing to emphasize key words and page numbers, as shown in Figure 9-2.

   The lead story consists of four distinct text frames.

5. The headline spans columns 3, 4, 5, and 6 of the underlying grid. Set the text in 30-point Palatino, with 34 points of space between lines. Left-align the text.

6. Set the author's byline in 12-point Helvetica. Format the text frame with a 2-point rule on the bottom edge. Notice that in order to print the rule across columns 3, 4, 5, and 6 of the underlying grid, you must use a text frame that extends across the four columns.

7. Set the body copy in 10-point Palatino, with 13 points of leading. Each paragraph except the first one begins with a first-line indent of 0.17 inch.

   You could create two linked text frames — one for each column of text. Instead, use the Frame Columns and Margins dialog box

Helping Hand: Text Frame Margins

When you use the Frame Margins and Columns command from the Layout menu to set up your text frames, remember that the size you specify for your frame margins influences how your text flows around pictures.

Publisher uses the top and bottom text-frame margins to determine how much space to leave between the text and the top or bottom border of overlapping picture frames. Likewise, the program uses the left and right text-frame margins to determine the amount of space to clear on either side of picture frames. If you create wide margins in your text frames, the pictures in your layout will have a wide berth. Conversely, if you create narrow margins or no margins in your text frames, the body copy will print very close to the picture frame.

to create two columns of text within a single text frame that spans columns 3, 4, 5, and 6. Also, in the Frame Columns and Margins dialog box, specify a margin of 0.15 inch on all four sides of the frame and a gutter of 0.20 inch between columns.

8. Create the fancy first letter by drawing a perfect ½-inch square text frame. Format the text frame with a 2-point border and a shadow.

   Set the capital letter *R* in 22-point Helvetica bold. Center-align the text.

9. Choose Ignore Background from the Page menu.

Creating a Consistent Design

As you study Figure 9-2, notice that the newsletter uses type and repeating elements to create a consistent design. For example, the frames for both the logo and the Contents use heavy rules at the top as decorative elements. All ancillary text, including drop caps and bylines, use the Helvetica typeface. As you complete the text design of page 2, pay special attention to how these design motifs repeat or are modified. For example, the logo and fancy first letter on page 1 use a shadow that also appears on page 2 in the fancy first letter, the running head, and the page number. Similarly, the menu sidebar on page 2 mimics the design of the Contents on page 1.

Hands On: Creating Consistent Type Designs

1. Using the Insert Page command on the Page menu, add a second blank page to the sample publication.

   Whenever you create a document that is more than one page long, place repeating elements — the page numbers and running headers — on the Background page.

2. Switch to the Background page. Draw a rectangle with a 2-point border. The rectangle should align with all four borders of the page.

3. Create a ½-inch square text frame in the lower left corner to hold the page number. Remember, if you want Publisher to add the correct page number to each page of your publication, you must use the Insert Page Numbers command on the Page menu.

Set the automatic page number in 14-point Helvetica bold. Center-align the text.

4. Create a text frame that spans columns 1, 2, 3, and 4 for the running header. Type the name of the newsletter, *Epicurean News,* and set it in 16-point Helvetica bold and format all except the initial letters (E and N) as small capitals. Add 5 points of extra space between each letter by using the Spacing Between Characters command, and add a 2-point border around the frame.

5. Return to the Foreground page.

   The elements you placed on the Background page automatically appear on page 2 (and any pages that you subsequently add to the newsletter). Now add the remainder of the text and note how many type specifications repeat from page 1.

6. Create a text frame, and type the headline. Like the headline on page 1, it spans four columns of the underlying grid, but it spans columns 1, 2, 3, and 4. Use the same type specifications you used for the headline on page 1.

7. Create the author's byline exactly as you did on page 1 — except that the text frame and its associated border should span all six columns.

8. Create a text frame that spans all six columns for the body copy, but use the Frame Columns and Margins dialog box to create three text columns instead of two.

9. Create a ½-inch text frame for the fancy first letter and type the letter *L.* Again, the specifications for the text frame and the type are the same as on page 1.

10. Create the menu sidebar by duplicating the text frame and its formatting from the Contents on page 1, including the border, the frame margins, and the fill pattern.

    Center the type in the narrow text frame. (The frame measures only 2 inches wide.) Set the text in 10-point Helvetica, with 12 points of leading. Use boldfacing to highlight each heading.

11. Using the Save As command on the File menu, save your work so far with an appropriate filename such as NEWLET.PUB — an abbreviation of "newsletter."

You're now ready to import pictures into your newsletter.

Importing Pictures

Before you import a picture into your publication, you should decide whether you need to draw a picture frame. If you want to import a picture to fit into a predetermined layout, you should draw a picture frame first so that Publisher will automatically size and proportion the image to match the waiting frame.

However, if you import a picture without first drawing a picture frame, Publisher imports the picture at its original size and shape and automatically creates a picture frame to fit around the image. This feature lets you maintain the original aspect ratio and minimize the chances of distorting your images. It is especially useful for working with bit-mapped images.

 ### Hands On:
Import Picture Command

1. Be sure that you're on page 1 in Full Page view and that no objects or frames are selected.

2. Open the File menu. Choose Import Picture.

3. When the Import Picture dialog box appears on screen, open the List Type of Files list box and select a bit-mapped format, such as Tagged Image Format (TIF), PC Paintbrush (PCX), or Windows Bit-Map (BMP).

Helping Hand: Substituting Clip Art

If you don't have access to an appropriate bit-mapped image, you can use one of Publisher's clip-art images instead. In fact, Publisher does supply a clip-art drawing of a chef (CHEF.CGM) and another of a woman (BOOKFEM1.CGM) in CGM format. Or, if you prefer to create your own image, you can create a BMP file using Windows Paintbrush.

The Picture Name list box displays only the files of the type you specified. If you had chosen to search for all file types, Publisher would display both bit-mapped and vector files.

4. Use the Directories list box to locate an appropriate image. (The following illustrations in this chapter use a scanned photograph created specifically for *Epicurean News*.)

5. Click OK to import the picture.

The sample photograph of chef Robbin Frances was scanned at 150 dots per inch, using 256 shades of gray. The display on screen does a poor job of showing the range of gray tones because the standard Windows palette contains only a few shades of gray. Don't worry: your laser printer will do a better job with the gray-scale information.

Picture Editing Tools

After you successfully import a picture into Microsoft Publisher, you can use the selection handles surrounding the picture frame to resize, or crop, the image. As you know, you can drag the frame handles to resize a picture. Or to maintain the correct aspect ratio as you resize a picture, you can hold down the Shift key as you drag a corner selection handle.

You can hide portions of a picture by using Publisher's Cropping tool. Think of the picture frame as a window. Using the Cropping tool is like pulling down the window shade. Although the view doesn't change, you can see more of the landscape when the window shade is up and less when it is down.

You can't fit the imported TIF image into your publication unless you employ Publisher's cropping and scaling functions.

Hands On:
Image Editing Tools

1. Select the picture of the chef (or whatever picture you imported).

Eight selection handles appear around the frame.

2. Click the Cropping tool icon on the Toolbar, or choose Crop Picture from the Format menu. (The Cropping tool icon looks like two

intersecting scissors.) When you place the Pointer over any selection handle, the Pointer changes to become the Cropping tool.

You use the Cropping tool to trim away parts of the picture that you don't want to use. The Cropping tool doesn't actually delete parts of the picture; it merely hides them from view. You can also use the Cropping tool to restore a picture to its original view.

3. Place the Cropping tool on the middle right handle. Move the pointer to the left until the picture frame touches the arm of the chef.

4. Repeat step 4 using the left, top, and bottom selection handles to delete the unimportant, visually distracting background from the photograph.

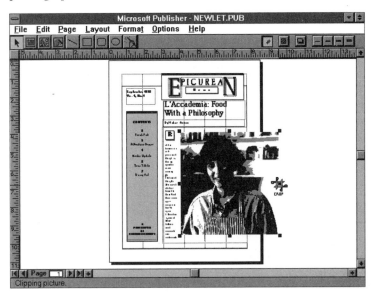

5. Deselect the Cropping tool by once again clicking the Cropping tool icon or by choosing the Crop Picture command.

6. Move and resize the photograph so that it spans columns 5 and 6 of the underlying grid. Remember to press the Shift key as you

move a corner handle. This procedure resizes the picture proportionally, so that you maintain the aspect ratio of the chef's face.

7. Use the move pointer to position the picture in columns 5 and 6 at the bottom of the page.

Picture Frame Effects

You can format picture frames in the same way that you format other Publisher frames. You can add shadow effects, place rules, create decorative borders with BorderArt, and even (in the case of vector images) add a pattern to the picture's background. You can access many of these options — including the Shadow attribute, the Shading dialog box, and standard weights for border rules — from the Toolbar. If you want to create more sophisticated effects with BorderArt or apply rules of different weights to each side of a picture frame, you'll need to use the Layout menu.

In the following exercise, you'll discover the importance of discretion. Framing a photograph with a decorative rule or a drop shadow can enhance its appearance. But too many effects distract the reader's attention from the picture. You will now enhance the photograph using BorderArt.

 ### *Hands On:* ### Formatting Picture Frames

1. Select the photograph of the chef.

2. Open the Layout menu. Choose BorderArt.

3. When the BorderArt dialog box appears on screen, select the Basic...Wide Outline border. Use the suggested size of 6 points.

4. Use the selection handles to resize the photo so that both the photo and the border fit within the column guides. Remember to hold down Shift and use the corner handle to resize the photo proportionally.

5. Click OK to return to the working screen.

Working with Text Wrap

After you position a picture in your publication, you must double-check to be sure that the picture doesn't disrupt the flow of text. Pay particular attention to how Publisher wraps the body copy around the picture frame to see whether the text needs adjustment on the page.

In your sample document, you placed the picture frame on top of the text frame which caused an automatic text wrap. The story no longer fits on this page. Don't make the common mistake of reducing the picture size to get everything to fit on one page. If you do, you'll have a crowded layout with cramped pictures. Instead of making the photograph smaller, jump the remaining text to another page in the publication.

When you add pictures to a publication, you change the flow of a story. Be sure to add supporting text to help the reader follow the copy. Add captions to pictures, and add continuation lines to stories that jump to another page.

Hands On:
Adding Supporting Text

1. Reposition the photograph to make room for a two-line caption at the bottom of the page.

2. Draw a text frame that spans columns 5 and 6. Make the frame approximately ½ inch deep.

3. Type the following caption. Format the text as 8-point Helvetica, with additional space of 0.25 points between characters.

   Robbin Frances in the kitchen of her restaurant, L'Accademia.

4. Add a second text frame directly above the photograph.

5. Type in the following text, and format it in the same style as the caption, adding right alignment:

   Continued on page 5

   Notice that the body copy flows around the text frame that contains the continued line. Publisher wraps text around picture frames and other text frames.

Instead of actually jumping the story to page 5, you can create a text frame in the scratch area to hold the overflow text. This lets you keep the text in a convenient location as you continue to work with your publication.

6. Create a text frame in the scratch area to the right of the page.

7. Select the text frame on page 1. Click the text frame button at the bottom of the frame.

Remember that the ellipsis indicates that the text no longer fits into the frame and that the additional text is stored temporarily as overflow. When you click the text frame button, the cursor turns into a cup. The cup remains upright until you place it over an empty text frame. Then the cup tips to indicate that you can "pour" text into the empty frame.

8. Position the cup over the empty text frame in the scratch area. Click once to link the two frames.

If you leave this text frame in the scratch area, it remains in view even when you turn to different pages in your publication. If you created all eight pages of this sample newsletter, you could easily move the text frame to a subsequent page. For now, leave it in place. Publisher saves the contents of the scratch area along with the publication.

The illustration on the next page shows the bit-mapped photograph in position on the page with the final border treatment.

Helping Hand: Rearrange the Layers

If the text flows over the picture frame instead of around it, you have layered the elements on your page incorrectly. Select the text frame that contains the body copy, and then choose the Send to Back command from the Layout menu. The text should now wrap around the picture frame.

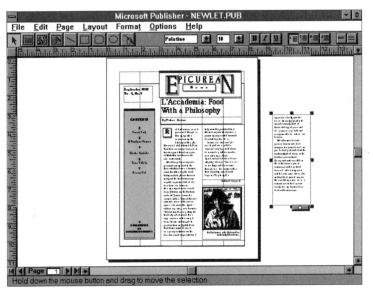

Managing Layers

You already used Publisher's image editing tools to add a photograph to page 1 of your publication in a straightforward manner. But you can also edit pictures to add drama. For example, on page 2 (Figure 9-1) of your sample publication, it appears that the picture of a grouper flies across the page. Likewise, the resized and cropped trout at the bottom of the page makes a big, bold statement.

Helping Hand: Substituting Clip Art

If you don't have access to an appropriate EPS file, you can use one of the CGM clip-art files included with Publisher. Publisher supplies a number of pictures of animals including CAT.CGM, COW.CGM, DOG.CGM, and FROG.CGM — but no pictures of fish. Choose a picture that works with the layout.

The following exercises will show you how to manage multiple layers of text and type to create sophisticated designs. In the process, you'll have the opportunity to review Publisher's cropping and scaling functions.

Hands On:
Layering Text and Pictures

1. Use the Page controls to move to page 2.

2. On page 2, draw a picture frame that spans columns 3 and 4. Make the frame approximately 3 inches deep.

3. With the frame selected, open the File menu and choose Import Picture.

4. Use the Directories and Drives list boxes to locate an appropriate image. The sample newsletter in this chapter uses an EPS picture of a Nassau grouper that is part of a clip-art collection available from Totem Graphics.

5. Click Preview to double-check the contents of the clip-art file.

6. Choose OK to import the picture into the waiting frame.

    The image on screen shows a low-resolution representation of the imported drawing. Use the low-resolution screen image to position the picture on the page. The EPS image will print as a high-quality, photo-realistic drawing of a Nassau grouper.

    However, you have inadvertently created a small problem. Even the low-resolution screen image lets you see that the proportions of the picture frame are wrong. Luckily, Publisher contains a special dialog box that lets you either return the picture to its original size or adjust the aspect ratio.

7. With the picture frame selected, open the Format menu. Choose Scale Picture.

When the dialog box appears, you can click the Original Size button to restore the picture to its full size. Or you can type scaling percentages to adjust the aspect ratio. As you can see in the following illustration, a proportional scaled picture always has identical height and width percentages.

8. To size this picture proportionately, type *75* in both the Scale Height and Scale Width text boxes.

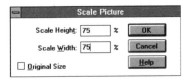

9. Click OK to return to the working screen.

The picture now has the correct aspect ratio. You can use the Shading dialog box to assign any of Publisher's tints and patterns to the background. The Clear fill, which is the default for EPS images, works especially well in this layout because it silhouettes the picture of the fish against the black rule.

10. Use the Move pointer to position the fish so that it overlaps the headline text frame, as shown in the illustration on the next page.

When you reposition the picture, the headline will probably wrap around the picture frame. You can sidestep Publisher's text-wrap feature by changing the stacking order of the frames. Publisher will not wrap text around a picture if the text frame is on top of the picture frame.

11. Select the text frame that contains the headline, and use the Bring to Front command to layer the text frame on top of the picture frame.

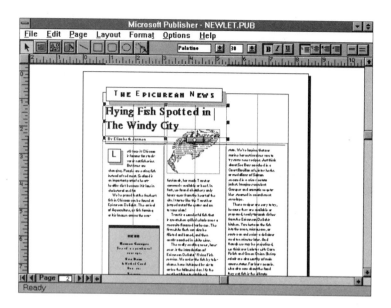

If you look closely at this illustration, you can see that the body copy flows around the illustration because the picture frame is layered on top of the text frame. However, the headline does not wrap around the illustration because the picture frame is layered below the headline text.

13. Complete the picture by drawing a text frame below the picture and adding this caption:

`Nassau Grouper is native to the coastal waters of Florida.`

Add a 2-point rule along the bottom edge of the text frame. Set the text using the same type specifications you used for the caption on page 1 — 8-point Helvetica, with an additional 0.25 point of character spacing. Remember to layer the caption text frame on top of the picture frame to avoid creating an awkward text wrap.

Automatic Text Wraps

When you work with Publisher's automatic text-wrap feature, you must pay attention to detail. For example, the second fish picture on page 2 extends halfway across the page. It covers three columns in the grid, consuming a large part of the center text column. As a result, when Publisher wraps the text around the picture, it must fit the text into a very narrow area.

The wrap works only because you originally set the text in a small typeface (10-point Palatino). If the text had a larger point size, you could fit no more than one word per line. To improve the appearance of this text block, you can use Publisher's Hyphenate command (on the Options menu) to break some words onto two lines.

To import and format the big fish, follow these instructions.

Hands On:
Improving Text Wraps Around Pictures

1. Open the File menu and choose Import Picture.

   Remember: if you don't draw a picture frame first, Publisher imports the picture at its original size and shape.

2. Use the Directories and Drives list boxes to find an appropriate picture file. The following illustrations show an EPS image of a lake trout that is part of a clip-art collection from Totem Graphics.

   You can import one of the CGM clip-art pictures supplied with Publisher instead. Publisher includes several pictures of animals, such as COW.CGM and FROG.CGM.

Helping Hand: Transparent Text Frames

If the headline text-frame obscures a portion of the picture, you need to adjust the text-frame shading. With the text frame still selected, open the Shading dialog box and choose the Clear option from the Style palette. You should now see the full picture.

3. Click Preview to double-check the contents of the clip-art file. Then click OK to import the image.

4. With the clip-art picture selected, open the Scale Picture dialog box from the Format menu.

5. Use the Scale Picture dialog box to enlarge the picture to 250 percent of its original size. Note that your CGM file will need to be scaled down, not up as here.

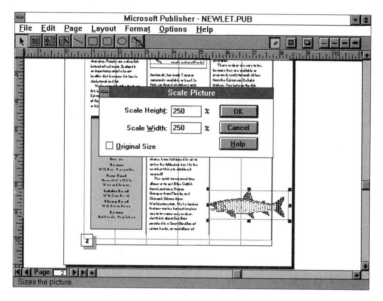

6. Position the picture so that the left side of the picture frame abuts the center guide.

7. Activate the Cropping tool by clicking the appropriate Toolbar icon. Grab the right center handle and crop the right half of the fish until the picture frame rests against the 2-point rule that surrounds the page.

8. Create a text frame that spans column 4 of the underlying grid, and enter the following caption:

```
Farm-raised Trout is now as plentiful as beef.
```

Format the text and text frame as you did the caption at the top of the page, except place the 2-point rule at the top of the frame and use left alignment. Be sure that you layer the caption on top of the picture frame to avoid creating an awkward text wrap.

Now you can complete page 2 by fine-tuning the way the body copy wraps around the picture.

9. Select the text frame that contains the body copy.

10. Open the Options menu. Choose Hyphenate.

You can use automatic hyphenation on an entire story or on all the stories in your publication. Publisher uses its built-in dictionary to propose the best hyphenation breaks. You can review and edit each hyphenation break by leaving the Confirm option turned on in the Hyphenate dialog box.

When you're finished, close the dialog box by clicking Cancel.

In the previous exercise, you used the Hyphenation command to create a better looking text wrap. In the next exercise, you'll modify the picture frame to create a better looking text wrap within the Contents on page 1. This technique takes advantage of the Cropping tool.

Hands On:
Improving Text Wraps with the Cropping Tool

1. Use the Page control to turn back to page 1.

2. Import the TROUT.EPS picture or another clip-art image and size it so that it fits within the boundaries of the Contents section.

In this instance, the picture of the trout functions as an icon. You'll notice that sizing the picture caused a logical and acceptable text wrap.

3. Now import the file ROSEMARY.EPS (or the image PLANT.CGM that is included with Publisher). Position it below the "Herbal Update" item.

As you can see in the following illustration, the narrow picture frame creates an awkward text wrap that you can't possibly read.

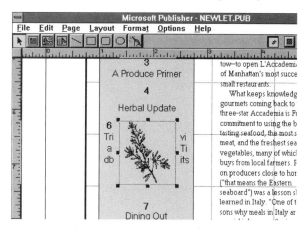

You can easily correct the problem by using Publisher's Cropping tool to increase the size of the frame — without increasing the size of the picture.

4. Select the picture of the plant. Choose the Cropping tool from either the Toolbar or the Format menu.

5. Use the Cropping tool to grab the middle selection handle on the right. Stretch the picture frame so that it touches the right edge of the text frame.

6. Use the Cropping tool to grab the middle selection handle on the left. Stretch the frame so that it touches the left edge of the text frame.

As you can see on the following page, the enlarged text frame forces Publisher to wrap the text.

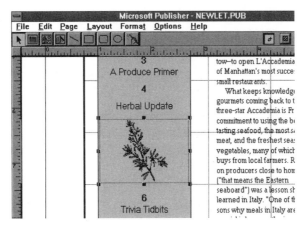

Now that the newsletter is complete, you can save and print the document.

What's Next?

At this point, you should feel confident incorporating pictures into your publications. Microsoft Publisher's cropping and resizing features let you highlight the most essential information contained in a picture — as you did when you eliminated unnecessary background from the photograph on page 1. Publisher's tools also let you take ordinary clip-art images and modify them so that they look like they were drawn specifically for your newsletter.

In Section III, you won't create design projects from beginning to end. Instead, you'll concentrate on advanced tips and techniques that you can apply to both text elements and imported pictures. By the time you finish the brief exercises in Chapters 10 and 11, you truly will have mastered Publisher.

ADVANCED TIPS
AND TECHNIQUES

Chapter 10

TEN HOT TIPS FOR TYPE

If you think you already know about all of Microsoft Publisher's type-handling functions, think again! This chapter presents ten additional ways you can use Publisher to fine-tune your text. All the exercises in this chapter assume that Publisher is already loaded. If you don't have Publisher open on the Windows Desktop, start it now.

Tip 1: Preformatted Text Frames

If you need to draw a series of identical text frames, you can save time by changing the default formatting options. Each frame that you draw will automatically assume the new parameters that you set. You can specify new default frame margins and columns, border rules, BorderArt, shading patterns, and automatic shadows. The trick is to specify the new defaults before you draw the first frame.

 **Hands On:**
Setting Frame Defaults

1. Select the Text Frame tool.

   Notice that when you first select the Text Frame tool (before you draw a text frame), the Toolbar displays frame formatting options for four line weights, an automatic shadow, and shading patterns.

2. Select the 1-point rule and the Shadow attribute from the Toolbar.

3. Choose Frame Margins and Columns from the Layout menu. In the dialog box, set up frame margins of 0.17 (⅙ inch) on all four sides. Click OK.

4. Draw a text frame.

   Each frame that you draw will have the attributes you just specified. To return to the original default of no rule, no shadow, and frame margins of 0.08 inch, you must either manually change the settings back again or restart Publisher.

Tip 2: Customize Your Text Wraps

Microsoft Publisher automatically wraps text around picture frames, WordArt frames, and text frames. The text always flows around the frame boundaries, creating a rectangular pattern. But you can wrap text more closely around the irregular edges of a picture if you layer objects — especially transparent objects. The following exercise lets you practice this technique with the newsletter you created in Chapter 9.

Hands On:
Layering Objects

1. Open the File menu, choose Open Existing Publication.

2. Locate the file NEWLET.PUB. Then click OK.

3. Select the picture at the bottom of page 2, move it up on the page a bit so you have room to work, and choose Send to Back from the Layout menu.

   The text frame now sits on top of the picture frame. The text flows over the picture.

4. Select the Picture Frame tool. Before you draw a frame, be sure these attributes are set: Clear for Shading and None for Border Thickness.

5. Draw a series of small picture frames on top of the text frame. The frames should follow the irregular outline of the underlying picture.

   Publisher displays the object boundaries of the frames you draw with a dotted line, so you will be able to see them on screen. However, because the small picture frames have no fill and no border, they won't show when you print your publication. And because you layered them on top of the text frame, the type flows around them, creating an irregular text wrap. The following illustration shows a publication with an irregular text wrap.

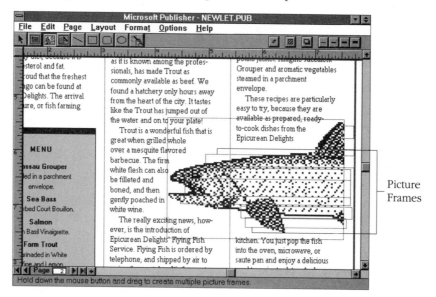

Picture
Frames

Tip 3: Making a Dash for It

Although Microsoft Publisher creates hyphens (which you use to divide or compound words) it doesn't support em dashes (which you use to punctuate sentences) — like this! Typesetters traditionally employ em dashes, which are the same width as the point size being set and were named because the capital letter *M* in early fonts was usually cast on a square body.

Using a hyphen instead of an em dash is a telltale sign of an amateur typesetter. However, you can manually create em dashes for many point sizes by using Publisher's inter-character spacing controls. Follow these instructions:

Hands On:
Creating Em-Dashes

1. Type two consecutive hyphens.

2. Highlight the first hyphen.

3. Choose Spacing Between Characters from the Format menu. In the dialog box, select Squeeze Letters Together.

4. Enter an amount between 0.25 and 9.75 points in the By This Amount text box and click OK.

The amount of space that you need to delete depends on the point size of your type. The following illustration shows type set at 14 points, with 1.5 points of space removed after the first hyphen.

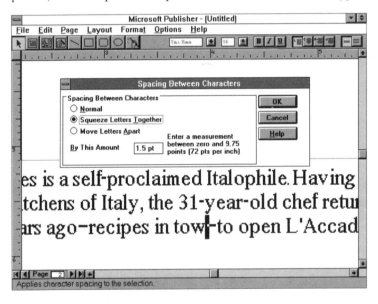

Tip 4: Expand the Alphabet

The typesetter's alphabet includes many more characters than the standard 26 letters. It also includes punctuation marks and extended characters, such as accented foreign language letters, copyright symbols, and international monetary symbols.

You can easily use these special characters in your Microsoft Publisher documents to produce publications that look professionally typeset. To insert extended characters into your text, you simply type a special code using the Alt key and the numeric keypad on the keyboard.

For a complete listing of the extended characters available to you, refer to your Microsoft Windows documentation. Also see the documentation for the type-management utilities (such as Bitstream Facelift) and soft fonts you use.

The samples in the following table all use an industry standard — the ANSI extended character set. Notice that the special character codes actually contain only three digits. Because Publisher requires a four-digit code, you must add a zero to the beginning of the number.

ANSI Code	Character	Example
233	é	sauté
231	ç	Provençal
169	©	© 1991
165	¥	¥200

Hands On:
Inserting a Copyright Symbol

1. Using the I-beam pointer, position the text insertion point where the special character should appear.

2. Hold down the Alt key. Using the numeric keypad, enter the four-digit code for a copyright symbol: *0169*.

3. Release the Alt key. The copyright symbol appears on screen.

Tip 5: Emphasize with Bullets

Bulleted lists let you organize information in a punchy, quick-read format. And you can improve your presentation by adding decorative bullets to each item in a list.

If you want to create standard square or round bullets, you can use Microsoft Publisher's Rectangle and Oval tools to draw the objects. However, if you want to create a variety of decorative borders, you can use BorderArt. To create a BorderArt bullet, you collapse a rectangle containing BorderArt both vertically and horizontally. In effect, you create a single point containing a fragment of the BorderArt pattern. To create the bullet in an appropriate size, you can specify the size of the BorderArt in points.

Hands On:
Creating a Bullet

1. Create a text frame and type in sample text. (Use a 16-point sans-serif typeface, such as Swiss.)

2. Highlight the text. Choose Indents and Spacing from the Format menu. In the dialog box, set the Left Indent to 0.5 inch. This leaves room for the bullet.

3. Using the Rectangle tool, draw a rectangle of any size.

4. Choose BorderArt from the Layout menu. In the dialog box, select any pattern that appeals to you. It's a good idea to pick a pattern with a strong corner motif. In the Border Size text box, type *16 pt* to match the point size of the text. Click OK.

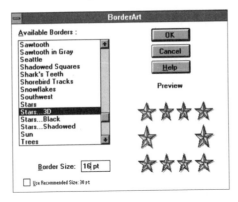

5. When you return to the working screen, use the selection handles to resize the rectangle, as follows:

   □ Pull up the bottom selection handle until it overlaps the top handle and creates a single line.

   □ Move the right selection handle until it overlaps the left selection handle and creates a point.

   You might find it easier to collapse the rectangle if you work in 200% view, with all Snap options turned off. After you collapse the rectangle both horizontally and vertically, you will have a decorative bullet.

6. Use the move pointer to position the bullet next to the text.

Tip 6: Hyphenate by Hand

Despite its small size, a hyphen is a powerful desktop publishing tool. Hyphens let you justify text and smooth ragged margins by breaking words at the ends of lines.

When you choose the Hyphenate command from the Options menu, Microsoft Publisher automatically suggests the best breaks using its built-in 100,000-word dictionary. However, you will sometimes need to employ manual hyphenation instead. Publisher's dictionary doesn't contain all words, particularly specialized medical and technical terms. Also, when you work with narrow columns or complex text wraps, you might want to force additional line breaks.

If you insert a permanent hyphen (by typing in a hyphen), you will need to manually delete it if you alter your text. Instead, insert an optional hyphen, which breaks a word only if it falls at the end of a line. If the word moves from the end of the line to a new position, Publisher hides the optional hyphen from view.

Hands On: Inserting Special Hyphens

1. To insert an optional hyphen, type Ctrl-hyphen.

   In these times of hyphenated last names and hyphenated company names, you also need the ability to insert nonbreaking hyphens into your text. A nonbreaking hyphen forces Publisher to keep hyphenated names and hyphenated words on a single line.

2. To insert a nonbreaking hyphen, type Ctrl-Alt-hyphen.

Tip 7: Searching and Replacing Text

Microsoft Publisher contains a powerful command — Find — that lets you locate specific words or phrases anywhere in your document. Another command — Replace — lets you simultaneously find text and change it to new copy. These File menu commands are especially useful when you edit long documents. For example, if you discover that you misspelled a client's name, you can search for each occurrence of the incorrect spelling and replace it with the correct spelling.

In addition to searching for standard letters and punctuation marks, you can use the Find command to search for nonprinting characters, such as tab stops and spaces. And you can use the Replace dialog box to insert nonprinting characters into your text.

For example, when you import a long text file into Publisher you might find that you need to delete extra space between sentences. Two spaces after a period may be good typing style, but it is *not* good typesetting style. Likewise, many people who work with word-processing programs start paragraphs with a tabbed indent. In Publisher it is usually much better to control paragraph indents using the Indents and Spacing command. Instead of manually scrolling through a long document to remove extra spaces or unnecessary tabs, you can use the Replace command to search for and delete or change nonprinting characters.

Hands On: Finding and Replacing Nonprinting Characters

To find or replace nonprinting characters type the appropriate code (as shown in the following table) in the Find or Replace dialog boxes.

Type this code	*To find*
(Spacebar)	A space
^-	An optional hyphen
^~(tilde)	A nonbreaking hyphen
^n	A line break
^p	The end of paragraph
^s	A nonbreaking space
^t	A tab stop

The Replace dialog box shown on the next page tells Publisher to search for paragraphs improperly indented with tab stops and to replace the tabs with end-of-paragraph markers.

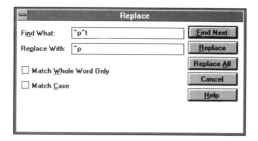

Tip 8: Overlapping Type

As you know, Microsoft Publisher automatically wraps text around other text frames. This can make it difficult to create logos in which letters overlap each other. To sidestep Publisher's automatic text wrap, you can use the Background and Foreground pages. Simply place one text frame on the Background page, and place the overlapping text frame on the Foreground page. This trick works best for single-page publications because any element you place on the Background page automatically appears on every page in your document.

Tip 9: Maintaining Consecutive Page Numbers

Most books number pages from beginning to end. But if you were creating a book using Microsoft Publisher, you wouldn't put the whole book into one document —you'd break it down into chapters or sections. Also, many periodicals number pages consecutively from issue to issue. This numbering scheme is valuable if readers want to bind all the issues of a publication into a single volume. You can use Publisher's Settings command to begin the pages in your publication with a numeral other than 1.

 ***Hands On:***
Setting a Page Number Other than 1

1. Open the Options menu. Choose Settings.

2. The Settings dialog box appears. Type the starting page number that you want to use.

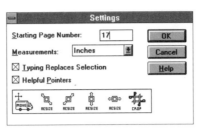

Tip 10: Change Your Typeface

If you want a new typeface to use in designing a logo but aren't ready to purchase a new font, consider this alternative. You can use Publisher's drawing tools to modify an existing typeface. This process works best on logos with only a few, large letters, but it can make a dramatic difference in your design.

Hands On:
Enhancing Type with Publisher's Drawing Tools

The logo in the following illustration shows white lines offset against black type. You can create this effect by following these steps:

1. Draw a text frame.

2. Type the following text, and set it in 60-point Swiss bold.

   EPICUREAN

3. Use the right mouse button to click the Line tool so you can create multiple lines. Before you draw the first line, use the Lines command from the Layout menu to change the Line Weight setting to 2 points and the Color to White.

4. Hold down the Shift key to restrain the line to a perfect horizontal. Draw white lines across the top third of the letters.

5. Finish the logo design by adding three black rules under the text.

Chapter 11

TEN HOT TIPS FOR PICTURES

In Chapter 9, "Picture Perfect," you learned about some of Microsoft Publisher's picture-handling features. Publisher offers several other sophisticated picture-handling tools. The ten tips listed here range from simple work-saving shortcuts to advanced functions that let you link your publication to external files and other Windows-based programs.

The exercises in this chapter assume that you have Publisher loaded. If Publisher is not open on the Windows Desktop, start it now.

Tip 1: Resolve Incompatible Graphics Formats

You might encounter a Windows-based program that doesn't save pictures in a format compatible with Publisher. As the following exercise shows, the Clipboard provides an easy way to circumvent this problem. (If you need help using the Clipboard, refer to Chapter 1, "A Window of Opportunity.")

 Hands On: Importing Pictures via the Clipboard

1. Open the application that you used to create the picture and load the file in which you stored the picture.

2. Select the picture (or a portion of the picture), and copy it to the Clipboard.

3. Use the Task List box to switch to Publisher.

4. Load your Publisher document.

5. Draw a picture frame.

6. With the picture frame selected, choose Paste Picture from the Edit menu.

Publisher pastes a copy of the picture into your document.

Tip 2: Update Pictures Automatically

The Paste Special command on the Edit menu lets you create links between the picture frames in your Microsoft Publisher document and files created in other programs and stored on disk. This process, which is technically called Object Linking and Embedding (OLE), lets Publisher automatically check the status of the external file each time you open your Publisher document. If the external file has been changed, Publisher will update the contents of the picture frame with the latest version of the file.

When you use the Paste Special command, Publisher treats the pasted image as a picture. However, the image itself could be a drawing created in Works, a table created in Word for Windows, or a spreadsheet created in Excel.

For example, suppose someone in your office created a chart in Excel that you want to paste into your Publisher document. If you use Paste Special instead of Paste, you will create a link between the chart stored on disk and the picture frame in your document. Whenever you open your Publisher document, Publisher checks the status of the source file — the Excel chart file. If the chart file has been changed by your co-worker, Publisher automatically imports the updated chart into the picture frame.

Linking ensures that your publication always contains the latest and most accurate version of the picture. You will find linking most useful when you work with pictures that are created or revised by other people. Linking also saves time if you produce publications that regularly update standard information, such as quarterly reports that show the latest statistics on sales and earnings.

To create a link to an external file, you must use Publisher in conjunction with a Windows-based application that supports this function as well — such as Microsoft Works or Microsoft Excel. As you can see in the diagram on the next page, after you establish the link, both the originating application (in this case, Works) and Publisher have access to the file. You can alter the file only in the originating application. Publisher has the ability only to import the contents of the file.

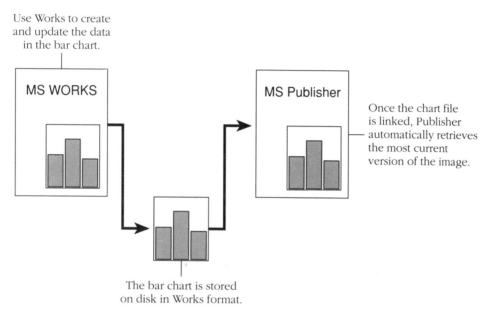

Use Works to create and update the data in the bar chart.

MS WORKS

MS Publisher

Once the chart file is linked, Publisher automatically retrieves the most current version of the image.

The bar chart is stored on disk in Works format.

To avoid problems, be sure to format the objects with the correct colors, typefaces, and point sizes before you link them to Publisher.

Before you establish links between Publisher and external files, you must know how to work with more than one Windows-based application at a time and how to use the Clipboard. For more information see Chapter 1, "A Window of Opportunity."

Hands On: **Linking Picture Frames to External Files**

1. Open Publisher and then Works or Excel.

2. Create a chart using Works or Excel.

3. Save the chart to a file.

4. Copy the chart to the Clipboard.

5. Using the Task List box, switch to Publisher.

6. Draw a picture frame in Publisher.

7. Open the Edit menu and choose the Paste Special command. Note that if you choose the Paste Picture command, you will import the picture instead of creating a link to the file.

   The Paste Special dialog box appears and gives you a choice of three formats: Native, Metafile, or Bitmap. You will insert the picture in Native format. You should import the picture as a Metafile only if you need to crop the image once it is inside Publisher. And, unless absolutely necessary, avoid inserting the picture as a bit map because you can seriously degrade the quality of the image if you resize it.

8. Select Native in the Paste Special dialog box.

9. Click the Paste Link button.

As you can see in the following illustration, the linked picture appears on screen, in place in your document. Notice that Publisher identifies the name of the source program in the Edit menu. Whenever you open this Publisher file in the future, the linked image will be updated automatically. One word of warning: don't change the location of the original file, or Publisher won't be able to find the picture to complete the update.

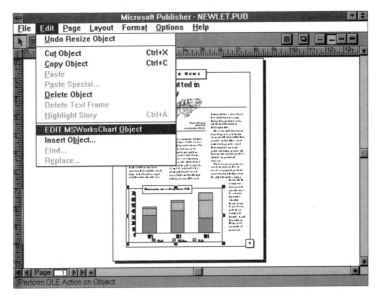

Tip 3: Invoke Programs from Within Publisher

In previous chapters, you learned that Microsoft Publisher can launch independent programs such as Help and WordArt. You can also launch other Windows-based programs — such as Works, Excel, and Word for Windows — from within Publisher. To do so, use the Insert Object command from the Edit menu.

When you choose the Insert Object command, you are using the OLE technology described in Tip 2. However, Insert Object provides direct access to all the functions of the external program — the Works spreadsheet, Excel's charting capability, and so on. This type of link makes it easy to revise the content of a picture from within Publisher.

Any picture you create with this technique is stored as part of your Publisher document. For example, if you insert an Excel spreadsheet, you will not be able to open it directly from Excel. Use the Insert Object command when you plan to use or edit the image only from within Publisher. If you want to share the image between programs, use Paste Special instead.

In the following exercise, you will substitute a Works spreadsheet for the main table of the quote form that you created in Chapter 3. By doing so you will turn a static fill-in-the-blank form into a live spreadsheet, complete with math functions.

 Hands On:
The Insert Object Command

1. Open the Quote template.

2. Draw a picture frame approximately the same size as the main table.

3. With the picture frame selected, choose Insert Object from the Edit menu.

   The Insert Object dialog box appears, which lists the types of objects that you can insert. Each object type is associated with a program that will load if you choose it. If you choose MS Works Chart, Microsoft Works will appear on screen in a separate, but linked, window.

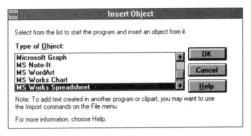

4. Select MS Works Spreadsheet, and click OK.

When you click OK, Windows loads Works, switches you to the
Works program window, and displays a blank spreadsheet. You
have access to all the spreadsheet functions: You can add columns
of numbers, calculate sales tax, and even insert and display formulas, as shown in the following illustration. It may seem strange to
think of a spreadsheet as a picture element, but that is how Publisher treats this object — so be sure that the spreadsheet typefaces
and rules appear exactly as you want them to print.

5. Type the sample data and complete the calculations.

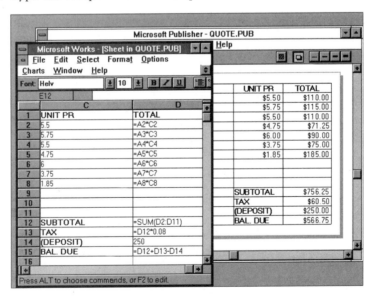

6. Choose the Exit command from the File menu in Works.

   The spreadsheet now appears in the picture frame you created in Publisher, but the picture is still linked to Works. To invoke Works so you can edit this picture, simply double-click the picture frame or choose the Edit Object command with the frame selected.

Tip 4: Movable Rulers

Microsoft Publisher's rulers are located along the left and top sides of the screen. The vertical and horizontal zero points align with the upper left corner of the working page (not with the corner of the screen).

When you work with multiple objects or with a complex drawing, you might want to reconfigure the rulers. You can easily change their position on the screen or move the zero point by using a simple trick: The left mouse button moves the rulers to a new position, and the right mouse button moves the zero points.

 ### Hands On:
Repositioning Rulers

1. Start in Full Page view. Select the Rectangle tool and draw a rectangle in the middle of the page.

2. Use the F9 key or the Page menu to shift to Actual Size view.

3. Move the pointer to the upper left corner of the screen where the rulers intersect. The pointer changes to a double-headed arrow. Using the right mouse button, drag the pointer until it aligns with the upper left corner of the rectangle.

   The zero point now corresponds to the corner of the rectangle.

4. Move the pointer to the ruler intersection. The pointer once again changes to a double-headed arrow. Now use the left mouse button to drag the pointer. Watch as the rulers move with the mouse.

   When the rulers align with the rectangle on screen, release the mouse button.

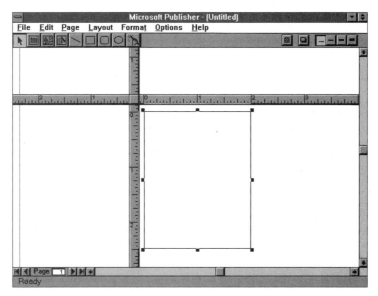

The position of the rulers on screen won't change, even if you change your view of the page. So be sure that you display the view you want on screen before you reconfigure the rulers. To return the zero points to their original position, double-click the intersection of the vertical and horizontal rulers.

Tip 5: Expand Your Palette

If you have a color printer, you can assign different hues to the objects in your publication. Although Microsoft Publisher's palette contains only eight colors, you can create the illusion of additional colors. To do so, choose one of the patterns found in the Shading dialog box. If you assign one color to the foreground, and another color to the background of the pattern, you will get the illusion of a third, blended color. Try it now.

Hands On:
Assigning Hues to Patterns

1. Draw a rectangle of any size on screen.

2. With the rectangle selected, open the Shading dialog box (either from the Toolbar or by choosing Shading from the Layout menu).

3. Choose a tightly woven, regular pattern. (The dot patterns work best.)

4. Click the Foreground drop-down arrow to display the list of colors. Select Cyan.

5. Click the Background drop-down arrow to display the list of colors. Select Magenta.

   The preview box now shows a purple rectangle.

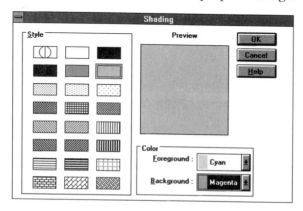

6. Click OK to return to the working screen.

Tip 6: Improve Black-and-White Printouts

If you use a color printer, the colored objects in your publications (including colored text) print in color. The shades you produce will vary depending on the capabilities of your color printer.

If you use a black-and-white printer, you can still take advantage of color. Windows automatically translates the colors contained in imported pictures, internally created drawings, borders, shading patterns, and WordArt designs (but not text) into shades of gray. You'll find that ink-jet and laser printers produce smoother gray tones than dot-matrix printers do. It takes some experimentation to determine which colors print best on a black-and-white printer. Even so, you'll enhance your black-and-white publications by turning them into black, white, and various shades of gray.

Tip 7: Save Display Time

Each time you modify a layout or change your view of the working page, Microsoft Publisher redraws the screen. If your layout includes many pictures — especially scanned bit maps — you will need to wait while Publisher redraws and displays each picture. This can be tedious, especially if you want to make only minor changes to the layout. To stop Publisher from redrawing the picture whenever you make a change, you can temporarily turn off the display of pictures. Publisher will display only the border or object boundary of the picture frame instead of drawing the entire image. Try it now.

Hands On:
Suppressing the Picture Display

1. Open the NEWSLET.PUB file that you created in Chapter 9.

   The first page contains a bit-mapped photograph that will slow the display.

2. Open the Options menu. Choose Hide Pictures.

   When you return to the screen, page 1 displays the picture frame without the picture. Publisher also hides the other pictures in the document. The hidden images include the WordArt elements in the logo and the pictures on page 2. Remember to display the pictures again before you print your publication.

Tip 8: Layer Pictures
to Create Special Effects

In Chapters 8 and 9, you learned how to layer picture frames and text frames to create sophisticated designs. You can also layer imported pictures, rectangles formatted with BorderArt motifs, and drawings created with Microsoft Publisher's drawing tools to create special effects. The illustration on the next page shows how you can turn a standard clip-art image into a unique illustration simply by stacking multiple copies of the image.

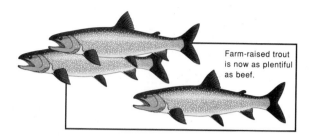

Farm-raised trout
is now as plentiful
as beef.

Hands On:
Layering Pictures

1. Open the File menu, and choose Import Picture.

   The sample illustration above uses a picture of a lake trout that is part of a clip-art collection available from Totem Graphics. You can use one of the CGM clip-art images included with Publisher, such as COW.CGM.

2. When the Import Picture dialog box appears, select a picture from the CLIPART directory, and then click OK.

3. Using the selection handles or the Scale Picture command on the Format menu, resize the image so you can fit three copies of the picture on your page.

4. With the picture frame still selected, copy the picture to the Clipboard.

5. Paste one or more copies back into your publication from the Clipboard.

6. Use the move pointer to reposition and overlap the pictures.

7. If necessary, use the Shading dialog box to assign a clear background to the picture frame. An opaque background could obscure portions of the pictures on the bottom of the stack.

8. Embellish the pictures with a unifying border — in this case a rectangle — and a caption.

Tip 9: Picture Frame Shortcuts

If your design includes many picture frames, you can save time by taking advantage of several shortcuts. For example, you can format all your picture frames identically by changing the default attributes before you create them.

 Hands On:
Changing the Default Attributes

1. Click the Picture Frame tool, but don't draw a frame yet.

   Use the Toolbar or the commands on the Layout menu to set new defaults.

2. Select a 2-point rule from the Toolbar.

3. Open the Shading dialog box. Choose a dramatic pattern, like the stripes or bricks. Click OK.

4. Open the Frame Margins dialog box. Set 0.2-inch margins on all four sides. Click OK.

5. Draw a picture frame.

   Each frame that you draw will have the attributes you just specified. To return to the original default of no rule, no fill, and no margins, either change the settings back again or restart Publisher.

6. To import a picture into the waiting frame, try this shortcut. Bypass the File menu and display the Picture Import dialog box by double-clicking the picture frame.

7. Select a suitable image from the CLIPART subdirectory. Click OK.

   If you work with templates containing dummy pictures, Publisher will detect the presence of an image and use the following dialog box to ask you if you want to replace the contents of the frame.

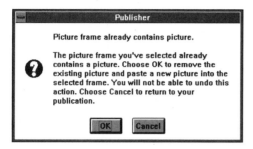

8. Click OK to delete the current contents of the picture frame and import a new image.

Tip 10:
Incorporate Electronic Notes

You can incorporate nonprinting notes into your publications to remind you — or your co-workers — of important information. These notes — called Note-Its — appear on screen as icons, complete with identifying captions. When you double-click a Note-It icon, the message displays.

You can use Note-Its for many purposes. For example, you can create a Note-It to remind employees using the official Epicurean Delights quote form (created in Chapter 3) to check on changing prices for seasonal and imported items. You can create a Note-It in one of two ways: by using a PageWizard or by using the Insert Object command from the Edit menu.

Hands On:
Creating a Note-It

1. Click the PageWizard icon on the Toolbar.

2. Draw a frame.

3. When the PageWizard dialog box appears on screen, choose Note-It. The PageWizard goes to work and presents a series of questions.

4. Choose the picture you would like to use as your icon.

5. Type in an appropriate caption and indicate the type size you want to use.

6. Type your message.

   If you prefer, you can create a Note-It by drawing a standard picture frame and then choosing the Insert Object command from the Edit menu. The Microsoft Note-It window appears, as shown in the following illustration. For more information on the Insert Object command, see "Tip 3: Invoke Programs from Within Publisher," earlier in this chapter.

   You will find Note-Its most useful if you position them in the scratch area of the page. But if you place Note-Its within the printing margins of your page, they will print as part of your publication. If you must place Note-Its within the printing area, be sure the message instructs the reader to move the icon before printing.

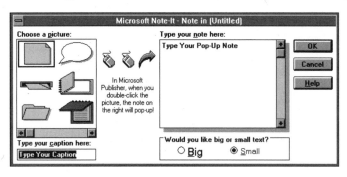

Section IV

APPENDIXES

Appendix A

INSTALLING MICROSOFT PUBLISHER

Before you can use Microsoft Publisher or complete the exercises in this book, you must install Publisher on your hard disk. Installing Publisher is a simple task because Publisher comes with a utility, called Setup, that guides you through the process. Setup gives you two installation options: Complete Installation or Custom Installation. Choose the Complete Installation option to install Publisher with all its tools and files. But if you want to control the directory location for Publisher's files, or if you want to install only selected portions of the program, choose the Custom Installation option.

 **Hands On:**
Complete Installation

1. Use the following checklist to be sure that you are ready to begin the installation procedure:

   □ You have properly installed Microsoft Windows. (For more information, see the *Microsoft Windows User's Guide.)*

   □ You have at least 6 MB of free space on your hard disk.

   □ You have chosen the disks that match your floppy-disk drive. Publisher arrives on two complete sets of disks — 1.2 MB capacity 5 ¼-inch diskettes, and 1.44 MB capacity 3 ½-inch diskettes.

If your computer system is equipped with only a 360 KB or 720 KB floppy-disk drive, you will need to send away for either a 360 KB or 720 KB Conversion Kit. The kit itself is free, but your application (which you will find in the Microsoft Publisher box) must be accompanied by your official product registration form.

You are now ready to begin the installation procedure. Publisher's Setup program runs within the Windows environment. If you need help working with the Windows interface conventions, such as mouse movements and dialog boxes, read Chapter 1, "A Window of Opportunity."

2. If Windows is not currently running, start it by typing the following command at the C> prompt:

```
win
```

The Windows Program Manager appears on your screen. Pay special attention to the menu bar, along the top of the screen.

3. Insert the Microsoft Publisher Disk 1 into your floppy-disk drive, which is designated either by the drive letter A or B.

4. Open the File menu, which is the first item on the menu bar, by clicking the menu name with the mouse.

5. Click the Run command.

6. When the Run dialog box appears on screen, you must enter the name of the program you want to run. Type the following command into the text box. (If you are using the B drive instead, substitute the correct drive letter.)

```
a:setup
```

Helping Hand: Conserving Disk Space

If you do not have enough available hard disk space to proceed with Complete Installation, Publisher will revert to Custom Installation. Using the Custom Installation procedure lets you conserve disk space by allowing you to copy only selected portions of the program to your hard disk. Alternatively, you can delete other unwanted files from your hard disk to make more room for the Publisher program.

The Publisher Setup screen appears. Take the time to read the information in the message box because, as you will see, installing Publisher is really as simple as responding to the on-screen instructions.

7. Click the Continue button.

8. A registration dialog box appears on screen. Type your name and company name into the appropriate text boxes. Then click OK to proceed to the next screen.

9. When the Setup Options dialog box appears, as shown in the following illustration, choose Complete Installation.

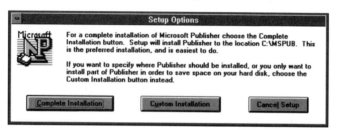

After you choose Complete Installation, the Setup program creates a number of directories on your C drive, including a directory called MSPUB. In addition, the Setup program automatically decompresses and copies the following files from the floppy disks to the appropriate subdirectories:

☐ Program files

☐ Help files

☐ Spelling Checker and Hyphenation files

☐ Word Processing and Graphics Formats Conversion files

☐ Templates

☐ Clipart

The Setup Program displays each filename as it copies the information from the floppy disk to your hard disk. In addition, a visual gauge informs you of the Setup program's progress. When the Setup program needs files from a different floppy disk, it prompts you to switch disks.

10. When prompted, insert Disk 2, containing the Program and Converter files, or Disk 3, containing the Help, PageWizards, Borders, and Templates files.

The Setup program completes the installation process by creating a program icon for Publisher and a program group for the MS Solution Series. The Microsoft Solution Series is a family of products that also includes Microsoft Works and Microsoft Money. (If you already have Works or Money, Publisher will be added to your Microsoft Solution Series group.)

A final dialog box asks you if you want to return to Windows or to run Publisher.

11. Choose Return to Windows.

12. Exit Windows by using the Alt-F4 keyboard shortcut.

Hands On:
Custom Installation

If you have less than 6 MB of hard-disk space, want to determine the location of the Publisher files on your hard disk, or want to install only portions of the program, use the Custom Installation option.

1. Follow instructions 1 through 8 for Complete Installation.

2. When the Setup Options dialog box appears, choose Custom Installation.

3. In the next dialog box, type the name of the directory where you want to store the Publisher files. Remember to type in a complete path statement, including the drive letter and any path or subdirectory information. For example, to install Publisher on drive D you might type:

```
d:\windows\mspub
```

The next dialog box to appear, shown in the following illustration, lists the files that come with Publisher. Each item is preceded by a check box. When an option box is selected (indicated by an X), the file will be copied to your hard disk. When an check box is deselected (indicated by an empty box), the file will not be copied to your hard disk.

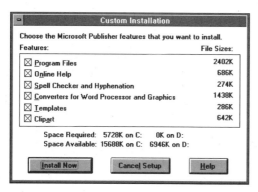

Publisher helps you decide which files to select by displaying several important statistics. The amount of space you need for each file is displayed to its right. In addition, the Setup program informs you of the disk space required to copy the files to your hard disk as well as the amount of disk space available on your system — even if you have more than one hard disk.

Deciding which portions of the program to copy to your hard disk is really as simple as deciding which tasks you need to perform. Obviously you must copy the Program files or Publisher can't run. You won't be able to import word processing files or picture files into your publications if you don't install the converters. However, you can easily save nearly a megabyte of disk space by deselecting the Templates (286 KB) and the Clipart items (642 KB). You can always run the Setup program at a later date to install only the Templates and the Clipart files if you find you need them.

4. Choose the items you want to install by selecting or deselecting each check box.

   If you need a more detailed explanation of a particular dialog box, click the Help button.

5. Click the Install Now command button to copy the selected files to your hard disk.

   The Setup Program displays each filename as it copies it from the floppy disk to your hard disk. In addition, a visual gauge informs you of the Setup program's progress. When the Setup program needs files from a different floppy disk, it prompts you to switch disks.

6. When prompted, insert Disk 2, containing the Program and Converter files, or Disk 3, containing the Help, PageWizards, Borders, and Templates files.

   The Setup program completes the installation process by creating a program icon for Publisher and a program group for the Microsoft Solution Series. The Microsoft Solution Series is a family of products that also includes Microsoft Works and Microsoft Money. (If you already have Works or Money, Publisher will be added to your Microsoft Solution Series program group.)

   A final dialog box asks you if you want to return to Windows or run Publisher.

7. Choose Return to Windows.

8. Exit Windows by using the Alt-F4 keyboard shortcut.

Installing Bitstream Facelift

You have now completed the installation of Microsoft Publisher. But you won't get optimal results from Publisher unless you also install scalable fonts. If you happen to own a laser printer, such as a PostScript printer or an HP LaserJet III, you can output your publications using the scalable fonts that are resident in the printer. (For more information on resident printer fonts see Appendix C, "Printing with Microsoft Publisher.")

However, if your printer provides only a limited selection of nonscalable fonts or if you want an accurate screen display of the type elements in your publication, you should make the extra effort and install a font manager, such as Bitstream FaceLift.

Several font management utilities on the market today will work in conjunction with Publisher (or any other Windows-based application). These utilities include Adobe Type Manager and Zenographics SuperPrint. However, there is one compelling reason to install Bitstream FaceLift — it's free. Microsoft is offering registered users of Publisher a free copy of Bitstream FaceLift (not including postage and handling) for a limited time only.

The following illustration clearly demonstrates how FaceLift can enhance the display of type on your computer screen. The image on the left is a standard Windows display without FaceLift; the image on the right shows the same display with FaceLift installed.

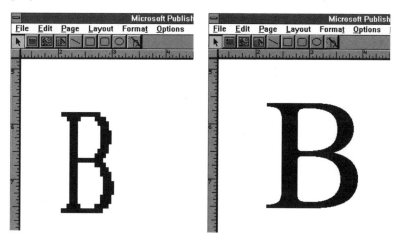

In addition to improving your screen display, Bitstream Facelift

- Provides 13 scalable fonts, including

  □ Dutch 801 in roman, italic, bold, and bold italic

  □ Park Avenue

  □ Brush Script

  □ Monospace 821

  □ Swiss 721 in roman, italic, bold, and bold italic

  □ Bitstream Cooper Black

  □ Formal Script 421

- Produces a WYSIWYG (What You See Is What You Get) screen display of these typefaces. As a result, you can see correct line breaks and accurately judge inter-character spacing in headlines.

- Prints its scalable fonts on any printer installed in the Windows Printer Control Panel, including the HP LaserJet and compatibles, ink-jet printers, and dot-matrix printers. The type will print at your printer's highest resolution.

- Makes it easy to install additional compatible Bitstream fonts.

Register as a Microsoft Publisher User

Before you move on to the exercises in this book, take a moment to fill out the Publisher registration card. Only registered users are entitled to product update information and free technical support from Microsoft Corporation.

KEYBOARD ALTERNATIVES

As you become familiar with Microsoft Publisher, you'll become more comfortable issuing commands with either the mouse or the keyboard. But simply stated: using the keyboard is faster than using a mouse for performing repetitive tasks, such as deleting objects, or for invoking frequently used commands, such as Save. Publisher provides many keyboard alternatives — methods of using keystrokes instead of the mouse to carry out commands. These keyboard alternatives are divided into two categories — shortcuts, which bypass menus completely, and equivalents, which mimic mouse operations.

Keyboard Shortcuts

Keyboard shortcuts let you bypass menus by issuing commands directly from the keyboard. For example, the Ctrl-P key combination lets you print your publication without opening the File menu. As you can see in the illustration of Microsoft Publisher's File menu on the next page, keyboard shortcuts are displayed at the right of the associated menu item. Using the mouse to open menus and then reading the entire entry for each command is a good way to learn the keyboard shortcuts for any Windows-based program.

File	
Create **N**ew Publication...	
Open Existing Publication...	
Close Publication	
Save	Ctrl+S
Save **A**s...	
Import Text...	
Import Picture...	
Print...	Ctrl+P
P**r**int Setup...	
E**x**it Publisher	F3

The following table provides a quick reference for Publisher's keyboard shortcuts. The keyboard shortcuts are organized under Publisher's menu headings, which is where you will find them listed within the program. Command descriptions preceded by an asterisk refer to command options that appear in a dialog box for the command or that can be executed directly via the mouse rather than with a menu command. (For example, there is no menu command to move to the next page in your document. You must click the Page Control arrow with the mouse.) In all cases a hyphen (-) indicates that you should hold down two or more keys simultaneously.

Publisher's Keyboard Shortcuts

Menu	*Command description*	*Key combination*
Menu commands		
File	Save	Ctrl-S
	Print	Ctrl-P
	Exit Publisher	F3
Edit	Undo last action	Alt-Backspace
	Cut object	Ctrl-X or Shift-Del
	Copy object	Ctrl-C or Ctrl-Ins
	Paste object	Ctrl-V or Shift-Ins
	Delete text frame	Ctrl-Del
	Delete object	Del
	Highlight a story	Ctrl-A or F8
Page	Actual Size view	F9
	Insert blank page	Ctrl-N
	Go to background/foreground	Ctrl-M

(continued)

continued

Menu	Command description	Key combination
Layout	Bring to front	Ctrl-F
	Send to back	Ctrl-Z
	Shadow	Ctrl-D
	Shading	
	* Transparent/opaque style	Ctrl-T
Format	Character	
	* Bold	Ctrl-B
	* Italic	Ctrl-I
	* Underline all	Ctrl-U
	* Subscript	Ctrl-=
	* Superscript	Ctrl-Shift-=
	* Plain text (Deselects all special character formatting)	Ctrl-Spacebar
	Indents and Spacing	
	* Center alignment	Ctrl-E
	* Justified alignment	Ctrl-J
	* Left alignment	Ctrl-L
	* Right alignment	Ctrl-R
	* Space between lines (1 line)	Ctrl-1
	* Space between lines (2 line)	Ctrl-2
	* Space between lines ($\frac{1}{2}$ line)	Ctrl-5
	* Space before paragraphs (0 pt.)	Ctrl-0
	* Plain paragraph (Deselects all special paragraph formatting)	Ctrl-Q
Options	Hyphenate	Ctrl-H
	Snap to guides	Ctrl-W
	Hide/show rulers	Ctrl-K
	Hide/show layout guides	Ctrl-G
	Hide/show object boundaries	Ctrl-Y
Help		F1

(continued)

continued

Menu	*Command description*	*Key combination*
Other commands		
	* Extend highlight of text across two text frames	Shift-Right arrow
	*Highlight text characters	Shift-Right arrow
	*Highlight a line of text	Shift-Down arrow
	* Go to next page	F5
	* Go to previous page	Ctrl-F5
	* Go to beginning of text frame	Ctrl-Home
	* Go to end of text frame	Ctrl-End
	* Go to next connected text frame	Ctrl-Tab
	* Go to previous connected text frame	Ctrl-Shift-Tab
	* Go to last text frame in chain	F8-Right arrow
	* Go To first text frame in the chain	F8-Left arrow

Keyboard Equivalents

In contrast to keyboard shortcuts, keyboard equivalents mimic mouse operations to open menus and select commands. This capability is a standard part of the Windows interface, so you can use keyboard equivalents to operate any windows-based application — including Publisher. For example, to print a file you would first press the Alt-F key combination to open the File menu, and then press the P key to invoke the Print dialog box.

Often there is more than one combination of keystrokes available to you to carry out a command. For example, there are actually four ways to close an active program window.

- You can press Alt-F to open the File menu, and then press the x key to Exit.

- You can press F10 to activate the menu bar, use the direction keys to highlight File, and then press Enter to open the File menu. Use the Down arrow key to highlight the Exit command, and press Enter to execute the Exit command.

- You can press Alt-Spacebar to open the Control menu, and then press C to choose the Close command and close the window.

- You can press Alt-F4 (which is a Windows keyboard shortcut).

You can manipulate the Windows interface (and operate Publisher) using the keyboard equivalents listed in the following table. The key combinations include a hyphen to show that you must hold down two or more keys simultaneously. In some combinations you must use a series of sequential keystrokes instead, in which case the series is indicated by a comma. For example, *Alt-Spacebar, c* means press and hold Alt while you also press the Spacebar, release both keys, and then press c. Several items in the table have both a keyboard shortcut and a keyboard equivalent. The keyboard shortcut is always listed first, followed by the keyboard equivalent.

Windows Keyboard Shortcuts and Keyboard Equivalents

Mouse operation	*Key combination*
Window management	
Activate the next application window or minimized icon	Alt-Esc
Switch to the next application window and restore applications that are running as icons	Alt-Tab
Move a window	Alt-Spacebar, m, arrow key
Minimize the current window	Alt-Spacebar, n
Maximize the current window	Alt-Spacebar, x
Restore a window	Alt-Spacebar, r
Open the Task List box	Ctrl-Esc *or* Alt-Spacebar, w
Close the active application window	Alt-F4 *or* Alt-Spacebar, c
Close the active document window	Ctrl-F4 *or* Alt-hyphen, c
Menu keys	
Open the Control menu for the current application window	Alt-Spacebar
Open a menu from the menu bar	Alt-the underlined letter *or* F10, Left or Right arrow, Enter
Invoke a command in an open menu	Press the underlined letter
Move among commands in an open menu	Up or Down arrow
Invoke the highlighted menu item	Enter
Cancel the selected menu	Esc

(continued)

continued

Mouse operation	Key combination
Dialog boxes	
Move forward from option to option within a dialog box	Tab
Move backward from option to option within a dialog box	Shift-Tab
Move the highlight between items within a list box	Arrow keys
Scroll up or down in a list box, one window at a time	PgUp or PgDn
Open a drop-down list box	F4 *or* Alt-Down arrow
Close a drop-down list box	F4 *or* Alt-Up arrow
Select an item in an open drop-down list box	Up or Down arrow
Select or deselect a list box item, a check box, or an option button	Spacebar
Execute the command	Enter
Cancel the dialog box without executing the command	Esc *or* Alt-F4
Program Manager	
Move between program groups	Ctrl-F6 *or* Ctrl-Tab
Move from icon to icon within a program group	Arrow keys
Start the highlighted program	Enter
Tile the open program group windows	Shift-F4
Cascade the open program group windows	Shift-F5
Close the active group window	Ctrl-F4
Exit Windows	Alt-F4
Help	
Open the Help program in the active program window	F1

Appendix C

PRINTING WITH MICROSOFT PUBLISHER

You can't claim to be a desktop publisher until you actually print a document. Whether you are producing newsletters, corporate reports, or greeting cards, paper is still the optimum delivery medium for your message.

Printing with the Default Settings

Getting your designs from the computer screen and onto paper is a straightforward process, especially if you are willing to accept the default settings in the Print dialog box. In fact, it requires only two mouse clicks — or one keyboard shortcut (Ctrl-P).

1. Open the File menu, and choose the Print command.

2. When the Print dialog box appears, click OK.

In some cases the default options (which include printing at the highest resolution of the current active printer and generating one copy of each page in your publication) are actually counterproductive. To print efficiently, you'll need to understand the printing options offered by both Microsoft Publisher and Windows.

Three dialog boxes within Publisher affect the printing process: the Print dialog box, the Print Setup dialog box, and the Page Setup dialog box.

The Print Dialog Box

When you invoke the Print command from the File menu, the Print dialog box appears. In the following illustration, the default printer, a PostScript printer, is currently selected.

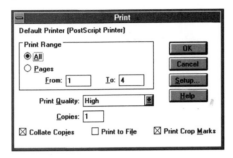

Setup

To change the currently selected printer, click Setup. This command takes you directly to the Print Setup dialog box. (For more information, see "The Print Setup Dialog Box," later in this appendix.)

Print Range

Use Print Range to print only a portion of your publication. You'll want to use this option when you are correcting a few pages in a long document. Instead of waiting for all of the pages to print, follow these steps to print only the pages you need:

1. Click the Pages option button.

2. Enter the specific page numbers you want to print. If you want to print only one page, enter that page number in both the From and To boxes.

Print Quality

When you print the final copy of your publication, you should always choose a Print Quality setting of High. This setting generates your document at your printer's highest resolution (measured in dots per inch).

However, sometimes speed is more important than quality — for example, when you are roughing out a design or want to proofread text. Follow these steps to speed up the printing process by lowering the Print Quality setting:

1. Click on the arrow to open the Print Quality drop-down list box.

   The options in the list box vary depending on the capabilities of the currently selected printer. For example, laser printers can typically print at Low (75 dpi), Medium (150 dpi), or High (300 dpi) resolutions.

   In contrast, many dot-matrix printers can print only at 180 dpi, even at the highest quality setting. And many dot-matrix printers substitute Draft mode for Low or Medium settings. Be warned: in Draft mode many dot-matrix printers cannot print pictures or other graphics, such as WordArt elements. For more information regarding printer resolution, see "The Windows Control Panel," later in this Appendix.

2. Choose the most appropriate quality setting: Draft, Low, Medium, or High.

Copies

It is generally faster to produce multiple copies of your publications using a photocopier. However, if it is important to maintain the highest quality for each and every copy (for pictures or documents containing small type sizes, for example) you can print multiples directly from Microsoft Publisher. Simply replace the default setting with the number of copies you want.

Collated Copies

Turn on the Collate Copies check box to have Publisher print each copy of your publication in the correct page order. Because Publisher must print each copy of the publication from beginning to end before it prints the next copy, it is usually faster to turn off this option and collate by hand.

Print to File

You might want to print your publication to a file rather than directly to a printer. For example, you may want to take advantage of a high-resolution or color printer that is not connected to your computer. And if you want to send your publication to a professional typesetter, printer, or service bureau for the highest possible reproduction quality, you need a way to transfer printer files (rather than publication files). In either case, you must first print your publication to a file, and then transfer the file to the target printer.

To take advantage of a printer that's not connected to your computer, you must be sure that the printer you will ultimately use is currently selected in the Print Setup dialog box — despite the fact that it is not physically connected to your computer. So if you have a dot-matrix printer at home, and an HP LaserJet in the office, you must install the laser printer as the current output device. After you install it, it will appear as one of the available printers in the Print Setup dialog box. (For more information, refer to the section on printer installation in your Windows documentation.)

To create a file to take to a service bureau, you must be sure that the currently selected printer is a PostScript printer. Only PostScript files are compatible with high-resolution, professional-quality output devices, such as Compugraphic or Linotronic typesetters. Because PostScript output is not device-specific, the same PostScript printer file can print on a PostScript-compatible laser printer at 300 dpi or a PostScript-compatible typesetter at 1200 or 2400 dpi.

When you print a publication to a file, you are translating Publisher's native file format into a format that is compatible with the selected printer. Therefore, you can print a file using a computer system that doesn't even have Publisher installed. Here are some more specific instructions.

 ### Hands On:
Printing to a File

1. In the Print dialog box, click Print to File.

2. Click OK.

3. When the Print to File dialog box appears, as shown in the illustration on the next page, type a filename that will clearly identify the publication. In this case, Publisher doesn't insert a PUB extension, so you should type an extension that will identify the file as a printer-ready document (for example, PRT).

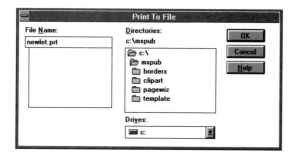

4. Use the Directories and Drives list boxes to specify where Publisher should store the file.

You'll probably want a copy of the file on a floppy disk so you can transfer the file to another computer system. However, if your publication includes several pages, software fonts, or numerous pictures, it probably won't fit on a single floppy disk. Publications printed to disk create large files because the print files must contain all the information in the document plus all the commands necessary to operate the printer. You should, therefore, create the print file on your hard disk and then copy it to a floppy disk.

5. Once the file has been successfully printed to your hard disk, transfer the PRT file from your hard disk to a floppy disk using one of the following methods:

   □ If the file fits on a floppy disk, use the Windows File Manager in the Main program group or the MS-DOS COPY command to copy the file. If you use the MS-DOS COPY command, be sure that you add the /v parameter to the command line; this will instruct MS-DOS to verify that the file has been copied accurately.

   □ If the file is too large to fit on a floppy disk, you can use the MS-DOS BACKUP command to copy the file onto several disks. If you use BACKUP, you must then use the same version of the MS-DOS RESTORE command to reconstruct the file on the computer system you'll use to print the publication.

   □ If the file is too large to fit on a floppy disk, you can also use a file compression utility (like PKZIP.EXE) to make the file smaller.

If you compress the files, you must use the companion utility (like PKUNZIP.EXE) to decompress the file on the computer system in which you will print the publication. (PKZIP and PKUNZIP are shareware utilities available on most bulletin boards.)

6. Transport the floppy disk to the computer system you want to use or to your service bureau. If you are printing the file yourself from another computer, you must copy, restore, or decompress the file to the hard disk of the computer system you want to use.

7. To print the file, use the Windows File Manager in the Main program group or the MS-DOS COPY command to transfer (or literally copy) the printer file to the output device. If you use MS-DOS COPY be sure to add the /b parameter to the command line. The /b parameter ensures that the entire file is printed, even if it contains multiple pages. A sample command line follows:

```
copy filename.prt lpt1:/b
```

Be sure to type the correct parallel port information for the computer system you are using. For example, the printer may be attached to the first parallel port (LPT1:) or to a second parallel port (LPT2:). If the printer is attached to a serial port (such as COM1:), you must reroute the port output before copying the file to the printer. See your MS-DOS manual for details.

Crop Marks

You can specify a custom page size that is smaller than your printer's standard paper size. Although you must trim off the excess paper manually, Publisher can help you by adding cutting guides, or crop marks, to the printout. Publisher requires at least ½ inch of free space to add crop marks. Turn off this option when your page size and paper size are identical. (For more information on setting a custom page size, see "The Page Setup Dialog Box," later in this Appendix.)

Cancel Button

You can escape from the Print dialog box by clicking Cancel. Even after you click OK, however, Publisher lets you stop the printing process at any time by presenting you with a special dialog box that also contains a Cancel button.

When you click Cancel, Publisher stops sending information to the printer. Any pages that have already been sent to the printer and stored in the printer's memory, however, will print.

The Print Setup Dialog Box

You can access Microsoft Publisher's Print Setup dialog box by choosing the Print Setup command from the File menu or from the Print dialog box. The options in this dialog box, shown in the following illustration, control the configuration of the printer itself.

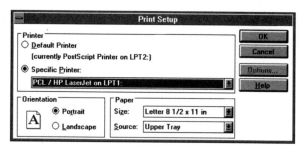

Printer

Publisher picks up information from the Windows Control Panel to determine what printers are installed on your computer system. Although Publisher assumes that you want to use the current default printer, you can create a publication using any other printer installed on your system.

Different printers offer different capabilities. For example, laser printers offer higher resolution output than dot-matrix printers. Some printers can produce color output, some can handle legal-sized or ledger-sized papers, and others provide a wide array of typefaces.

To create a publication using a printer other than the current default printer, follow these instructions.

1. Click the Specific Printer option.

2. Click the downward-pointing arrow to open the drop-down list box. Select the printer you want to use.

    In the previous illustration, Publisher will print to the HP LaserJet, even though the default printer is a PostScript printer.

Orientation

The Orientation option lets you determine whether the page will print vertically (Portrait) or horizontally (Landscape) on the paper. A small icon to the left of the option buttons lets you preview the paper orientation. Be sure to choose the best orientation for your document. For example, choose Portrait orientation for a standard business letter, but choose Landscape orientation to print the envelope.

Paper

Your choices of both Paper Size and Paper Source are determined by the currently selected printer. To see the choices that are available to you, simply open the associated drop-down list boxes.

Using these two options can help you produce a wider variety of publications. For example, if you choose a larger paper size, you have more latitude in determining the page size of your publication. A larger paper size is especially helpful if you use a layout that prints two or four pages to each sheet of paper. And if you choose Manual for the Paper Source, you can feed non-standard papers, such as envelopes, odd-sized sheets of paper, and heavier paper or card stocks, through your printer.

The Page Setup Dialog Box

The Page Setup command from the Page menu also influences the printing process. The layout options in the Page Setup dialog box let you print more than one publication page on each sheet of paper.

As you can see in the illustration on the next page, the Preview to the right of the Layout Option section shows how many pages of your publication will print on each piece of paper. For example, when you select the Side-fold Greeting Card option, Microsoft Publisher prints four pages on a single sheet of paper and prints two of the pages upside down. This arrangement, or imposition (the technical word for the arrangement of multiple pages on a larger sheet of paper), ensures that the four pages of the greeting card will appear in the correct order when you fold the paper.

Helping Hand: Nonprinting Margins

Most printers are alike in one important way — they reserve a portion of the page to grip the paper and feed it through the printing mechanism. This portion of the page cannot contain any printed image or text.

To determine the nonprinting margin for your printer, follow these simple steps:

1. Open a new publication in Publisher.

2. Use the Print Setup dialog box to select the printer and paper size. (Select the largest paper size your printer can accommodate.)

3. Use the Page Setup dialog box to be sure that the page size matches the paper size.

4. Using the Rectangle tool, draw a rectangle that covers the entire page.

5. With the rectangle selected, open the Shading dialog box from the Layout menu, and choose any style other than Clear.

6. Open the File menu, select the Print command, and then click OK.

   When the page prints, the area around the edge that is not shaded constitutes the nonprinting margins. Whenever you plan a publication, be sure you set page margins that are at least as wide as the nonprinting margins.

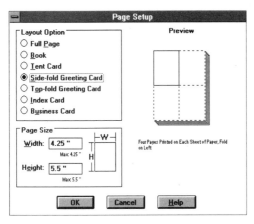

Similarly, the Book option prints two publication pages on each sheet of paper and arranges the pages in spreads so that you can bind the book in sequential page order. For example, the first and last pages of your publication will appear on the same sheet of paper to form the front and back cover. The following diagram shows how Publisher prints a four-page publication. Notice that although the pages are arranged properly, they are on separate sheets of paper. You must photocopy pages 2 and 3 onto the back of pages 1 and 4 before you can fold and trim the publication and bind it into a book.

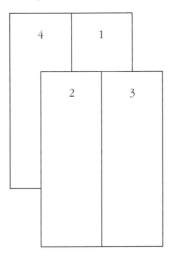

The Windows Control Panel

The Windows Control Panel helps you configure your computer hardware. Control Panel settings let you change your screen colors, alter the appearance of the Windows Desktop, and install printers. For a complete description of the Windows Control Panel, refer to your Windows documentation. The following section explains how the Control Panel settings can improve overall printing performance and influence the way your publications print.

Default Printer

When you begin a new publication, Microsoft Publisher assumes you want to use the printer designated as the default printer in the Windows Control Panel. And when you create a publication using a PageWizard, the Page-Wizard also assumes you want to use the default printer. To change the default printer, follow these steps:

1. Double-click the Control Panel icon in the Windows Main program group.

2. When the Control Panel appears on screen, double-click the Printers icon.

3. When the Printers dialog box appears, as shown in the following illustration, double-click one of the printer names listed in the Installed Printers box. The printer that you choose with a double-click becomes the default.

Print Manager

When you select Use Print Manager, Publisher routes your publication through the Windows Print Manager instead of sending it directly to the printer. The advantage is simple: Publisher sends the file to the Print Manager at high speed, and the Print Manager then sends the file out at the slower speed required by the printer. Because the Print Manager handles all the communication with the printer, you can continue to work while your document prints.

You can also continue to send files to the Print Manager even when it is busy printing another file. The Print Manager stores all the files in a queue and prints them in order. You can open the Print Manager to view the print queue, change the order in which the files will print, pause the printing process, or delete files from the queue.

To access the Print Manager while it is active, simply double-click the icon that appears on the Windows Desktop. To access the Print Manager when it is inactive, click its program icon, which is part of the Main program group.

Memory

The performance of a laser printer is highly dependent upon the amount of printer memory you have installed.

A laser printer must create an entire page in its memory before it prints the page. A full page of 300 dpi graphics (not text) requires at least 1 MB of printer memory. If the page contains complex pictures, it might require even more memory. If your printer does not have enough memory available, it might print half the page on one sheet of paper and the other half on a second sheet of paper, or it might not print at all. And although text pages usually require less printer memory, you should be aware that downloaded fonts must also be stored in the printer's memory.

If you run into a printer memory shortage, you can try one of the following solutions:

- Reduce the number of downloaded fonts in your publication.

- Substitute hardware-resident fonts or cartridge fonts (which don't require printer memory) for downloaded fonts.

- Substitute WordArt elements, which print as pictures, for downloaded fonts.

- Lower the resolution of the printout. A page of graphics at 150 dpi requires half as much printer memory as the same page printed at 300 dpi. But be warned, the quality will be noticeably poorer.

- Use the Print Range option to print only one page of a long document at a time.

- Open the Options menu, and choose the Hide Pictures command. This option prints only the text of your publication and is obviously acceptable only for printing proofs.

If you have persistent memory problems, you should consider adding more memory to your printer. (Refer to your printer's manual for specific instructions.)

Fonts

The printed appearance of the text in your publications is largely determined by the quality of the fonts available to you. Computer-generated fonts are available in two formats: bit-mapped (or raster) fonts and outline (or scalable) fonts. A bit-mapped font is defined as a complete alphabet in a particular type-face, weight, posture (or obliqueness), and point size. For example, 14-point Dutch, bold, italic describes one bit-mapped font. To use various point sizes of a bit-mapped font, you must have access to a complete alphabet at each new size. Obviously, creating and storing a wide variety of point sizes eats up valuable hard-disk space. If you do not generate a complete alphabet for each point size you need and instead attempt to resize a bit-mapped font, you will seriously degrade the quality of the printed letterform. Bit-mapped fonts have the advantage of printing very quickly.

An outline, or scalable, font is defined as a complete alphabet in a particular weight and posture. Notice that size is not included. The size of an outline font is variable, which is why it is referred to as a scalable font. Outline fonts have two advantages. You can resize an outline font without degrading the quality of the final printed letters. And outline fonts take far less storage space on your hard disk.

In addition to the two basic formats, computer-generated fonts are available from four sources: as resident fonts, in cartridges, as downloadable fonts, and from type managers. When you start mixing and matching the font formats with the possible font sources, you will begin to understand the complexity of the current state of font technology.

Resident hardware fonts are built into your printer. Some printers, like dot-matrix printers or the HP LaserJet Series II, store bit-mapped fonts as resident fonts. Other printers, like the HP LaserJet III or PostScript printers, store scalable fonts as resident fonts. When you install your printer, Windows makes the resident fonts available to you based on the information in the printer driver. Hardware fonts, especially bit-mapped hardware-resident fonts, print very quickly.

Cartridges are another source of hardware-based fonts. Font cartridges plug into the body of your printer. Your printer can then use the fonts in the cartridge as if they were resident fonts. Cartridge-based fonts can be stored in either a bit-mapped or an outline format.

Before you can use a font cartridge, you must be sure that your printer is compatible with the cartridge and that you can alert Windows to the presence of the cartridge. The Windows Control Panel lists many standard font cartridges for popular printers like the HP LaserJet family of printers. To alert Windows to the presence of a standard font cartridge, follow these steps:

1. Double-click the Control Panel icon in the Main program group.

2. When the Control Panel appears on screen, double-click the Printers icon.

3. When the Printers dialog box appears, click the name of the printer you want to configure.

4. Click the Configure button.

5. In the next dialog box, click the Setup button.

6. The dialog box shown in the following illustration appears. Use the Cartridges list box to select additional hardware fonts for your printer.

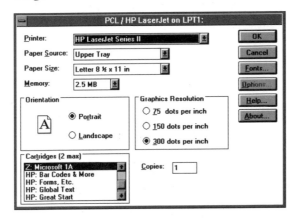

Downloadable, or soft, fonts are generated by font installation programs. Although you store fonts on your computer, you must transfer them to the printer for each work session. Depending on your printer, downloaded fonts can be either bit-mapped or scalable. You can use the Printers option on the Windows Control panel to install downloadable fonts. Although downloadable fonts give you a wide choice of high-quality typefaces, they require permanent storage on your hard disk, and they eat up printer memory. Downloadable fonts generally take longer to print than hardware-resident fonts.

Type managers are an alternative source of software-generated fonts. These memory-resident programs, which include Bitstream FaceLift, Adobe Type Manager, and Zenographics' SuperPrint, run within the Windows 3 environment, and all are compatible with Microsoft Publisher. They perform three basic functions:

- Type managers supply a number of scalable fonts to any Windows-based application, and they provide an easy mechanism for installing additional fonts.

- After the type manager scales the type, it prints the image to any printer installed in the Windows Control Panel, including laser printers, ink-jet printers, and dot-matrix printers.

- In addition to scaling the font outlines for the printer, type managers scale font outlines for your screen display. These screen fonts ensure a close match between the screen display and the final printed page.

Type managers have only one disadvantage. Because they use your computer's resources to scale the font outlines, they can slow down the performance of both your computer and your printer.

Mixing and Matching Fonts

It may seem like it's more trouble than it's worth to sort through all of the various font options. However, understanding how font formats and font sources interact can help you get the most out of Publisher. For example, these three performance problems can all be avoided if you understand the benefits and limitations of each font technology:

- You cannot use the greeting card or tent card layout options in conjunction with hardware-resident bit-mapped fonts. Most hardware bit-mapped fonts have a specific orientation (usually portrait) and cannot be rotated to print upside down.

If you must print your publication to a printer (such as a low-end dot-matrix printer) that uses built-in bit-mapped fonts, your options are limited. Either you can use the book layout to print only upright pages, or you can create all the type in your document using the WordArt module (which is sent to the printer as a picture, not as text).

■ Most laser printers can print white type reversed against a black background. However, many dot-matrix printers cannot duplicate this effect if you create it using Publisher's text frames. The reason, once again, is related to the limitations of bit-mapped hardware fonts. If you cannot print reversed type in a text frame, use the WordArt module to create the type instead.

■ Publisher always attempts to give you a WYSIWYG (What You See Is What You Get, pronounced *wizzywig*) screen display. In fact, if you turn off the display of object boundaries and guides, your screen image should provide a fairly accurate preview of the printed page.

This works better in theory than in practice, however, because Windows often cannot accurately represent fonts on screen. The reason is simple — Windows relies on bit-mapped screen equivalents of your printer fonts. Windows supplies a number of standard bit-mapped screen fonts for many standard printers. But if you don't have the correct point size for the screen font, Windows simply enlarges the bit map, which creates a distorted screen image of the font.

You can avoid this problem in two ways. Both solutions rely upon soft fonts, and only one solution is really acceptable:

□ When you generate bit-mapped soft fonts for your printer, you can generate a duplicate set of fonts for your screen. You'll have to generate an entire alphabet of screen fonts in each point size that you might use in your publication. This solution is sometimes unacceptable because it requires an enormous amount of disk space to store both printer fonts and screen fonts.

□ You can install a type-manager utility that generates accurate screen fonts on the fly, without eating up disk space. Type managers have the added advantage of providing an accurate screen display for all sizes of type, at all levels of magnification.

Appendix D

GLOSSARY OF TERMS

Actual Size view. In Microsoft Publisher, screen view that shows document at its actual size. The entire document can be viewed by scrolling up, down, left, or right.

aliasing. In computer graphics, the effect produced when display resolution is too coarse to minimize the jagged, or "stairstep," appearance of certain design elements, such as diagonal lines, curves, and circles. Aliasing occurs because pixels (dots on the screen) are arranged rectangularly, in rows and columns. If this grid is not fine enough (as in bit-mapped images), pixels sometimes cannot be darkened (or lightened) in a pattern that the viewer will perceive as a smooth diagonal or curve. Aliasing is clearly visible on low-resolution screens or when a small portion of a graphic is enlarged to display the individual dots that constitute it.

alignment. The placement of type relative to the margins. Also the placement of an element relative to the margins or to another element.

anti-aliasing. Gradual color transitions in gray-scale or color bit-mapped images that use intermediate shades or colors to trick the eye into seeing smooth lines.

ascender. That portion of a lowercase letter that rises above the main body (x-height) of the letter, such as the long strokes of *b, d,* and *h.*

aspect ratio. In computer displays and computer graphics, the ratio of width to height of a screen or an image; for example, an aspect ratio of 2:1 indicates that the width is equal to twice the height. Aspect ratio generally refers to the image area (the frame that holds the image) rather than to the image itself. It is an important factor in maintaining correct proportions when a graphic is printed, resized, or incorporated into another document.

ASCII files. Plain text files that do not contain any formatting codes. ASCII files are used to exchange information between applications and operating systems that would otherwise generate incompatible file formats.

attribute. A formatting characteristic of an object. An attribute can indicate style, color, or position. For example, boldfacing is a possible attribute of type.

autoflow. The fastest mode for text placement in which an imported text file flows continuously from column to column and page to page until the entire file has been placed.

background color. In a vector graphics file, the background is often defined as a separate plane — with a specific color. In Publisher, you can change the background color on both internally created objects (such as rectangles) and imported vector files (such as CGM or EPS pictures).

Background page. The Background page contains any text or design elements that appear on every page of a publication, for example the running head and folio. When the page is viewed or printed, Publisher combines the Background page with the Foreground page to complete the layout.

bad break. A line break that creates an awkward hyphenation, such as the breaking of one word of an already hyphenated compound; or a line break that is visually jarring, such as a page that begins with the second half of a hyphenated word.

bad rag. A visually jarring shape of a text block created by very irregular, uneven line breaks in ragged-right text.

baseline. In the printing and display of characters, an imaginary horizontal line with which the base of each character, excluding descenders, is aligned.

bit-mapped graphics. Computer graphics that are stored as collections of bits in memory locations corresponding to pixels on the screen. Bit-mapped graphics are typical of paint programs, which treat images as collections of dots rather than as defined shapes.

bleed. An extra amount of printed image that extends beyond the trim edge of the page. A bleed either extends smoothly across two facing pages (because the image extended beyond the trim on the inside page edge) or prints to the very edge of the page (because the image extended beyond the trim on the outside page edge).

body copy. The main text of a story excluding ancillary text such as headlines, pull quotes, and captions. Also called body text or running text.

boldface. A type style that makes the text to which it is applied appear darker and heavier than the surrounding text. **This sentence is printed in boldface**.

border. A printing boundary edge that can surround text, graphics, or an entire page. In Publisher, text and graphics are contained within frames. You can choose to apply a border to frames. Borders can range from simple hairline rules to decorative graphic elements.

bullet. A small shape, such as a dot or a box, used to set off a block of text or each item in a list.

byline. The text line that credits the author of an article.

callout. A label that identifies an element in an illustration.

cap height. The height of a capital letter in a particular font and size.

center alignment. The alignment of characters or an object around a point located in the middle of a line, page, or other defined area; in effect, the placement of an element or text an equal distance from each margin or border.

centerfold. The centermost, two-page layout in a multiple-page document. A centerfold is easily created using Publisher's Book option in the Page Setup dialog box.

character. An individual letter or symbol. A character is not necessarily visible, either on the screen or on paper; a space, for example, is a character.

clip art. A collection — either in a book or on a disk — of proprietary or public-domain photographs, diagrams, maps, drawings, and other such graphics that can be "clipped" from the collection and incorporated into other documents.

Clipboard. A special memory resource maintained by an operating system such as Microsoft Windows. The Clipboard temporarily stores a copy of the last information that was "copied" or "cut." A "paste" operation passes data from the Clipboard to the current program.

column guides. In Publisher, vertical guidelines that set boundaries for text frames and help you position design elements. Column guides let you easily create multiple frames of exactly the same width.

Computer Graphics Metafile format. Often abbreviated as CGM. A standard file format that describes a picture graphic as vector information (a set of drawing instructions). CGM files are supported by many illustration and desktop publishing programs, including Publisher. CGM clip-art images are provided with Microsoft Publisher.

condensed font. A font style that reduces the width of each character and then sets the characters closer together than their normal spacing.

continued line. A line of text indicating the page on which an article continues, or the carryover line on a page that identifies the article being continued. Also called a jumpline.

copyright. Ownership of a work by the writer, artist, or publisher. A copyright symbol — © — is also a character in the extended alphabet used by professional typesetters.

copy. To duplicate information and reproduce it in another part of the same document, or in a different application or file. A copy operation can affect data ranging from a single character to large segments of text, a graphic image, or multiple objects. In Windows you copy elements to the Clipboard.

copy fitting. The process used to adapt a story to a layout or page design. Methods include editing the actual content, changing the text attributes, or modifying the document design.

crop. In preparing graphics or photographs, to cut off or hide part of the image. You can delete unneeded sections of a picture such as extra white space around the borders or unnecessary background. You can use Publisher's cropping tool to edit pictures you import into a document.

crop marks. Intersecting lines that mark where paper will be trimmed to form pages in the final document.

crossbar. Intersecting lines resembling a plus sign that act as a pointer to locate the specific coordinates of a mouse. Also called a cross hair.

cut. To remove part of a document, usually placing it temporarily in memory (on the Clipboard) so that the cut portion can be inserted (pasted) elsewhere.

cut and paste. A procedure in which the computer acts as an electronic combination of scissors and glue for reorganizing a document or for compiling a document from different sources. In a cut-and-paste operation, the portion of a document to be moved is selected, deleted to the Clipboard, and later reinserted into the same or a different document.

default. The choice made by a program when the user does not specify an alternative. Defaults are built into programs if some values or options need to be assumed in order for the program to function. For example, the default type style in Publisher is 10-point Times Roman.

deselect. To cancel the selection of text, graphics, or options within a dialog box.

descender. That portion of a lowercase letter that falls below the baseline, such as the long strokes of *g* or *y*.

dialog box. In a graphical user interface, a special window displayed by the system or application to solicit a response from the user.

display type. A typeface suitable for headings and titles in documents, distinguished by its ability to stand out from other text on the page. Sans-serif faces, such as Helvetica or Swiss, often work well as display faces.

dot-matrix printer. Any printer that produces characters made up of dots using a wire-pin print head. The quality of output from a dot-matrix printer depends largely on the number of dots in the matrix, which might be low enough to show individual dots or might be high enough to approach the look of fully formed characters. Dot-matrix printers are often categorized by the number of pins in the print head — typically 9, 18, or 24.

dots per inch. Abbreviated dpi. A measure of screen and printer resolution that is expressed as the number of dots that a device can display or print per linear inch.

downloadable font. An individual font that you can install in your desktop publishing system. You must send (or download) the font information from your computer system to the printer's memory before you print a document. Also called a soft font.

drag. To move an element, such as a picture, a text block, or a window from one place on the screen to another by "grabbing" it and pulling it to its new location. With a mouse, *drag* means to hold down a mouse button while moving the pointer to a new location on the screen.

drop cap. An enlarged initial letter that drops below the baseline in the first line of body text. Publisher refers to drop caps as Fancy First Letters.

drop shadow. A special effect that places a black or gray duplicate of a selected object and offsets it slightly. In Publisher, you can add drop shadows to frames by issuing the Shadow command. You must use WordArt to add drop shadows to individual text characters.

dummy copy. Placeholder text that occupies a space in a layout.

ellipsis. A set of three dots (...) usually used to indicate omission. An ellipsis in printed text indicates the omission of one or more words. In software with a graphical interface (as in many Windows-based programs), an ellipsis following a menu command indicates that choosing the command will display a dialog box. See also *dialog box*.

em dash. A punctuation mark (—) generally used to signify a change or an interruption in the train of thought expressed in a sentence or to set off an explanatory comment.

en dash. A punctuation mark (–) used to indicate a range of dates or numbers (for example, *1980–90*) or to separate the elements of a compound adjective, one part of which is hyphenated or consists of two words (for example, *pre–Civil War*).

Encapsulated PostScript format. Abbreviated EPS. A file format that contains vector information (a series of drawing instructions). EPS images print with smooth rather than jagged edges but can be viewed on screen only as low-resolution bit-mapped images. EPS files can be created in graphics programs that produce PostScript code. EPS images do not print on non-PostScript printers. See *header*.

expanded font. A font style that increases the width of each character and then sets the characters farther apart than their normal spacing.

extended characters. Characters in the typesetter's alphabet other than the characters found on the keyboard. They include accented foreign language letters and copyright symbols. See Chapter 10, "Ten Hot Tips for Type," for instructions on accessing extended character sets.

fancy first letter. Also called a drop cap. In Publisher, an enlarged initial letter that drops below the baseline in the first line of body text.

fill. In computer graphics, to "paint" the inside of an enclosed figure, such as a circle, with a color or a pattern. The portion of the shape that can be colored or patterned is the fill area.

flush. Aligned or even with, as in flush left or flush right text.

flush left. Aligned along the left margin.

flush right. Aligned along the right margin.

folio. A printed page number.

font. A set of characters of the same typeface (such as Times), style (such as italic), weight (such as bold), and — in the case of bitmapped fonts — size (such as 12 points). A font is not to be confused with a typeface. *Typeface* refers to the entire family of a letter design. Times is a typeface, but 32-point Times Bold is a font. Fonts are used by computers for on-screen displays and by printers for hard-copy output. In both cases, fonts are created either from bit maps (patterns of dots) or from outlines (as defined by a set of mathematical formulas). For more information about font technology see Appendix C, "Printing with Microsoft Publisher."

footer. One or more identifying lines printed at the bottom of a page. A footer might be printed on the first page, all pages, every even page, or every odd page, and it might be centered or aligned with the left or the right margin. It sometimes includes the folio (page number) and might also show the date, author or title of a document. A footer is sometimes called a running foot.

foreground color. In a vector graphics file the foreground is often defined as a separate plane — with a specific color. In Publisher, you can change the foreground color on internally created objects (like rectangles).

Foreground page. In Publisher, the Foregound page contains text and design elements that are specific to an individual page. When you view or print a page, Publisher combines the Foreground page and Background page to complete the layout.

format. The overall appearance of a publication, including page size, binding method, page layout, and design elements such as margins, number of columns, headline treatment, and so on. Standard formats for publications such as newsletters and catalogs are typically stored in templates. As a verb in desktop publishing, to format text or graphic elements means to change the appearance, or specifications, of the selected object. See *formatting.*

formatting. The elements of a style that determine the appearance of text, graphics, and pages in a publication. For example, when you format text you apply character and paragraph styles to the copy. When you format graphics you apply attributes such as drop shadows, fill patterns, line weights, and colors to simple geometric shapes. When you format pages you apply global attributes such as page size, page orientation, and page margins.

frame. In Publisher, a space or box in which you place text or graphic images. You can assign formatting attributes, such as drop shadows, borders, and margins to Publisher's frames.

graphic. As used in this book, a graphic is an object or a design created with Publisher's built-in drawing tools, as opposed to a picture, which is an image imported into Publisher. In general terms, a graphic is a representation of an object, such as a graph, chart, illustration or picture, on a two-dimensional surface.

gray scale. A progressive series of shades ranging from black through white. Gray scales are used in computer graphics to add detail to images of all kinds. The number of shades of gray depends on the number of bits used to describe the "color" of each pixel (dot) in the image. The more bits used in coding shades of gray, the more gradations are possible. For example, using two bits per pixel produces four unique shades of gray. Six bits per pixel produce 64 distinct shades on a gray scale, and eight bits produce 256 shades of gray. The way in which gray-scale images are represented on the screen and on paper varies with the capabilities of your monitor and printer as well as the functions of the application program.

greeking. In traditional design, randomly generated text — and even nonsense words — used as dummy type in the early stages of the design process. In computer graphics, greeking also refers to the screen display of text that is too small to be drawn properly. Instead of displaying fully formed letters the graphics program presents a screen display of symbols or gray lines.

grid. The division of a page into regular rectangular areas to aid in arranging, measuring, and aligning text and picture elements.

grouping. A process that lets you select multiple elements and treat them as a single element. In Publisher, you can move, cut, copy, and paste a group of multiple elements.

gutter. The space between two columns, or the margin between two facing pages.

hairline rule. A very thin rule. In desktop publishing, the thickness of a hairline rule varies depending on the resolution (measured in dots per inch) of the printer.

halftone. The printed reproduction of a photograph or other illustration as a set of tiny, evenly spaced spots of variable diameter that, when printed, visually blur together to appear as shades of gray. Many printers used in desktop publishing, notably laser printers and digital imagesetters, are able to print halftone images. In traditional publishing, halftones were created by photographing an image through a meshlike screen; the darker the shade at a particular point in the image, the larger the spot in the resulting photograph. In desktop publishing, halftone spots are created electronically by mapping each gray level onto a collection of printer dots (called a halftone dot or linescreen setting) printed by the laser printer or imagesetter.

handles. The small solid squares that surround a selected object. Selection handles are used to resize and reshape objects.

hanging indent. A paragraph style in which the first line extends to the left of subsequent lines, as in this glossary.

hard return. A line break that signals the end of a paragraph, created by pressing the Enter key to insert a carriage return.

header. One or more identifying lines printed at the top of a page. A header might be printed on the first page, all pages, or every even or odd page, and it might be centered or aligned with the left or right margin. A header usually includes the folio (page number) and might also show the date, author, or title of a document. Also called a running head. A very specific use of the word *header* refers to a descriptive section of an EPS file. Because you cannot view an EPS picture on-screen at high resolution, a low-resolution, bit-mapped representation of the image is usually stored in the file in what is called a header. If the EPS header does not contain a bit-mapped image, the EPS file will appear on screen as a simple box with an identifying filename.

headline. The title of a story.

hypenation. Breaking a word with a hyphen after a syllable and continuing the word on the next line. Used to create fully justified text or to create a more visually appealing rag.

I-beam pointer. In a graphical user interface, a special pointer shaped like a capital *I* that is used for positioning the insertion point and selecting text.

indent. Moving a line of type to the right to indicate the beginning of a new paragraph. Alternatively, adjusting the position of the left and right text margins.

import. To bring information from one system or program into another. The internal format or structure of the data being imported, particularly documents containing images, must be supported in some way by the system or program receiving the information.

imposition. The arrangement of several pages on a larger sheet of paper in the proper order for printing and binding.

initial cap. A first letter set in an enlarged and sometimes decorative type for graphical emphasis.

ink-jet printer. A nonimpact printer that fires tiny drops of ink at the paper. A well of liquid ink is either a part of the print head or connected to the print head with a tube. Ink is vibrated or heated into a mist and sprayed through tiny holes in the proper patterns to form characters or graphics on the paper.

insertion point. A blinking vertical bar on the screen that marks the location at which inserted text will appear. The position of the insertion point is set by clicking the mouse to place the I-beam pointer on the page.

inside margin. The space between the binding edge of the page and the text.

italic. A type style in which the characters are evenly slanted toward the right. Italics are commonly used for emphasis, foreign-language words and phrases, titles of works, technical terms, display type, and captions. *This sentence is printed in italics.*

jaggies. Also called aliasing. The "stairsteps" that appear in diagonal lines and curves drawn at low resolutions.

justified. Type that is flush, or even, along both the right and left margins. Computer programs justify text along the left and right margins by inserting extra space between the words in each line. The spacing, if it is excessive, can be evened out either by rewriting or by hyphenating words at the ends of lines.

justify. To align lines of text evenly along both the left and right margins of a column or page. Some desktop publishing programs also allow you to justify text vertically, creating columns of equal length.

kerning. The process of adjusting the distance between pairs of letters. Typically kerning is applied to make the spacing around letters more balanced and proportional in order to increase legibility. Some pairs of letters that are usually kerned are AV, WA, and YO.

kicker. A phrase preceding a headline that provides identifying information about the story.

landscape orientation. The horizontal orientation of a page in which the width of the page is greater than its height.

laser printer. An electrophotographic printer that is based on the technology used by photocopiers. A focused laser beam and a rotating mirror are used to draw an image of the desired page on a photosensitive drum. This image is converted on the drum into an electrostatic charge, which attracts and holds toner. A piece of electrostatically charged paper is rolled against the drum, which pulls the toner away from the drum and onto the paper. Heat is then applied to fuse the toner to the paper. Finally, the electrical charge is removed from the drum and the excess toner is collected. By omitting this final step and repeating only the toner-application and paper-handling steps, the printer can make multiple copies. Laser printers typically have a resolution of 300 dpi.

layout. The arrangement of text and graphics on a page.

layout guides. In Publisher, nonprinting vertical and horizontal rules that are used to position and align text frames and graphic objects on the page.

leader. A row of dots, hyphens, or other such characters used to lead the eye across a printed page to related information — for example, to connect chapter titles with page numbers in a table of contents. Also, a rule that moves the eye from a callout or label to the part of the illustration it describes.

leading. Pronounced "led-ing." The distance, expressed in points, between lines of type, measured from the baseline (bottom) of one line to the baseline of the next; derived from the traditional typesetting practice of inserting thin bars of lead between lines of metal type.

left alignment. The alignment of characters or an object at the left margin or the left boundary of a defined area.

letterspacing. The amount of space between letters.

line weight. The thickness of a rule, measured in points.

Linotronic. A specific brand name of high-resolution, professional-quality imagesetters capable of printing 1200 or 2400 dots per inch.

margin. The distance from the edge of the paper to the image area occupied by text and graphics. In Publisher, you can also set margins for individual text and picture frames.

masking. The process of blocking out a portion of an object by layering another object on top of it and filling the top object with the same color as the background.

mechanical. A camera-ready pasteup of artwork. A mechanical includes type, line art, and position-only stats keyed to art that is to be stripped in (added to the film that is used to create the printing plate) by the printer. Also called a keyline, a pasteup, or a camera-ready page.

mirrored pages. A layout effect in which the background page elements, such as the headers and folios, are positioned at opposite sides on facing pages.

moiré. A distracting pattern that results when two geometrically regular patterns (such as two sets of parallel lines or two halftone screens) are superimposed, especially at an acute angle. Usually the result of scanning a previously screened halftone.

monospace font. Also called a fixed-width font. A font (set of characters in a particular style and size) in which each character occupies the same amount of horizontal space regardless of its width — an *i,* for example, taking as much room as an *m.*

nonprinting guides. Also called layout guides. In Publisher, nonprinting vertical and horizontal rules that are used to position and align text frames and graphic objects on the page.

Note-Its. A note that can be incorporated into a Publisher document. Note-Its appear as icons on the screen. Double-clicking the icon reveals the hidden message.

Object Linking and Embedding. Abbreviated OLE. A protocol supported by the Windows environment that allows you to create links between two application programs. Objects can be either linked or embedded. When an object is linked, the data file for the object and the source application are referenced by the receiving application. When an object is embedded, the data for the object is stored in the document in which it is embedded, and only the source application is referenced. Within Publisher, an OLE can be established either by using the Paste Special command (which creates a link) or the Insert Object command (which embeds an object). When you use the Paste Special command, each time you open the Publisher document, Publisher automatically checks the status of the linked file. If the linked file has been changed, Publisher automatically updates its copy of the file with the new version. When you embed an object into a Publisher document by using the Insert Object command, Publisher loads the associated program in a separate but *dependent* window, which lets you easily edit the object, such as a spreadsheet or chart, directly from *within* Publisher.

object-oriented graphics. Also called vector graphics. Computer graphics that are based on the use of "construction elements" such as lines, curves, circles, and squares. Object-oriented graphics describe an image mathematically as a set of instructions for creating the objects that make up the image. Because objects are described mathematically, object-oriented graphics can also be layered, rotated, and magnified relatively easily. Object-oriented graphics enable the user to manipulate objects as entire units — for example, to change the length of a line or enlarge a circle — whereas bit-mapped graphics require repainting individual dots in the line or circle.

optional hyphen. Indicates a location at which to break a word if necessary to justify text or create a better rag. The hyphen does not take effect unless the word occurs at the end of a line and will not fit completely. Also called a discretionary hyphen.

orphan. The first line of a paragraph printed alone at the bottom of a page or column of text, or the last line of a paragraph printed alone at the top of a page or column. Orphans are visually awkward and thus undesirable in printed materials.

outside margin. The space between the outside trim (page boundary) and the text.

page size. Also called trim size. The dimensions of a publication's pages. In commercial printing, the size of the page after it is cut during the binding process. In Publisher, the page size can be equal to or smaller than the paper size.

paragraph spacing. Distance from the baseline of the last text line in a paragraph to the baseline of the first text line in a subsequent paragraph, measured in points.

paste. To insert information that has been cut or copied from one document into a different location in the same or a different document. A paste operation can affect data ranging from a single character to large segments of text, a graphic image, or multiple objects. In the Windows environment, you paste elements from the Clipboard.

PC Paintbrush format. Abbreviated PCX. A standard file format for bit-mapped pictures. PCX files typically contain 2, 16, or 256 colors or shades of gray.

pica. A unit of measure equal to 12 points, or approximately ⅙ of an inch. Picas are used to specify page measurements such as paragraph indents, text line length, column width, and margin size.

picture. As used in this book, a picture is any artwork imported into Publisher, as opposed to artwork created within Publisher.

pixel. Short for picture element. The smallest dot or display unit on a computer screen. The clarity of screen resolution depends on the number of pixels per inch on the monitor. A typical VGA monitor displays 72 dots per inch. If a pixel has only two color values (usually black and white), it can be encoded by 1 bit of information. If more than 2 bits are used to represent a pixel, a larger range of colors or shades of gray can be represented: 2 bits for four colors or shades of gray, 4 bits for sixteen colors, and 8 bits for 256 colors.

point. A typographical unit of measure equal to approximately ¹⁄₁₂ of a pica, or approximately ¹⁄₇₂ of an inch. Points are often used to indicate character height, character spacing (kerning), and the amount of space (leading) between lines of text.

portrait orientation. The vertical orientation of a page in which the height of the page is greater than its width.

PostScript. A graphics language developed by Adobe Systems, Inc., that is both resolution and device independent. The same PostScript file can be printed to a 300 dpi laser printer and a 1200 dpi Linotronic imagesetter.

proportional spacing. A form of character spacing in which the horizontal space each character occupies is proportional to the width of the character. The letter *w,* for example, takes up more space than the letter *i.*

pull quote. A quotation copied from the body of an article, often set in a larger point size and emphasized by rules or boxes. Also called a teaser or a lift out.

rag. The shape created by the uneven line breaks in text that is aligned along only one margin. A rag complements flush alignment. For example, word-processed letters and other documents are commonly set flush left with ragged-right margins. Ragged-left text is used infrequently — typically, in advertisements — for visual effect.

ragged left. Text alignment that is even, or flush, on the right margin and uneven on the left.

ragged right. Text alignment that is even or flush on the left margin and uneven on the right.

RAM. Pronounced "ram." An acronym for random access memory. RAM is where the computer stores information temporarily while you're working with it. If you lose power or shut down before saving your work, whatever is in RAM at the time is lost.

recto. Publishing term for a right-hand page. A recto is always an odd-numbered page.

resident font. A font that is stored in the permanent memory of the printer.

resolution. The clarity of detail visible on screen or in the final printout, expressed as dots per inch. In printed material, the resolution is dependent on the printer's capacity. For example, laser printers typically print at 300 dpi.

right alignment. The alignment of characters or an object at the right margin or the right boundary of a defined area.

roman. An adjective describing a typeface or typestyle in which the characters are upright.

row guides. In Publisher, horizontal guidelines that set boundaries for text frames and help you position design elements. Row guides let you easily create multiple frames of exactly the same height.

rule. A line printed above, below, or to the side of an element, either to set the item off from the remainder of the page or to improve the look of the page. The thickness of a rule is typically measured in points. (A point is approximately $\frac{1}{72}$ of an inch.)

running foot. A line at the bottom of the page that might include information such as title, author, chapter, issue date, and page number. See also *footer*.

running head. A line at the top of the page that might include information such as title, author, chapter, issue date, and page number. See also *header*.

sans serif. Literally, "without stroke." Describes any typeface in which the characters have no serifs (the short lines or ornaments at the upper and lower ends of each letterform). A sans-serif typeface usually possesses a more straightforward, geometric appearance than a typeface with serifs and typically lacks the contrast between thick and thin strokes found in serif faces. Sans-serif typefaces are used more frequently in display type, such as headlines, than in large blocks of text.

scalable font. Any font that can be scaled to produce characters in varying sizes. Examples of scalable fonts are stroke fonts (such as Script) that are part of the Windows environment, outline fonts common to high-end laser printers (such as the HP Laserjet III and PostScript compatible devices), and fonts generated by font-manager programs (such as Bitstream Facelift).

scale. As a verb, to enlarge or reduce a graphic object, such as a vector drawing, a bit-mapped photograph, or an outline character font. When you change the width and the height of an object by the same percentage, you maintain the original aspect ratio, or size, of the object proportionally.

scanner. An input device that uses light-sensing equipment to scan paper or other mediums (such as 35-mm transparencies), translating the pattern of light and dark (or color) into a digital signal — or bitmap — that can be manipulated by graphics software.

scratch area. In Publisher, the area outside the perimeter of your working page. Using the scratch area lets you experiment with special effects without disrupting your work area. Objects in the scratch area don't print because they fall outside the page boundaries.

screen. The process of creating tonal variations by printing percentages of black or another color. In traditional printing, meshlike screens were used to convert continuous tone images (such as photographs) into a regular grid of dots that could be reproduced on a printing press. When a specific frequency screen (which refers to the fineness or coarseness of the dot pattern) is applied to a photograph, it creates a halftone picture. When a screen is applied to a solid color it creates an area with an even, or flat, tint.

script. A typeface that simulates handwriting.

serif. Describes any of the short lines or ornaments at the upper and lower ends of the strokes that form a character in a typeface; also describes any face with serifs. A serif face is usually considered to be easier to read — especially in large blocks of text — than is a sans-serif face.

service bureau. A commercial business that processes computer files on a high-resolution typesetter, such as the Linotronic.

shading. In traditional graphic arts, a particular color variation produced by mixing black with a pure color. Also called a value. In computer graphics, a color-mixing method that varies the intensity or brightness of a color. In Publisher, the shading command that lets you assign colors and patterns to objects.

sidebar. A smaller, self-contained story inside a larger one, usually boxed with its own headline to set it apart from the main text. Also a block of text placed to the side of the main body of text in a document, often set off by a border or other graphical element.

small caps. A font of uppercase letters that are smaller than the standard uppercase letters in that typeface.

soft font. A font generated by software installed on your computer system that you must download to the printer's memory before printing the publication.

spine. Also called a backbone. The back of a bound book connecting the two covers.

spread. Two facing pages in a publication.

subhead. A subordinate title or headline.

tab. A nonprinting character used to align text and numerals in columns on the screen and on the printed page. A tab is visually indistinguishable from a series of blank spaces entered by repeatedly pressing the Spacebar, but tab characters and space characters are different to a computer. A tab is a single character and therefore can be added, deleted, or overtyped with a single keystroke. In addition, the position and alignment of a tab stop can be specified by using the Tabs dialog box. For example, you can align numerical data on the decimal point.

Tagged Image File Format. Abbreviated TIFF. A standard file format commonly used for scanning, storage, and interchange of bit-mapped, gray-scale, and color images.

template. In desktop publishing, a ready-made design of a publication that provides the necessary layout grid and type formats. Publisher comes with a library of templates for many different kinds of documents. You can make your own templates by creating a publication from scratch and selecting the Template option in the Save As dialog box.

text. The body matter of a page or document, as distinguished from the headings or titles.

tint. A percentage of black or another color to create tonal variations. Also called a tone.

toggle. To switch back and forth between two states, or modes.

trim. In commercial printing, the size of the page after it is cut during the binding process.

typeface. A specific, named design of a family of fonts. A typeface is not the same as a font, which indicates a specific style, weight, and in the case of bit-mapped fonts, size of a typeface, such as 12-point Helvetica Bold or 10-point Times Roman Italic. An example of a group of related typefaces would be Helvetica, Helvetica Bold, Helvetica Oblique, and Helvetica Bold Oblique.

type size. The size of printed characters, usually measured in points. (A point is approximately $\frac{1}{72}$ of an inch.) Thus, a line of text in 18-point type is twice the height of a line of text in 9-point type in the same typeface.

typestyle. Either the obliqueness (slant) of a typeface or a reference to the overall design of a typeface or typeface family. In the first meaning, which is the correct technical usage, *style* specifies the degree of slant. In most typefaces, the style is either upright (normal) or slanted (italic). In the second meaning, *style* can refer to either the design of a specific typeface, such as Helvetica Oblique, or the design of a typeface family, such as Helvetica, Helvetica Bold, Helvetica Oblique, and Helvetica Bold Oblique. Increasingly, typestyle refers to the collection of character and paragraph formatting attributes that determine the appearance of text on screen and on the page.

vector graphics. A method of generating images that uses mathematical descriptions to determine the position, length, and direction in which lines are to be drawn. In vector graphics, objects are created as collections of lines, rather than as patterns of individual dots (pixels).

verso. Publishing term for a left-hand page. A verso is always an even-numbered page.

weight. The density of letters, traditionally described as light, regular, bold, extra bold, and so on. Also the thickness of a rule, measured in points.

widow. A single word, a portion of a word, or a few short words left on a line by themselves at the end of a paragraph or column of type on a page. A widow is considered visually undesirable on the printed page. Because it is short, a widow can generally be eliminated by editing or rebreaking preceding text.

Windows Bit Map format. Abbreviated BMP. A standard file format in which pictures are stored as a collection of pixels or bits. BMP files typically contain 2, 16, 256, or a full range (16 million) colors.

Windows Metafile format. Abbreviated WMF. A standard file format that is common to Windows-based programs. WMF files store information as a series of drawing instructions.

word spacing. The amount of space between words.

wraparound text. Text that wraps around a graphic. Also called run-around text.

WYSIWYG. Acronym for "What You See Is What You Get," which refers to screen displays that can generate an accurate preview of the printed page. Pronounced "wizzy-wig."

x-height. In typography, the height of the lowercase letter *x* in a particular font. The x-height represents the height of the body of a lowercase letter, excluding ascenders (such as the top of the letter *b*) and descenders (such as the tail on the letter *g*). The bottom of the x-height is the baseline.

INDEX

Special Characters

... (ellipsis), 15, 16
(number sign), 149

A

active window, 75
Actual Size view, 48, 175
aliasing, 256
alignment, WordArt elements, 209–11
alignment icon, 59
Annotate command, 38
ANSI extended character set, 287
antialiasing, 256
application programs. *See also* Clipboard;
    Help program; Microsoft Works; pro-
    gram groups; Program Manager;
    WordArt program
    Calculator, 91
    loading, 24–26
    Microsoft Money, *xiv*, 21, 312, 314
    Microsoft Write, 24–25
    multiple, 2–29
    switching between, 26–29
Arch effects, 212, 215
arrows, two-headed, 13, 53
ASCII format, 117, 220
aspect ratio, 160, 274
automatic hyphenation, 122–23, 278
automatic page numbering, 148–49, 186–87
automatic text wrap, 22–24, 276–80, 291

B

Background pages
    automatic page numbering, 186–87
    mirrored, 150–51
    overlapping type, 291
    overview, 102–3
    placing objects on, 146–50
    turning off, 167–68
BACKUP command, 327
Best Fit option, 208

bit-mapped fonts
    hardware-resident, 177, 335–36, 337–38
    overview, 335
    screen display, 338
bit-mapped images, 255, 256–57
Bitstream FaceLift
    fonts, 177, 178, 179
    installing, 314–16
Blank Page button, 45–46
BMP filename extension, 252, 255
body copy
    choosing font, 188–91
    formatting, 196–98, 221–24
    importing, 191–93, 220–21
    newsletter, 106
    overview, 188
    spelling checker, 198–99
    word processing filters, 194–95
boldface type, 59, 195
book layout, 142–43, 168–69, 332
Bookmark command, 38
BorderArt
    bullets, 287–88
    dialog box, 234–36
    tools, *xiv*
borders. *See also* margins
    creating, 90, 92
    window, 12, 13
boundaries, objects, 63–64, 79
Bring to Front command, 61
bullets, 287–88
Business Forms PageWizard, 70, 7–78
Button effect, 212, 215

C

Calculator, 91
Cancel button, 328–29
captions, newsletter, 106
cartridges, hardware fonts, 336
Cascade command, 28
cascading, windows, 27–28
CGM filename extension, 108, 252, 255,
    257, 272

Luisa Simone

Luisa Simone is a New York-based consultant, teacher, and journalist specializing in computer graphics. For the past three years, Miss Simone has been a contributing editor for *PC Magazine,* writing about desktop publishing programs, presentation graphics packages, illustration software, and multimedia computing.

Her work has also appeared in magazines that run the gamut from computer journals — such as *PC Computing,* and *PC Sources* — to trade publications aimed at design professionals — such as *Photo/Design* and *How* magazine. Miss Simone's credentials include teaching at the Pratt Institute in New York and speaking at the New York Computer Graphics Show.

The manuscript for this book was prepared and submitted to Microsoft Press in electronic form. Text files were processed and formatted using Microsoft Word.

Principal word processor: Sean Donahue
Principal proofreader: Carla Thompson
Principal typographer: Debra Marvin
Interior text designer: Kim Eggleston
Principal illustrator: Luisa Simone, Lisa Sandburg
Cover designer: Celeste Design
Cover color separator: Color Control

Text composition by Editorial Services of New England, Inc. in Garamond Light with display type in Futura Extra Bold Condensed, using the Compugraphic 9400 laser imagesetter.

Printed on recycled paper stock.